SAGE was founded in 1965 by Sara Miller McCune to support the dissemination of usable knowledge by publishing innovative and high-quality research and teaching content. Today, we publish over 900 journals, including those of more than 400 learned societies, more than 800 new books per year, and a growing range of library products including archives, data, case studies, reports, and video. SAGE remains majority-owned by our founder, and after Sara's lifetime will become owned by a charitable trust that secures our continued independence.

Los Angeles | London | New Delhi | Singapore | Washington DC | Melbourne

INDIA'S URBAN HOUSING AND POVERTY

INDIA'S URBAN HOUSING AND POVERTY

Feasible and Sustainable Housing Development Interventions

M. MAHADEVA

SAGE

Los Angeles | London | New Delhi
Singapore | Washington DC | Melbourne

First published in 2022 by

SAGE Publications India Pvt Ltd
B1/I-1 Mohan Cooperative Industrial Area
Mathura Road, New Delhi 110 044, India
www.sagepub.in

SAGE Publications Inc
2455 Teller Road
Thousand Oaks, California 91320, USA

SAGE Publications Ltd
1 Oliver's Yard, 55 City Road
London EC1Y 1SP, United Kingdom

SAGE Publications Asia-Pacific Pte Ltd
18 Cross Street #10-10/11/12
China Square Central
Singapore 048423

Typeset in 10.5/13 pt Berkeley by AG Infographics, Delhi.

Library of Congress Cataloging-in-Publication Data

Name: Mahadeva, M., author.
Title: India's urban housing and poverty : feasible and sustainable housing development interventions / M. Mahadeva.
Description: Thousand Oaks, California : SAGE Publications Inc., 2022. | Includes bibliographical references and index.
Identifiers: LCCN 2022023177 | ISBN 9789354794070 (hardback) | ISBN 9789354794155 (epub) | ISBN 9789354794193 (ebook)
Subjects: LCSH: Public housing–India. | Housing–India. | Urban poor–India.
Classification: LCC HD7361.A3 M34 2022 | DDC 363.5/0954–dc23/eng/20220525
LC record available at https://lccn.loc.gov/2022023177

ISBN: 978-93-5479-407-0 (HB)

SAGE Team: Amrita Dutta, Shipra Pant and Kanika Mathur

To my mother,
Late Devamma.

Bulk Sales

SAGE India offers special discounts for purchase of books in bulk. We also make available custom editions for institute specific requirements as well as excerpts from books for media reviews.

For orders, enquiries or to subscribe to our mailing list, please write to us at **marketing@sagepub.in.**

This book is also available as an e-book.

CONTENTS

LIST OF TABLES

LIST OF ABBREVIATIONS

ACA	Additional Central Assistance
AHF	Affordable housing finance
ASs	Apex societies
CAS	Central assistance scheme
CBOs	Community-based organizations
CFAs	Central financing agencies
CI	Corrugated iron
CMPs	City master plans
COMP	Cities with one million and above population
CSR	Corporate social responsibility
DNSP	Draft National Slum Policy
EHSs	Employees' housing societies
EWS	Economically weaker sections
FAR	Floor area ratio
FDI	Foreign direct investment
GI	Galvanized iron
GIC	General Insurance Corporation
GIS	Geographical information system
GJRHFS	Golden Jubilee Rural Housing Finance Scheme
GoI	Government of India
GRHFC	Gujarat Rural Housing Finance Corporation
HDFC	Housing Development Finance Corporation
HDMA	Housing Development Monitoring Authority
HFCs	Housing finance companies
HFI	Housing financial institutions
HFM	Housing finance market

HFS	Housing finance system
HIGs	High-income groups
IAY	Indira Awas Yojana
IDSMT	Integrated Development of Small and Medium Towns
IF	Insurance fund
IHM	India's housing market
IHSDP	Integrated Housing and Slum Development Programme
IMDP	Integrated municipal development plan
ISEC	Institute for Social and Economic Change
JNNURM	Jawaharlal Nehru National Urban Renewable Mission
LIC	Life Insurance Corporation
LIGs	Low-income groups
LPG	Liquefied petroleum gas
MCF	Municipal coverage fund
MF	Mutual fund
MFIs	Microfinance institutions
MIGs	Middle-income groups
MRTS	Mass rapid transit system
MSW	Municipal solid waste
NABARD	National Bank for Agriculture and Rural Development
NBO	National Buildings Organization
NCHFI	National Cooperative Housing Federation of India
NGOs	Non-governmental organizations
NHB	National Housing Bank
NHFIP	National Housing Finance Inclusion Plan
NHHP	National Housing and Habitat Policy
NHP	National Housing Policy
NRIs	Non-resident Indians
NSDP	The National Slum Development Programme
NSP	National Slum Policy
NSSO	National Sample Survey Office
NUHHP	National Urban Housing and Habitat Policy
NULM	National Urban Livelihood Mission
OMP	One million population
PF	Provident fund
PHSs	Primary housing societies

PIIs	Public interest institutions
PMAY-HA	Pradhan Mantri Awas Yojana-Housing for All
PPP	Public–private partnership
PPPMAH	Public–Private Partnership Model for Affordable Housing
PRI	Panchayati Raj Institutions
PSL	Priority sector lending
RAY	Rajiv Awas Yojana
RBC	Reinforced block concrete
RBI	Reserve Bank of India
RCC	Reinforced cement concrete
RERA	Real Estate Regulatory Authority
RGRHC	Rajiv Gandhi Rural Housing Corporation
RHF	Rural housing fund
RRBs	Regional rural banks
RRS	Regular refinance scheme
SCBs	Scheduled commercial banks
SCM	Smart City Mission
SDF	Slum development fund
SFB	Small finance banks
SFCs	Slum-free cities
SFCPA	Slum-Free City Plan of Action
SHBs	State housing boards
SHG	Self-help groups
SPV	Special purpose vehicle
SSFPA	State Slum-Free Plan of Action
SUHHP	State Urban Housing and Habitat Policy
UCB	Urban cooperative banks
UHF	Urban housing fund
UIDSSMT	Urban Infrastructure Development Scheme for Small and Medium Towns
ULBs	Urban local bodies
UN	United Nations
UNCHS	United Nations Centre for Human Settlements
UT	Union territory
UTI	Unit Trust of India

FOREWORD

Providing housing accommodation to all the eligible families has been an everlasting challenge in all the countries. The problem of homelessness is more severe and acute in relatively economically poorer countries, especially due to limited actions for housing development. The governments which have been targeting to provide houses to the poor and disadvantaged homeless families have ended with little success. The other facilitating endeavours towards the homeless families are equally very limited. The limited actions have contributed substantially to increase the quantitative and qualitative dimensions of housing poverty. Even the technological advancements in building cheaper houses has not been able to address this critical problem, which has been a social development indicator. If this is the case of homeless families, getting decent housing by all the eligible households would be a distant dream. Owing to the public resource crunch and lack of development of affordable houses by the housing market, a good number of eligible families have rendered themselves homeless in India. More so, the poor families, owing to their challenging economic situations, resort to dwell an abysmally substandard life in environmentally challenging segments. It is the case of major urban centres of the country, although the problem is not entirely different in other centres. It is estimated that 46 lakhs families in urban India (4.6 million) have been facing the shortage of houses. Similarly, over 37 per cent of the families live in one room accommodation only. About 21 per cent of urban families live in environmentally challenging slum settlements. It is unfortunate that urban growth has paved way for the growth of informal settlements or slums and has become an integral part of urbanization over the years. Growing economic prosperity, coupled with enormous employment opportunities in the urban centres, has resulted in increasing housing poverty for the poorer sections.

As a first, Dr Mahadeva has captured these problems of Indian housing and their relationship with poverty in an impressive way in this book. He has lucidly covered the topic, designing his book in a systematic way and, over all, he has succeeded to present the same in a coherent manner. One gets a clear depiction of housing market by reading the book. The demarcation of urban growth from all perspectives stimulates the interest of the readers of the book. As he has pointed out, development of the other tier towns and cities should ease the existing urban housing problems apart from decongesting major urban centres as part of sustainable urbanization. Dr Mahadeva has clearly brought out the quantitative and qualitative perspectives of housing poverty and has suggested various remedial measures to overcome this. Accounting the severity in the growth of the slums, public development interventions, success and failures have been an added dimension of the analysis. A critical review of ad hoc regime, National Housing and Habitat Policy, Shelter for All Policy, National Urban Housing and Habitat Policies and Affordable Housing Development Strategies has found critical evaluation in this book.

Dr Mahadeva works out neatly the policies which are required for a pragmatic urban housing sector. He clearly discusses the compartmentalized and need-based housing policy and points out that rejuvenation of the cooperative housing movement can tackle the challenge of urban housing very effectively. Overall, he suggests that the housing strategy must be sustainable in nature. It should focus on efficient allocation and utilization of available and accessible resources. He works out the strategy to combine government, private and cooperative resources to solve the problem. He points out, 'Time has now come to put forth the idea of establishing direct linkages between financial institutions and primary housing societies in order to expedite the process of housing loan approvals and to achieve cost efficiency in the operations.' Various financial strategies needed to address the challenge of urban housing are well depicted by Dr Mahadeva in this book. He advocates for strengthening cooperative movement in every nook and corner of the backward regions to solve this gigantic problem. Whether cooperative method alone can solve the housing problem is a moot question. He laments that the government has never laid emphasis on strengthening housing cooperatives with network and potentials to mobilize the homeless to tackle this problem. Dr Mahadeva's lengthy discussion in this regard in the book will surely be an eye-opener to the government. The government on its part speaks of 'shelter for all' and better quality of life to all citizens, whereas the author points out that the government itself shall live up to its own responsibility of housing the poor. The government can also harness the unused potentials in the public, private and household sectors for housing development activities.

Overall, this book fills an important research gap in the area of India's urban housing. It is a very useful addition to urban economics. I wish all the best to the author and hope he fills many more gaps in this area.

C. K. Renukarya
Director, Post-Graduation Centre
PBM Mahajana Education Centre
Professor of Economics (Retd)
University of Mysore

PREFACE AND ACKNOWLEDGEMENTS

The issues of housing poverty and housing of the homeless in general and poor in particular in all the countries have been widely discussed from the 1970s. Till then, the public actions were very limited under ad hoc interventions. The community actions through cooperatives and market interventions have been centred around the developing regions, including the backward regions, rather than being widespread. Simultaneously, the experiences of not having an adequate policy and public commitments to develop housing as a critical social infrastructure and as a social development indicator have also been brought to the debate. When the issue of importance for the development of housing for the homeless and poor was less realized or focussed, the United Nations (UN) initiatives played an extremely significant role in sensitizing the member nations. The first-ever conference on Human Settlements in 1977 at Vancouver (Canada) laid the foundation to establish the Habitat–United Nations Centre for Human Settlements (UNCHS) in Nairobi, Kenya. Within a decade, the year 1987 was declared as the International Year of Shelter for the Homeless (IYSH) by the United Nations General Assembly (UNGA), which led to the establishment of new shelter policies or strategies in 55 countries for the first time. In 1988, the Global Strategy for Shelter to the Year 2000 adopted by the UNGA emphasized on the need for better production and delivery of shelter and new national housing policies and enabling strategies. The second conference on

Human Settlements of 1996 held in Istanbul (Turkey) focussed on sustainable human settlement development in an urbanizing world with adequate shelter for all. It emphasized on the need for solutions to the challenges faced by cities, towns and villages with regard to housing. One of the interesting developments is that these declarations have enormously influenced public policymaking in the field of housing and habitat in many countries. In the Indian context, not only have there been many positive changes in the housing sector from the mid-1980s, but it has also led to the implementation of watershed programmes thereafter.

I had developed interest over this book from the time of my doctoral study in the University of Mysore. My research topic leading to a doctoral degree, which was guided by Professor C. K. Renukarya, Department of Economics, University of Mysore, Mysore, from August 1987 to July 1992, has also nurtured my interest. During this period, ad hoc approaches were dominating the housing sector from the time of the First Five-Year Plan of the country. The academic freedom at the Institute for Social and Economic Change (ISEC) between the period October 1992 and August 2010 prompted me to undertake further research on one of the prominent social infrastructure and social development indicators. I am indebted to Professors V. K. Nataraj, former director, Madras Institute of Development Studies; B. S. Sreekantaradhya, professor of economics, University of Mysore; and Abdul Aziz, professor of economics, ISEC. Without their timely motivation and help, I would have missed the opportunity to join ISEC as a faculty of economics.

The impact of the housing development interventions largely through the social housing schemes was the initial point of my research in the backdrop of this relatively less researched area in India. Incidentally, the first-ever presented official database by the Census of India has helped my understanding of the Indian housing scenario in two distinctive contexts of the rural and urban areas. Having born and lived in a hut in my initial childhood days, I have evinced serious interest to see the precarious housing situation and changes in the housing dynamics over the years in the country. At this stage, similar concerns were shared with me by Justice Shri E. S. Venkataramaiah, former Chief Justice of Supreme Court of India and Chairman, Board of Governors, ISEC, which brought a great deal of enthusiasm to my work. Further, I am indebted to the encouragement of the management and administration at the Institute of Finance and International Management (IFIM) for giving me the opportunity to start my second stint as professor and dean research. My sincere thanks also go to Shri Sanjay Padode, Chairman of the Centre for Developmental Education. Professor M. Viswanathaiah, Director, IFIM, was indeed a great source of inspiration for me and facilitated with all support to finalize this book for publication. My earnest gratitude to him and his secretary, Ms Syeda Almas Bano.

Almost at that same point of time, the concern of the international community on the development of housing for all the homeless people and for the poor in particular in the developing and backward countries was at its peak and coincided with the UN declarations. The expression of public commitment for the development of housing in India in the early 1990s has had international concern and a little influence, with the passage of the National Housing and Habitat Policy (NHHP) by the Parliament of India in the late 1990s. By then, the whole nation was convinced that India's housing problem could not be solved solely by the government or public efforts, but the development of the housing market was indeed necessary. As part of the foundation as well as watershed in the housing development, the National Housing Bank (NHB) was established by the Parliament with two major responsibilities to develop the full-fledged housing finance market and to encourage the establishment of public and private sector subsidiaries to supply housing finance to all the housing needy and the homeless poor. In view of meeting the critical finance for housing across the length and breadth, the NHB has evolved a number of refinancing interventions to boost the finance with loans, subsidies and other packages. These interventions with public support have upscaled the confidence among the housing finance supplying institutions in meeting a principal housing input. At the same time, the increasing scale of India's urbanization during the economic reforms period has prompted enormous migration, owing to the multifarious economic expansion and innumerable economic opportunities in the urban context of the country. This shift has resulted in a number of challenging implications, especially related to human settlement issues like housing—a basic necessity of mankind and housing amenities—a lifeline of all human beings.

This book is an earnest effort to throw light on the overall challenges before the nation on the human settlement front of urban India. These critical challenges have been assessed and examined within the emerging urban set-up, which, in all measures, gives a realistic impression about the national development scenario in general and the settlement environment in particular. The urban expansion in terms of geographical areas and development disparities between the major urban centres and other urban areas have undoubtedly proved expensive. Institutional contours in urban development, households' growth, housing stock by type, nature and distribution of housing poverty, deprivation of housing amenities, growth of informal settlements, solid waste management failure and other issues have been the real challenges. These issues have been highlighted in the book in greater details with the help of public and secondary information. Based on these realities in the urban areas, the book has also offered a number of pragmatic policy implications for effective public interventions in order to bring about effective and orderly urbanization with improved urban life in the country.

While putting these issues into the public discourse, I have received academic and other support from different sources, which I must sincerely remember and acknowledge. I am indeed grateful to Professor H. G. Devaraj, Kuvempu University, to have taken the risk of reading the first draft of this book and to have offered good number of constructive suggestions for revision of the book. I am fortunate to be supported by Shri S. Narendra, former senior manager, GRUH Homes Ltd, with copy-editing work of the book, in spite of his other compelling engagements. The insights of his work experience from the housing market for over three decades were especially the source of improvement for this book. I am deeply honoured that Professor David Hulchanski, director, Centre for Urban and Community Studies (CUCS), University of Toronto, Canada, has consented to write the foreword to this book. My common academic interest with Professor David has bonded our relationship with the award of Indo-Shastri

Canadian Fellowship and my stay in the University of Toronto. They have helped me in this project at different stages, and I am immensely benefitted with their guidance, encouragement and support. It is a matter of great privilege and honour to be with them for more than 30 years. My sincere thanks to my non-biological mother Smt Sharadamma Suryanarana Rao for holding my family's hands when we were in deep financial stress during the family formation and fellowship time.

Several of my dear friends have helped me in sustaining the momentum of the work and in the collection of the latest data on trend and progress of housing and contributions of the cooperative housing movement. Particularly, Shri Siddaiah, IAS, former principal secretary of Higher Education, Commissioner of Bruhat Bangalore Mahanagara Palike, Bangalore Development Authority, and secretary to three different chief ministers, Government of Karnataka, has been a great source of strength. I am the beneficiary of many discussions held with Shri Siddaiah on several issues concerning human settlements for the poor in informal settlements. I am grateful to his constant support to my work. I remember and appreciate the service of Professor A. Somashekaramurthy, former principal, Dr Ambedkar Institute of Education. Without the several contacts he provided in the state government secretariat, I would not have been successful in collecting information. Mrs Pargabha, Dr P. Lakshmi and Dr Gitanjali are great sources of inspirational help for me, especially while collecting information on the new initiatives of the Government of India, like Smart Cities Mission, Real Estate Regulatory Act, Public–Private Partnership (PPP) Model for Affordable Housing and Pradhan Mantri Awas Yojana (PMAY). Dr S. Baskaran, professor of management studies, Dr Ambedkar Institute of Technology, has provided wonderful computational support to this book. He has tolerated all the inconvenience, for which I am grateful to him. Dr C. R. Mahesha, associate professor, Dr Ambedkar Institute of Technology, has been a big help in this work, which I acknowledge with special thanks. Shri M. Mahadeva, chief librarian, IFIM, was instrumental in motivating me to explore the possibility of publication of this book with SAGE. In fact, the credit of suggesting the people concerned in SAGE should go to him, for which I am indebted forever. My sincere thanks to the peer reviewers and their meticulous reading of the manuscript. I should admit that the peer recommendations over the earlier draft have improved the quality of this book. Ms Amrita Dutta, commissioning editor at SAGE, has been a great source of support at every stage of preparation of the manuscript for publication. In all measures, I am indeed grateful to her. I must say that she has been a constant motivator and is an asset to the publishing house.

Finally, my family members have tolerated my non-availability with them as well as my preoccupation with manuscript preparation. My sincere thanks to all of them for supporting me in various ways. Needless to say, I am alone responsible for anything missing and shortcomings in this book.

India's Housing Problem and the Housing Market

1

Housing has acquired a multidimensional importance in any society—be it developed or developing, rich or poor, or rural or urban. It is not merely a physical structure with walls, roof and interior provisions required for the family members, but it also has been a symbol of identity in society universally. The significance of housing is beyond the basic needs that come after fulfilment of food and clothing. Individuals or family members draw strength from their housing unit to undertake economic activities and to take part in political activities at all levels. Owing to these factors, owning a house has been one of the dreams for all the households, irrespective of the size, as part of the settlement strategy and plan. A standard, substandard or deficient housing structure gives happiness to all the family members as they dwell, cook and live together as long as possible. By owning a house, everybody can protect themselves from all the climatic conditions such as winter, summer and rainy seasons. Also, it is a common feature that the permanent or temporary housing structures protects all the belongings of the mankind. Further, housing has acquired the characteristics of an economic good, since the same is being constructed only with the given amount of investment, and its value appreciates uninterruptedly. Similarly, it is a social good and facilitates permanent settlement in a particular place and gives social identity. By constructing a house for self-occupation, the mobility of the family or family members to any other place could be restricted. Housing is considered as a private good if it is constructed by individuals or family members with their own resources and as a public good when it is constructed by public authorities. It is also a welfare good when it is constructed for the poorer sections with government supports such as grants, assistance and subsidies in any form of the principal housing inputs such as land and finance.

Every family dreams of owning housing unit with all the features narrated in poverty—inflicted societies in the place of their convenience and at an affordable cost, depending upon the resource accessibility. Each family constructs or owns a housing structure of their choice, given their access to financial resources—initially, with a limited structure and then gradually to a comfortable house and finally to a luxury housing structure. It has also registered that all the three methods of housing construction—some relatively small in numbers construct with their own land and finance, some in majority construct with the support of the housing markets that supply housing inputs such as serviced land and finance. A substantial number of individuals construct housing units only with government or public support, as they neither have their own capacity nor have access to the input markets. However, from a development perspective, we are not concerned about the first two categories where individuals can meet their housing goals by their own efforts, but we are concerned about the last category, as they are basically poor without a guaranteed income to purchase the principal housing inputs. This category is poverty- stricken and looks for government support to fulfil their housing dream and need. Until the government fulfils this critical need, this category of dole seekers always lives in minimum housing with little or no comforts and without any family privacy. They generally and obviously opt to dwell in deficient housing structures, as they cannot afford to construct safe houses like the substandard units or the standard structure. It goes without saying that it is these sections living in deficient housing that face housing insecurities like building collapse, mostly during the precipitation period. Fire accidents are also very common among huts and similar structures during the summer season. The fact is that these sections would not have undertaken housing repairs at frequent time intervals or would not have replaced the life-threatening housing structures owing to their poor status.

The housing situation is not entirely different in India and is similar to other part of the societies that have been facing the problem of poverty in general and housing poverty in particular. Poorer households or families in India are living insufficiently and with lack of adequate resources and lead a subnormal or uncomfortable life. Because of this major lacuna, poor families generally lead a subhuman way of life with almost no access to most of the basic needs, let alone other comforts. Largely owing to their precarious situation, even after 75 years of India's independence, poor families have failed to earn three square meals a day and shelter. Housing, which is one of the basic needs, is a common requirement to protect oneself and one's belongings and to take shelter during night, rains, winter, etc. It is a social as well as an economic good, as discussed, in the sense that anybody, particularly homeless, needs economic means to fulfil housing. Those who are homeless often resort to live in public places to protect themselves from the changing climatic conditions and external aggression. In fact, it is mostly the poor households that lack a decent roof over their heads and face all forms of poverty and life threats. Perhaps poorer sections are among the first to face destitution, as they cannot afford home ownership by themselves, owing to non-fulfilment of critical housing inputs such as serviced land and housing finance. In the absence of secured housing, India's poor, especially in the urban areas, have resorted to congested and crowded dwelling with other families. Besides dwelling in dilapidated structures, facing all forms of life threats has been the commonest practice of poor families. Economically weaker sections (EWSs) are the first among the poor who generally live in unauthorized settlements like slums and in public housing (Saluja 2004, Sanchayeeta and Deb 2004). Low-income groups (LIGs) are marginally better among the poor, and they mostly live in old city settlements, some in public housing and others in slums. Middle-income groups (MIGs) live largely in old city areas and in unauthorized colonies (Jain 2016). But a good number of them also dwell in publicly built-up housing and in private housing units, as they can afford to do so. These are typical examples of how poor families have been housing themselves in urban settlements in light of the limited public action towards the poor ever since the independence. The housing market, which has been organized from the watershed period and commenced from the late 1980s, has been uncaring for the cause of the poor. These apart, fractured community action in general and dwindling cooperative actions in particular to mobilize the poor for meeting the housing needs are serious concerns. It may not be wrong to say that housing the poor has almost been left in the lurch with all the suppliers remaining indifferent, which in turn has given rise to informal settlements in urban areas of the country with a challenging dwelling environment.

The current housing problem or challenge faced by the poor families in the country is poised between overcrowd and deficient stock, and their incidence is almost in equal numbers. Undoubtedly, the current housing shortage, which has accumulated over the last several decades, is due to supply deficit and defective housing policies. If the supply of new houses was proportional to the total market need, crowd dwelling or housing adjustments would not have existed. Similarly, if redevelopment and renovations of the existing housing units, particularly the dilapidated ones, were undertaken at regular intervals, deficient dwelling and housing threats would not have been the reality. Thus, the management of the existing stock is as important and beneficial as constructing new housing units (Cancellieri et al. 1990). The official information reveals that as many as 26.46 million families are in need of housing units, which is roughly 11 per cent of the total families (Census 2011). A noticeable reality is that the incidence of housing shortage in rural areas is fourfold more than the urban areas. Also, the families facing housing problem in the countryside is more than two times. In absolute terms, 21.86 million (82.62%) families in rural areas and 4.60 million (17.38%) families in urban areas have been hit by housing poverty. It reflects on the fact that the incidence of housing poverty is undoubtedly severe in absolute terms in rural areas than in urban areas. This is mostly because of the relegation of the rural housing issue from the development interventions, due to the urban-centric housing development strategies since independence and the complete neglect shown by the housing market (Mahadeva 2019). The incidence of housing poverty has also not spared any region, including the union territories (UTs), in the sense that every state and UT has been inflicted with housing poverty at varying degrees. Like their small geographical areas, the, UTs have also registered housing poverty to be a little over 1 per cent in total, with 0.27 million families or 6.44 per cent. But the striking fact is that housing poverty is equally poised between congested or overcrowded dwellings and dilapidated or deficient dwellings. If poverty exists in rural areas in the same scale and volume across the two types at 10.93 million each, urban areas have recorded a marginal difference at 2.25 and 2.35 million, respectively. It only compels that poverty needs to be mitigated both by supplying new housing units and by upgrading the existing dilapidated or deficient units. Interestingly, the latter is more cost-effective than the former, as it does not involve the cost of basic inputs like land. Presuming the ground reality that the current homelessness is only of the poor, not only has there been a need to open the eyes of public to step up its interventions to mitigate, but there is also a need to facilitate financial institutional packages for the homeless.

The literature on housing development in the Indian context has focussed largely on the overall housing scenario, housing growth by types and public interventions, including social housing programmes and incidence of housing poverty and distribution. Most of the literature has not attempted to analyse the policy change and approach for the development of affordable housing for various income groups, including the unaffordable sections. Moreover, the pragmatic strategies supported with financial packages of the national government targeting only the poor households have hardly been analysed and reviewed. Therefore, this section reviews and examines how the development of affordable housing strategies is beneficial for homeless families, who have been incidentally the poorer strata of society facing housing insecurity and housing threats. While doing so, it examines all the three major policy initiatives (Pradhan Mantri Awas Yojana-Housing for All (PMAY-HA), Public–Private Partnership Model for Affordable Housing (PPPMAH) and Refinancing Schemes for Affordable Housing) of the national government by analysing every aspect affecting the housing conditions of the poor. The chapter has made use of all the official details and information made available by the official authorities, and the arguments and implications are based on this information.

This book is an outcome of the academic and research works of the author, spread over two and a half decades in higher education. The book has six independent chapters as detailed, including the introduction with an overview of the housing market. These chapters have been carefully designed to reflect the overall situation of the urban world of the country. Each chapter is different in its own way and depicts the emergent picture of the urban areas, the institutional players in the urban growth and public policy changes with a focus on the poor, human settlement issues and degraded environment. Apart from these important components, the book attempts to quantify the nature and type of housing poverty; deprivation of amenities; and prevalence, distribution and management of slums in urban areas. Lastly, the future thrust of the policy and development alternatives for the non-reversible urban context of the country are discussed. As such, although the emerging urban India is not vibrant in terms of its social life, it has been the centre of economic opportunities, high-income earning and a development centre of socio-economic infrastructure in the state capitals and other important centres. Unfortunately, this is generally not the case of the rest of the urban centres (second tier and other cities) of the country. At the same time, these segments of human settlements have also been known for the disparities within themselves in terms of development and deprivation of even the basic amenities and, above all, known as centres of degradation with the prevalence of slums. These emergent features could be termed as development disparities.

The arguments and findings of this work are based on various databases, as presented by public authorities, from time to time, in the country. The comprehensive database on households and houses in general and in the urban slums in particular for the decade 2001–2011 presented by the Census of India has been a prominent source. Similarly, statistical statements related to the cooperative movement in India—Part II (non-credit societies), which have been published by the National Bank for Agriculture and Rural Development (NABARD), are an authoritative source to capture the role of the cooperative sector in housing development. Five-Year Plan documents brought out by the then Planning Commission of India have been extensively used to reflect on the public policies on housing development as well as on the investment in the housing sector by different sources. As the housing market has taken a definite shape from the mid-1980s under the aegis of the National Housing Bank (NHB), its publications of the trend and progress of housing India have been a useful source to capture various institutional dynamics of the housing sector and housing market. Lastly, various policy guidelines of the United Nations Centre for Human Settlements (UNCHS) have been a major source to capture the international influence on the housing policymaking in the country in general and for the poor homeless households in particular. But for these various sources of data, this book would not have taken this shape. Further, the book has five different objectives: (a) to ponder over the urban development and disparities in India in terms of the geographical expansion, demographic growth, urban households, housing stock and access to various housing amenities; (b) to account for the major contours of development in the housing sector with regard to the institutional growth, their operations in response to the housing need, development governance, etc.; (c) to review the housing policies in two regimes of the pre-watershed period of 1950–1987 and during the watershed from 1987 onwards; (d) to assess the dimensions of housing poverty and deprivations of amenities in the regional context and in urban slums; and (e) to propose pragmatic approaches for urban housing development to ensure an effective and responsive housing administration.

By virtue of the socio-economic features and dynamics and development scales, India's society is divided into two segments—rural and urban. The main factor that divides the Indian society is the primary occupation of the people for livelihood—agriculture is the main occupation in rural society and non-agricultural occupation in the urban set-up. The latter one is fully supported with all forms of developmental institutions, presence of government establishments and, above all, existence of the market that produces goods and services for consumption. Contrarily, the former is the pursuit of people on a voluntary basis, which is roughly supplemented by public actions of the state. The latter occupation is also known for housing all the financial institutions, including existence of all forms of markets ever since India's independence (1947). With these advantages in its basket, the urban housing market has never made constructive efforts to organize a full-fledged housing market for the entire country to supply adequately prominent housing inputs to the needy nor has there been a sufficient supply of the constructed homes to the people in need and the homeless families. In the absence of such effective mechanisms, the needy in general and houseless families have been totally left in lurch for roughly four decades of the development planning period. The plight of the home seekers in general and the poorer strata has been a misery, having been the homeless or resorting to dwelling in life-threatening housing structures. This has been largely due to either apathy of the governments or due to a lack of political will to promote orderly human settlements through effective public actions or through a well-organized market in the country. In the absence of these strategies, the limited public actions or ad hoc interventions have been aiming to meet the immediate housing needs of people under stress and in emergency situation for several decades. Obviously, these limited public interventions have not touched even a fringe of the homeless people. Leaving the backward regions and rural areas to themselves or untouched has been a serious setback for orderly housing development of the country, having been focused all the public actions towards the urban areas. The other major setback of the housing development history is that the country had never attempted to understand the housing dynamics of the people till the early 1980s. This is due to the lack of public information and understanding the characteristics and magnitude of the homeless people. However, it was only from the mid-1980s that public information on the housing needs was made available through the census operations. The census operations assessed and brought to the fore the housing realities for the first time, which paved the way for bringing watersheds in the housing sector. Another deficiency is the ad hoc approach employed, which has impeded any serious attempts to understand the problem of housing from its totality and on sustainable perspectives in the development history. Unfortunately, this ad hoc approach has been in practice even to date in one or more perspectives, as the country has not created self-sustainable mechanisms to supply the finished products as well as the housing inputs in accordance with the requirements of the homeless people.

If this is the overall history of development in the housing sector, realization of having the so-called India's housing market (IHM), including the development of the critical sub-markets, is still a distant dream in the development discourse. In this regard, the housing policies enunciated in the late 1980s and early 1990s have expressed the interest to evolve the housing market, although they did not attempt to organize the market professionally. Because the housing market, among many other factors, plays a critical role in ensuring sociopolitical identity in the first instance, it minimizes housing-linked deprivations such as electricity, sanitation and better environment and brings about regional development, especially in the backward regions. However, the public expression of interest and subsequent policy discourses in the housing sector have not conclusively contributed to the development of a long-awaited and well-designed housing market, let alone being effective and inclusive. However, the first decade of the 21st century is appearing to be positive for the Indian housing sector, as there are attempts to contemplate optimistic policies. The policymakers have separately brought out exclusive policies for rural and urban areas to guide and promote housing activities in the respective areas by keeping the housing dynamics of the two distinctive ends in view. Correspondingly, these policies have rightly identified the role of the independent sub-markets as the 'special action areas' to promote housing activities across the affordable and unaffordable sections of the people. This long-awaited development is a welcome change, although it will certainly affect the market in a very limited sense. But leaving the sub-markets to themselves and therefore to a largely unorganized environment is again a serious concern, which calls for policy and administrative corrections at the earliest. This apart, the emerging IHM is undoubtedly in the infant stage of its development according to its functions, and it needs to be more expansive to be effective and to achieve inclusive development in housing. Going by the declaration of the first-ever public policy of the housing sector in India (National Housing and Habitat Policy—NHHP—1998), the housing market is young at 30 years and is yet to take a proper shape and deeper roots across the length and breadth of the country. In other words, this policy expressed its intention to develop a full-fledged housing market to supply not only the final products of housing but also the critical inputs for housing development corresponding to the housing needs of various segments. But in its virtual form of existence, the needed change in terms of its characteristics, functional style and operations is yet to be realized, especially in the backward regions and rural areas. It needs no explanation for the poor and disadvantaged houseless families in the neglected rural and interior parts of the country. Today, if poverty-linked homelessness exists, it is largely due to the uneventful or inelastic housing market conditions, apart from the failure of the market players to supply critical housing inputs adequately and at affordable prices. To make the market more responsive, it is extremely important to highlight the functioning style of the housing market of the country and to call for corrective action and reorganization of the market.

Housing market is a highly specialized market that deals with long-term products and services and caters mostly to affordable consumers in developed, developing or even backward economies. The housing market supplies critical housing inputs such as serviced land and credit and skilled workforce for housing development activities of various housing consumers. Moreover, many times, the housing market supplies finished products like constructed homes to many affordable consumers for occupation and dwelling. The housing market, irrespective of its existence, plays a critical role in realizing the housing dreams of the needy, thereby protecting the consumers from changing climatic conditions and their material belongings. Despite these positive features of the market, it is disheartening to say that the housing market as such largely caters to affordable sections and drops unaffordable sections from its ambit and throws them to limited public or voluntary actions. As the literature identifies (Fallis 1990; UNCHS 1998), the housing market performs three critical jobs or supplies: (a) finished products like ownership housing and rental housing produced by a number of players; (b) public and voluntary players supply low-income housing and subsidized housing to mostly targeted unaffordable sections; and (c) the input market deals with serviced land, affordable finance and skilled workforce as the fundamental requirements for constructing houses.

The housing products and housing inputs are generally scattered across different places with different environments, and according to their locations, the unit prices are determined. In other words, unlike other markets where goods and services are available in a particular place and at a particular price, the housing market stands apart in terms of the availability of products and inputs in one place. The housing market is a critical part of the overall housing sector development of any country, which can be organized or unorganized. The importance of housing market with good access can be further placed with the supply of affordable housing units in arresting the housing needs of the people. An accessible and effective housing market mirrors the housing situation of any nation—affordable housing surplus if an effective market exists, and housing poverty and deprivation if the market does not exist. If the developed nations are taken as an example for having an organized housing market to promote decent but affordable housing, the situation is entirely different in most of the developing nations. By and large, in many countries, including India, the housing market is either non-existent or unorganized. Especially, in the Indian situation, the housing market is a typical example of exclusiveness from its functional style as well as being undeveloped in terms of its regional perspective according to its characteristics and traits. Moreover, the Indian housing market at the same time has been producing housing surplus and experiencing housing glut by constructing unaffordable houses in urban areas. As a result, unoccupied houses, especially in the sky-rise dwelling structures, are high, as the number suggests. It goes without saying that there is a lack of assessment of the affordable needs based on the situation. Unsustainable capital formation and investment in the urban housing supply are other features. Unfortunately, this is not the case for the backward regions since the market has never existed, which is an example of development divide.

Before diagnosing the IHM, it is indeed necessary to note similar markets elsewhere, mainly to know the differences in the Indian market. Like the rest, IHM has three important sub-markets for the supply of principal housing inputs, namely developed or serviced land, finance and labour for housing development activities across all the three sectors—public, private and cooperative. These sub-markets have been functioning independently without any interlinkages between each other and have not been well knitted/integrated or functioning under one roof; moreover, they are not controlled by any single authority. The home builders are expected to independently mobilize the critical inputs from different sources. Each of the major players supplies the input according to their time and convenience. Public sector players (mostly specialized institutions) have been playing the role of an initial promoter, and they have played a critical role in the provision of the developed land for housing and subsidized finance. But they do not supply construction workers/labourers under any circumstances. Given the housing poverty scenario of the unaffordable sections and poor families since independence, the role of public institutions is all the more important, as these targeted consumers are not catered by the private sector/builders. It is a reality as well as an unfortunate truth that the political will to meet the total commitment of the targeted sections has never been exhibited hitherto in this regard. Instead, over the years, the public sector chose to confine itself to meet the social housing commitments of the targeted sections and that too inadequately. Second, the cooperative sector as a community movement, with over a century-old existence in the housing market, is no better than the public sector in terms of volume, frequency, effectiveness and coverage in the supply. The cooperative movement (all-the-way cooperatives, co-venture and flat ownership, house mortgage and house building; Naik 1971, 1976) is not widespread across the length and breadth of the country but is confined to the urban areas even to date. Particularly, the movement has not adequately penetrated into rural areas and backward regions in the supply of the inputs and has left the needy people untouched (NABARD 2006). Third and distinctly, in the absence of an effective supply mechanism on the part of the public and cooperative sectors, the private sector has established its control over the supply of the inputs, covering a wide range of housing consumers largely in urban areas because of its economic prospects. In contrast, the presence of land developers and builders in the supply of serviced land for housing activities is not widespread in the countryside. Apart from this broad imperfect market situation, the functioning style of the sub-markets is not entirely different. Neither the public institutions nor the cooperative sector has achieved functional efficiency; they have also not covered the entire needs of the various sections of consumers and their areas of operations. If public institutions have made some inroads in the supply of finance, the private sector has achieved some degree of success in the supply of serviced land. But the cooperative movement, as the third sector, has not achieved its supremacy either in housing finance or in the supply of serviced land for housing. Even more startling is the crippling nature of the cooperative movement in rural areas, as far as its spread and functions are concerned. Having earned abnormal distinction, the existence of the cooperative sector is in question, as these organizations have been downplaying their roles by under-performing their functions.

Restraining business tradition of the general finance market in the rural and backward areas has been one of the well-known traits from the days of the development planning era and independence. It is more so in the case of scheduled commercial banks (SCBs) even after imposing social responsibility through their nationalization in 1969. However, the strategic intervention of financial resource deployment to promote rural economic activities through priority sector lending (PSL) has brought some respite and achieved limited success than meeting the overall needs and impacting conspicuously. Unfortunately, the operational rigidities and low impact of strategic interventions are the hard realities even to date, despite having a strong (supposed to be) financial system with the SCBs. It can be said that the social responsibility attached to the SCBs through their nationalization has been belied. Second, a majority of the underprivileged sections such as marginal farmers, local traders, Scheduled Castes (SCs), Scheduled Tribes (STs) and women have continued to be the unserved communities of the financial system (RCFI 2008). It can be said that the financial abandoning of these unserved sections have straight away thrown into informal financial operations, which is uneconomic and high costs. If this is the overall situation, less said the better with regard to the housing finance system (HFS). Undoubtedly, the HFS is a by-product of the general finance system, and its functional style is totally unsatisfactory. The system led by the NHB has a very limited impact on the housing needy or shelter-less people (NHB 2010). The availability of housing financial services is not widespread across the needy, and its exclusion is very conspicuous in rural areas (Mahadeva 2009). As a result, the financial exclusion of the homeless has pushed them into informal/doorstep lending for minimum improvement. Lastly, considering the market ruling price as a determinant factor, the housing labour market (skilled and unskilled workforce) is highly unorganized in the country. Because of these traits, the labour component constitutes a very significant portion in the total cost of construction, and it becomes a frequent source of worry to the unaffordable sections. Thus, in a nutshell, the IHM does not function under one designated public authority to supply all the inputs for housing. In addition, the market with unorganized features has many limitations due to which realizing housing dreams of the needy is quite difficult, especially by the unaffordable sections. Public failures have also added their own dimensions of miseries to the already worsened market situation. With this backdrop, the specific features of each market are discussed in the following paragraphs.

Land market: Land is an integral ingredient for house construction activities of the needy—rich or poor and rural or urban. In fact, the volume of availability of land determines the housing development in any place. To be precise, higher the availability of serviced land, higher is the housing development activities across different sections and vice versa. With this perspective, it may not be out of context to mention that if housing poverty of the homeless people exists today in the country, it is not only due to the non-availability of the serviced land at an affordable price but also due to the non-development of habitations in rural and urban areas at regular intervals. Moreover, there is no common land market for the entire country, encompassing all the housing dynamics of the needy in terms of institutional arrangements, scale of development, plot size, affordable price, etc. It must be noted that urban areas benefit from the availability of all the key players in land development—private developers, cooperative societies and public development authorities, and each one of them supplies serviced land for housing at different costs at different points of time. In contrast, in rural parts of the country, the land market does not exist at all, let alone the different players. Promoters and builders, who are the key suppliers of serviced land for housing, are conspicuously absent in rural areas as they confine themselves to core and main urban areas. At the same time, individuals developing land for housing are also missing altogether in rural areas. As a result of this conspicuous lacuna, the housing needy in rural areas must depend entirely on redevelopment of the existing dwelling structure, irrespective of the increasing number of dwellers and additional pressure on the existing in-house facilities. Under many circumstances, the needy resort to farmhouse dwelling, which is generally away from the core rural residential areas. Second, and visibly, the development of new habitations/settlements in the countryside is continuing to be a distant dream even today, despite the need for the same. This situation is largely due to the lack of developers/builders in the backward regions. Community initiative of the people for habitation development is almost non-existent. Cooperative activities in habitation development are unheard of unlike the rural credit stream. At the same time, the local government (PRI), which assumes the role of a public player for the purpose of habitation development, is marred with financial constraints. It only points to the fact that housing development cannot be expected in the absence of a land market to supply the serviced land. Unless these constraints are addressed in rural and backward areas, sustainable and orderly housing development to mitigate the rural–urban differences would be a difficult proposition.

Financial market: Housing financial stress is the main trait in backward regions, and it is a major concern even today. Vulnerable and poorer sections, who have been generally facing housing poverty in the country, especially in rural areas, are the sections that face stressful situations and have to deal with housing financial exclusion. In the absence of a conducive institutional mechanism to promote financial management culture (deposits, savings, borrowings, etc.), people have resorted to various practices for meeting financing needs, including high-cost doorstep borrowing from moneylenders. It is especially true in the case of house construction and housing improvement activities. In reality, the excluded and marginalized people in the backward regions generally employ three methods to meet their financial needs. First, disposal of farmland or other property is the commonest practice for the construction of new housing units or for redevelopment of the existing dilapidated dwelling. This trend is increasing in recent days due to other reasons such as farm distress, non-remunerative income, change in occupation of the siblings and non-availability of agriculture labourers. At the same time, all those landless and homeless families have resorted to social housing schemes—the only source to realize their housing dreams. Second, informal financing for housing (Bai 2003; Jorgensen 1977; Sharma 1989) is the other common source of finance for the homeless families that is not only available at their doorsteps but also at higher costs. The availability of finance from this source is subject to the repayment (capital and interest) ability of the borrowers, which is further determined by the land, other asset holdings and social order. Generally, defaulters would stand to lose the property pledged against the informal borrowings. Last but an optimistic practice in recent days is savings-linked borrowings from the people-led self-help groups (SHGs) and community-based organizations (CBOs). It must be noted that in recent days, there is a shift in the purpose of borrowings from SHGs and CBOs from short-term consumption to medium-term asset development. Thus, borrowing for housing purposes from these sources is slowly catching up, although the volume of finance is meagre to meet housing extension expenditure or to repair the existing houses. But it is certainly not sufficient to meet the total cost of new construction. Because of these reasons, some segments of homeless families prefer to be homeless or resort to poor housing than to be in the debt market.

Labour market: Construction labourers are entirely different from the other labour communities, namely industrial labourers, agricultural labourers or other. Construction labourers generally form a unique category, as they are highly skilled or semi-skilled, which would have been inherited or imbibed over the years/decades but not by receiving formal training to become a specialized workforce. This category of labourers can be classified into specific groups: (a) construction assistants who have graduated to masons and (b) other labourers who have become even more specialized in electrical work, plumbing, carpentry, floor laying, painting, etc. This is a typical characteristic of the workforce, and it goes without saying that each form of labour commands different labour costs, especially the secondary category. These labourers generally work in a group or under a contractor and work either on contract or on piece work basis. Another feature of this category is that these labourers work generally for 8 hours unlike their counterparts who work for more than 8 hours for lower wages. This workforce, having hailed from rural areas, migrates temporarily or permanently to the nearby urban centres where the prospects for construction work are more, and they frequently commute between their residence and work area. It must also not be forgotten that construction labourers have two other features: first, to have changed the occupation (mostly from the agricultural sector) in rural areas, and second, for having largely contributed to migration in urban areas. Attractive wages, conducive work environment (number of working days and working hours) and entertainment are some of the pull factors for the growth of construction labour market, while rural and farm distress, lower wages, underemployment and other factors are some of the push factors (Chandrasekhar 2005).

From the development perspective, the housing market of India can be characterized as undeveloped, unorganized and unpenetrated with regard to the land, labour and financial markets, respectively. The housing sector has been given least importance without developing the supportive market in the country, more so in rural areas. Unlike urban areas, there exists hardly any exclusively designated supplier of serviced land for housing activities; moreover, there have been no attempts to develop one in the devoid areas. Thus, in the absence of such a market, housing activities have been guided by private and voluntary sectors to a greater extent, according to the whims and fancies of the homeless families. Further, the other biggest supply-side deficit is the lack of a database at the local government level, pertaining to the availability of land at their jurisdiction and land-use planning, let alone the development of public land for habitation purposes. The case of the labour market is no different from that of the land market. The construction labour market can be characterized as 'unorganized' in all measures, and the registry of labour details and segregated labour according to their core specializations has the biggest gap. The details of labourers employed, underemployed or unemployed have been altogether missing at the regional level. The absence of such vital information affects not only planning the local and regional development activities but also public asset building activities through public employment interventions in rural areas. Significantly, the housing finance market (HFM) consisting of housing finance companies (HFCs) and other financial institutions such as SCBs, regional rural banks, microfinance institutions and cooperatives is organized under the overall authority of the NHB. The HFM has been functioning in its own operational style unlike the housing land and housing labour markets. It has confined its financial operations to urban areas, covering only the income class as its clientele. It has never attempted to cover the underprivileged sections and unserved ones, especially in backward and rural areas. Non-penetration of the housing financial institutions (HFIs) and non-availability of financial services for housing activities to the majority of the needy are conspicuous features of the HFM (Mahadeva 2008). Traditional financial institutions like banks have been reluctantly operating in rural areas, with all possible operational constraints. The lack of the presence of over a century-old housing cooperatives has not only marred the overall housing development of the vulnerable communities but has also thrown housing thrift—one of its founding principles—into air. If this is the pathetic condition of the most responsible cooperative institutions, then it is less said better about HFCs, which are very important outlets of the HFM. These companies have been mostly urban centric in their operations and are hardly found in the countryside. Clearly, the skewness in the operations of the HFM has resulted in unchecked growth of the informal financial market and informal borrowings for housing from rural moneylenders at a high cost. Further, the development of housing thrift and customized financial products for housing has continued to be a distant reality for rural communities.

The housing market is indeed a backbone and necessarily an undefined institutional mechanism that plays a critical role in the supply of various inputs for housing development. This specialized market assumes importance due to two very important reasons. In the changing economic scenario, which has minimized the role of the government and public authorities, the market becomes an alternate player and assumes unparalleled significance in the supply of goods and services, including housing inputs. Particularly, it is very much true in the case of serviced land for various segments for housing purposes, as public authorities have almost become non-performing institutions. Second, when the role of other player(s), like cooperatives and community organizations, becomes ineffective, the market's intervention becomes inevitable to meet the supply gaps for housing. Because the market is a parallel mechanism to public and cooperative actions, it is difficult to visualize effective housing development without a supply chain arrangement in housing. The housing market is all the more a necessity in the Indian scenario, given the ineffective role of the public authorities in the supply of inputs and for eliminating the existing condition of housing poverty quantitatively and qualitatively (Mahadeva 2005). Undoubtedly, the national housing policies have emphasized to organize the supply of critical housing inputs (land, finance and labour), as facilitating agents for housing, with the existing institutional mechanisms in both rural and urban areas. But this arrangement has a number of limitations. First, it is clear that the vulnerable communities have been made to depend entirely on the government and public action in rural–urban areas than exposing them to the market operations and realization of their housing dreams effectively. To do so, the 'housing market' itself needs to be well organized with two principles—inclusion and affordability—as it happened in many urban pockets. Second, the framework of policies and the public arrangements have obviously targeted only the defined vulnerable groups and left the other housing needs in lurch. Instead, a full-fledged housing market as a parallel mechanism with a number of players (government, public authorities, cooperatives, private sector and individuals) can cover the entire homeless and needy. Particularly, the role of individuals in housing production needs a special mention. This is because only individuals have helped themselves in fulfilling their housing needs, be it a new construction or renovation, without the support of the public authorities and the market. Therefore, unlike the past, there is a serious need to integrate individual actions with the emerging market with tailor-made products in the backward regions. In addition, such a market with customized strategies would encourage all the homeless people to minimize public dependence owing to its ineffective supply. Third, village panchayats in rural areas have entangled with financial stress and difficulties, as they have been wholly depending on upper-level governments for grants and transfers. Needless to mention that the revenue earnings of the panchayats are inadequate to meet their own financial commitments. Under these circumstances, expecting panchayats to develop new rural settlements or habitats would be a far-reaching reality, unless people's participation is strongly promoted and financial grants/transfers are enhanced for adequate development. Otherwise, meeting the total housing needs of the vulnerable communities, if not all, orderly housing development and minimized rural and urban housing differences would continue to be a distant dream. Fourth, given the exorbitant price, economic value, social barriers and the stigma, earmarking of a serviced land or a portion of the floor area for the benefit of EWS/LIG strata of homeless in the private sector housing projects is a difficult proposition in urban areas. Moreover, knowing the growing unethical approval procedures (violations, corruption, favouritism, etc.) of housing projects, the expected compliance by the public authorities is far from the reality. Finally, with almost no presence of financial institutions either from the public or from the private streams and people-led organizations, financial inclusion of the homeless in general and vulnerable communities in particular is next to impossible. Non-participation of rural-based organizations like post offices and CBOs would further distance the process of financial abundance that needs serious considerations.

The aforementioned presentation and discussion suggest a number of plausible policy inputs for public policymaking and to ensure an effective housing market in the country and the countryside in particular. At the outset, a viable and effective market should be developed to promote housing development and to alleviate housing poverty of the vulnerable sections of the society. For this purpose, private sector institutions should be encouraged to cover a wide range of excluded people with their innovative strategies for both resource mobilization and investment in the backward regions to achieve an inclusive market. Similarly, a housing cooperative movement should be promoted and strengthened in every nook and corner of the backward regions to promote thrift for the development of housing inputs. The housing cooperative federations at the state level should take lead in this regard to spread the movement with cooperative education and philosophy, especially in the backward regions. The government should design operational incentives to the private and cooperative sectors in the process of the development of an inclusive market. For this purpose, the following four credible and specific policy inputs can be offered for effective policymaking. First, mere establishment of the financial institutions in the backward regions would not suffice the financial needs of the homeless. Instead, what is pertinently needed is their inclusion strategies of financial operations like savings and loans for various purposes. For this purpose, the financial institutions need to design tailor-made saving options, including products like pigmy deposits on a daily or weekly basis to inculcate the habit of thrift among the LIGs, especially for their housing activities. This strategy gives opportunities to know about the financial behaviours of the customers. At the same time, the thrift promotion not only builds up a resource base for the institutions, but the institutions can also use the accumulated thrift/savings as the basis for loans. Second, governments at the national and sub-national levels should not see lower-tier government or gram panchayats (GPs) as mere outlets of various welfare schemes, including social housing schemes. Instead, GPs should be encouraged to prepare innovative human settlement plans for various sections and rural communities, based on the resources like land and finance at their command. Governments at the higher level should transfer the development funds based on the actual local needs rather than as a ritual or on a half-hearted basis. This would certainly facilitate the GPs to meet the total housing needs of the vulnerable communities rather than on a piece meal basis. Third, strict imposition of earmarking of the serviced land and floor areas in the private sector housing projects by the approval authorities for EWS/LIGs, irrespective of the socio-economic backgrounds, appears to be a reasonable solution to promote decent housing culture among these sections and to ensure social mixing. It is indeed an indirect method to pay back by the private sector, by the private sector having received many public services like connectivity (chiefly roads, water, electricity, etc.). This should be carried out without conceding to pressures and unethical methods in order to allow the private sector to take part in resolving housing issues of the vulnerable groups. Further, monitoring the implementation of this provision by the concerned party is equally important, given the track record of violations by the promoters. However, a significant setback for the EWS/LIGs is the capacity to pay/afford the maintenance and other hidden charges, which needs to be addressed by the promoters possibly through their participation. Furthermore, the success of land earmarking for the urban vulnerable sections and social mixing is entirely dependent on the spatial and financial incentive packages of the governments and local bodies to the private builders and private developers. Higher the incentives, larger is the inclusion process, and vice versa; therefore, given the need and necessities, higher packages are required. Fourth, to augment the process of financial inclusion and availability of financial services to the excluded sections, cooperative housing societies (CHSs) shall be encouraged in large numbers in the backward regions besides popularizing the post offices, not only to promote housing savings but also to lend financial services to housing. This would go a long way in minimizing the role of high-cost local moneylenders. Finally, the development of a database by GPs and urban local bodies (ULBs) about the natural and human resources in their command is the need of the hour. This database is very important for EWS/LIGs homeless households, workforce by occupation, construction workers by specializations and their employment status, financial penetration, financially excluded sections and many other development-relevant aspects. It goes without saying that this database would facilitate local-level development discourse besides helping to prepare development plans.

This book has seven independent chapters, including the nature and dynamics of the housing problem with a detailed understanding of the housing market as discussed already. These chapters have been carefully designed to replicate the overall urban growth and development in the country. The urban areas are altogether a different segment within the country, owing to the scale of economic advancement and development. Each chapter is different in its own way and depicts the emergent picture of the urban areas, institutional players in the urban growth and public policy changes with a focus on the poor, affordable housing strategies as contemplated recently, human settlement issues and degraded environment. Apart from these important components, the book has attempted to quantify the nature and type of the housing poverty; deprivation of amenities; and the prevalence, distribution and management of slums in urban areas. Finally, it also discusses the future thrust of the policy and development alternatives for the non-reversible urban context of the country. As such, although the emerging urban India is not vibrant in terms of social life, it has been the centre of economic opportunities through high-income earning and development centres of socio-economic infrastructure in the state capitals and other important centres. Unfortunately, these centres have recorded a degradation in their environment, with the prevalence of slums and informal settlements. In the case of the rest of the urban centres, human settlements are known for development disparities within themselves, and they are deprived of even basic amenities.

This research has evidently documented the urban disparities in the geographical growth across the different sizes of urban classes in the backdrop of urbanization taken place in the country. A good number of critical parameters are used to capture the realities. They include urban agglomerations, total areas, population by different sizes of agglomerations/towns, and households by sizes and density of the population. It must be noted that the development of urban growth is highly tilted only towards the major centres than across all the cities and towns. This has resulted in urban congestion and supply shortage of even basic amenities apart from homelessness. It is also true that second- and other-tier urban areas have been starving of development, especially in terms of lower-rung towns, which are evidently losing out due to the lack of business promotions, lowest preference of the people and lack of economic opportunities. It is further evident that urban areas of major cities have expanded in comparison to rural areas. Invariably, these disparities have emerged from the growth of the population and its density. One of the highlights in the decade between 2001 and 2011 is the expansion of households at almost equal volumes between the rural and urban areas. While the number of households in rural areas is dwindling, there is an equal increase seen in urban areas due to household preferences and migration by newly formed families. This may be because of a variety of reasons, including economic prospects, discussed later. Another typical feature of the decade is the growth in nuclear families as against the conspicuous fall in joint families, especially in households with six to eight and more than nine members. At the same time, households with three or four members have been gaining momentum. An interesting feature of the decade is with regard to the housing stock, which has facilitated a positive growth in the overall stock as well as the good/standard stock, largely in urban areas. This success is also due to an upgrade in the substandard/liveable stock apart from constructing new houses. However, the disappointing reality is the continued existence of the dilapidated housing stock almost at the same number and volume. This means that the unaffordable poor families have continued dwelling in such structures, as they could not replace/upgrade these structures. It also reflects on the volume of new construction for the poor under various social housing schemes.

Given the emerging urban realities, Chapter 2 discusses urban development realities in part 1 in terms of changes in the urban agglomerations and towns, growth in geographical areas, urban population, households distribution, households and housing stock. It is also attempted in the second part to capture access to housing amenities chiefly drinking water, toilet facility, drainage connectivity, source of lighting and cooking fuel in a comparative framework between the urban areas and urban slums.

The urban housing development has been extensively discussed with four major contours in Chapter 3. First, the role of the oldest player in the housing market 'cooperative housing movement' pioneered by primary housing societies (PHSs) existing for over a century has been captured. It goes without saying that the cooperative housing movement was the only option to realize the housing dreams of the homeless. The movement has existed much before the independence, the introduction of development planning or the organization of the full-fledged housing market in the country. The evolution of the CHSs—primary and apex—their spread across the country, performance in terms of capital formation, lending operations of the movement and houses constructed have been discussed in detail. With over 100,000 PHSs, it is highly noteworthy that the movement has facilitated construction of independent houses and tenements to the order of over 2.4 million units. It is a testimony in itself that out of sheer cooperative spirit, the movement was organized much before the independence. Second, the debate around the what, why and how the HFS emerged is indeed necessary not only to understand the model's evolution elsewhere but also to analyse various mechanisms or practices of housing finance. The commonest practice around the world has been an exclusive market for financing economic activities, including housing activities, in the most advanced and industrialized countries. But for the limitations and deficiencies of the governments and public authorities, an exclusive financing market would not have been popular and widespread. Public financing of housing has been the second commonest method in countries facing extreme weather conditions for protecting homeless people through social housing programmes. The other method has been financing from the market and government on a limited scale, which has been adopted by the developing world. If the government fulfils the social housing commitments, the market at the same time will cater to affordable sections. It is unfortunate to mention that none of these sources have met the total housing finance. Apart from these sources, informal financing for housing is another source, which has been very popular in countries like India, and its modus operandi is presented subsequently. It must be noted that informal financing practices are sustainable not only for the lack of HFS but also due to their skewed operations, besides the limited role of the government. Third, one of the major and positive changes that took place in the late 1980s was the establishment of the NHB by an Act of Parliament. As a subsidiary of the Reserve Bank of India (RBI), the NHB is responsible for developing and supervising the HFS in the country. With its own approved resource mobilization strategy, the NHB has evolved refinancing policies for the housing finance segments, which include SCBs, subsidiaries, private companies, trusts, etc. The last part of the chapter is about the four recent initiatives of the government towards the urban housing sector. Smart City Mission (SCM) with ₹1 trillion expenditure is intended to develop 100 cities. SCM is a special purpose vehicle (SPV) and is intended to improve the urban lifestyle such as decongestion, degraded environment, acute shortage of water, sanitation deficiencies and pathetic housing conditions of the poor. In five different phases of the selection, 99 cities have been selected for the implementation of the SCM. PPPMAH is another innovative policy that aims to address the problem of housing in urban areas on input cost-sharing basis among the stakeholders. The Real Estate Regulatory Authority (RERA) came into being to become the law to protect home buyers and to boost investment in the housing sector at the same time. Functional road map and compliance of the guidelines are seen as safeguards for housing developers as well as home buyers. PMAY-HA is an ambitious scheme with 60:40 fund sharing between the Central and state governments. It includes in situ development of slums, subsidy for individual housing and credit-linked subsidy between ₹300,000 and ₹600,000 for LIGs and MIGs.

Chapter 4 highlights the urban housing policies that were designed keeping in view the poor from the period of the First Five-Year Plan till the making of an exclusive policy for the country as a whole. Understanding the housing development history and the policies assumes paramount importance from the viewpoint of the paradigms or transitions that have taken place. This section essentially captures the policy changes at different points of time in the country. The first stage of the public housing commitment of the government is spread over 40 years from 1950 to 1991. This period can be clearly considered as a 'Period of Adhocism' in the sense that public actions were necessarily in response to a particular situation/need of a particular group and of a given place. In other words, the development approach was not necessarily in response to the total problem of homelessness in the entire country. The development approach was obviously limited since the thrust was extremely limited, and even the public expenditure was grossly limited. In all, the approach that aimed at addressing the total housing problem of all the homeless people of the country was altogether lacking. It must be noted that during this period, housing interventions were made only to different target groups through social housing programmes rather than focussing on the quantitative and qualitative needs holistically. Also, after the creation of state housing boards (SHBs) in the 1950s, the development of industrial housing, slum clearance and rehabilitation, land acquisition, etc., were initiated, but their success was very much limited on account of inadequate public financing. The research showed that apart from the subsidiary allocations for housing during the plan period (I–VII), public financing was evidently dwindling substantially against the overall increase in the plan allocations by multiple times. But the irony was that despite garnering most of the plan allocations for housing meant for the entire country, the resources have not fully met the housing need nor has urban housing surplus been achieved. The other serious lacuna of the period was that the redevelopment of the deficient housing or dilapidated housing stock was never emphasized, as if this aspect was not critically affecting the poor. The second important stage was the making of the first-ever National Housing and Habitat Policy (NHHP)—1998 in response to the United Nations declaration of International Year of Shelter for the Homeless (1987). This policy focussed on three major issues, namely motivate the homeless people to construct dwelling units, encourage housing investment and eliminate constraints in housing development. The NHHP has clearly defined the roles of the Central government, state governments and local governments in housing development. The policy has also declared land and finance as the critical inputs for housing and directed the NHB, Housing and Urban Development Corporation, HFCs and HFIs to mobilize resources from the provident fund (PF), insurance fund (IF) and mutual fund (MF) for housing purposes. The government was directed to offer fiscal incentives and concessions to the people for housing. The third policy development was the influence of the Global Shelter Strategy (UN Habitat 2000) of the United Nations General Assembly on Indian soil. It strongly suggested the member nations to factor population growth, migration and economic development in assessing the housing demand; promote investment in owner housing and rental housing; develop HFS and credit; promote affordable housing; provide subsidized housing for the poor; evolve region-based housing prices for land and rents in different regions; and other factors. These guidelines have subsequently helped in designing an exclusive policy for the urban areas. The National Urban Housing and Habitat Policy (NUHHP) (2007) is an exclusive policy designed keeping in view the urban housing dynamics like living environment and healthy environment. Interestingly, it aims at the creation of housing surplus in urban areas with shelter options with well-defined responsibilities of the Central–state–local governments, banks and HFIs, cooperative societies and the private sector. It has recognized eight specific areas for action, such as land, finance, legal and regulatory framework, infrastructure, employment in the housing sector, technology support, slum improvement and sustainability. Yet a marked difference in the housing policy debate is the strategies pertaining to affordable housing contemplated recently for the first time in the housing development history. Three different schematic interventions under the affordable housing programme, namely PMAY-HA, PPPMAH and Refinancing Scheme for Affordable Housing (RSAH) of the NHB, have been extensively discussed. It includes the intended target groups (EWS, LIG and MIG), financial packages (subsidy-linked credit and interest), purpose of financial assistance (new construction, renovation and reconstruction) and terms of assistance.

Chapter 5 of the book deals with the flip side or development failures pertaining to India's urban human settlements that specifically include the housing poverty according to its types and deprivation of housing amenities in urban India. While doing so, the research has categorically pointed to the fact that the housing poverty has both quantitative and qualitative dimensions. This proves the fact that housing development interventions have neglected the qualitative dimensions, which have currently become an integral and critical part of the housing poverty. It has been attempted to highlight categorically, the distribution of housing poverty in the regional context. The analysis shows that how the case of 13 major states have been the centers of the housing poverty with around 86 per cent of the total incidence of the country. About 7 per cent of the families are facing homelessness in these states, and the incidence is certainly above the national average. It is also true that the quantitative and qualitative dimensions of housing poverty exist almost equally, which calls for the supply of new housing units as well as redevelopment of the dilapidated/deficient units at the same volume of scale. Similarly, families deprived of critical housing amenities (drinking water, toilet and lighting) still form a considerable portion at over 5.6 million or a little over 7 per cent in the country. This indicates that the provision of the housing amenities has a direct relationship with the standard and quality of housing. The present order of deprivation of amenities at the household level is not due to their lack of connectivity but because they cannot be provided with the existing dilapidated dwelling stock. Thus, it needs to be emphatically noted that the housing amenities cannot be provided at different points of time or outside the housing premises but should be integrated within the premises.

Further, the ugliest feature of urban India is the presence of slums or informal settlements formed by those sections that cannot afford the mainstream urban life. It is not only a serious problem but also an important concern from the viewpoint of the dwelling parity and development disparity. This is because the dwellers in such an environment have been living in subhuman conditions by compromising on settlement standards. It is important to note that dwelling in subhuman conditions is very common across the length and breadth of urban India. This research points to the fact that except for the state of Manipur and three other UTs, about 21 per cent of the urban households are living in slums. The incidence is even above the national average in the case of seven major states of the union. The research has also identified 27 cities with one million population (OMP) as the centres of slums and pointed out that about one-fourth of their population live in subhuman conditions. Similar to that for urban housing development, slum development also had an ad hoc approach for 40 years, immediately after the independence (1956–1996). A pragmatic approach for in situ development of slums is being followed only in the last two decades with the draft guidelines of the National Slum Policy (NSP), 1996. It has emphasized the need to provide additional Central assistance (ACA) to state governments for providing shelter upgrading, water supply, storm water drains, community latrine and bath, widening and paving existing lanes, streetlights, sewers, etc. As a follow-up, Rajiv Awas Yojana (RAY) was introduced with three-pronged critical objectives: (a) to tackle the problem of shortage of urban land and housing the poor; (b) to remove constraints for slum development and put an end to the creation of new slums; and (c) to subsume slums with rest of the urban system, after achieving parity in basic amenities. While dreaming to achieve slum-free cities, RAY has come up with two action plans, namely State Slum-Free Plan of Action (SSFPA) and Slum-Free City Plan of Action (SFCPA). Based on the survey of slums, mapping of slums and preparation of the development road map, state governments have to respond to this requirement mandatorily to realize the dream of slum-free cities (SFCs). Interestingly, the official reports have evidently pointed to the positive impact over the slums and the subsuming process. The interesting part is that the research has captured the changing dynamics of the slums between 2002 and 2009 based on the national sample surveys. It has portrayed some ray of hope in the overall improvement of the slums in terms of the quality of housing, declining deprivation of housing amenities, environmental improvement and the dwindling number of slums, if not substantially. Finally, the generation and collection of solid waste is a serious issue in urban India, and the research points to the municipal failures in this regard. It is brought to the fore that over one-third of the solid waste is disposed of in public places, which has dented the image of the urban governance besides causing environmental distress. The survey estimated that solid waste generated to the extent of 37 per cent of the households is not being collected at all. The incidence of no collection is highly conspicuous at more than half of the households sheltered in kutcha structure than in any other types of households.

Chapter 6 discusses the need and necessity of evolving pragmatic strategies in the urban governance in general and in the urban housing sector in particular, based on the findings of the research. It must be noted that urbanization is a continuous process, which can be neither reversed nor stopped and is generally caused by natural growth as well as rural migration. Moreover, urban facilities and advantages have always motivated people to migrate from different rural parts mainly due to push factors like distress. Having accepted these realities, the best way is to respond to the emerging urban affairs and put in place the development governance. Specifically, human-related issues that have assumed paramount importance need responsive and effective administration. It must also be realized that urban and human settlement issues cannot be left to themselves, as has happened in the past couple of decades. Prospective understanding of the urban growth in terms of area expansion, corresponding population and responsive administrative planning is an essential need. In particular, a well-thought-out road map for the development of the second- and other-tier urban centres should be in place to ensure sustainable and orderly urban life. Having characterized the nature of housing poverty, the research strongly emphasized the compartmentalized as well as the need-based housing development approach in the country. The three very important forms of housing poverty (crowded, deficient and pavement) can be appropriately alleviated and eradicated if the approach is sustainable. This will also call upon to give up the hitherto followed approach of supplying only new housing units and embrace the development of the deficient or dilapidated housing units, given the cost-effective advantages. It also proposes to evolve mechanisms to supply temporary housing units to the pavement dwellers in all the urban areas under the administration of ULBs. Further, the chapter has also focussed on identifying the supply-side deficiencies of the critical housing inputs like land and finance. The growing indolent attitude of the public authorities towards the supply of developed residential land to the needy and a number of deficiencies pertaining to the HFS have been pointed out. From the demand-side perspective, mobilization of the poor for affordable housing to make them partners in realizing the housing dream is imperative with the suggested measures.

Given the enormous contribution of the cooperative housing movement in terms of the creation of housing stock, the case for rejuvenating the movement is made very strongly for network advantages. The cooperative way as an alternative cost-effective method of housing production appears responsive as compared to the market forces and the government and public inefficiencies. In doing so, the cooperative method would go a long way, given their tenets and advantages associated. Organization of housing cooperatives among the poor from the apex societies (ASs) is a specific intervention needed as an alternative to the government inefficiencies and indifferent market. Keeping the onset trend of urbanization in the country, evolving sustainable development strategies and inclusive policies are indeed warranted to create an adequate space for all and importantly for the poor. Because urban areas offer opportunities for the prospects of the poor and their linkages with the rest of the income classes, they need to be properly facilitated for their settlements. Although the ongoing strategies and schematic interventions for the poor are highlighted, special emphasis should be laid on additional impetus for the benefit of the poor by partnering with the corporate world to ensure a decent housing environment with all the housing amenities.

Urban India

The World of Development Disparities

2

Understanding about India's urbanization and the corresponding development is of paramount importance from the development point of view, as it has several facets. First, it exposes the changes and patterns of urbanization over a period of time, which in turn showcases the urban face as well as urbanization levels of the country. Second, it manifests the urban expansion in terms of geographical areas, household growth, housing status of the people, urban world within, etc. Third, it unmasks the urban realities, which further helps to design public interventions. This chapter throws light on these issues for public understanding as well as public policymaking to facilitate achieving an orderly urban society. These issues are discussed in two parts for clear comprehension.

PART I
DEVELOPMENT DISPARITIES

Many scholars have opined that India's urbanization ever since it commenced has not only had an uneven momentum (Rao 1983) but is also concentrated in major urban centres like megacities and metropolitan areas (Crook and Dyson 1982). These observations are even truer in the urban growth and expansion in recent times. The characteristics of urbanization between the decades of the 1990s and 2000s have evidently mirrored the trend. An all-round urban growth, especially in terms of number of towns, geographical areas, population and density, is presented in Table 2.1, which portraits three major trends in India's urbanization. First, cities, urban towns and agglomerations being the living places of the urban population have increased in numbers to 5,161 in 2001 from 4,615 in 1991. This means that the urbanization

Table 2.1 *Glimpses of Urbanization in India (1991–2001)*

Urban Class by Population Size	*Class I (100,000 and above)*	*Class II (50,000–99,999)*	*Class III (20,000–49,999)*	*Class IV (10,000–19,999)*	*Class V (5,000–9,999)*	*Class VI (<5,000)*	*All Class*
Number of urban agglomerations and towns							
1991	322	421	1,161	1,451	971	289	4,615
2001	441	496	1,387	1,564	1,042	231	5,161
Change	119	75	226	113	71	–58	546
Total area (square kilometres)							
1991	24,022 (38.92)	6,306 (9.82)	14,177 (22.01)	12,806 (19.90)	5,426 (8.03)	1,099 (1.32)	63,836
2001	30,985 (39.62)	8,827 (11.29)	17,283 (22.10)	14,090 (18.02)	6,193 (7.92)	822 (1.05)	78,200
Change	6,393	2,521	3,106	1,284	767	–277	14,364
Population by size of town (million)							
1991	122.3 (56.67)	28.8 (13.35)	35.3 (16.36)	21.1 (9.77)	7.4 (3.43)	0.9 (0.42)	215.8
2001	178.2 (62.28)	34.5 (12.06)	42.1 (14.72)	22.6 (7.90)	7.9 (2.76)	0.8 (0.28)	286.1
Change	55.9	5.7	6.8	1.5	0.5	0.1	70.3

(Table 2.1 Continued)

(Table 2.1 Continued)

Urban Class by Population Size	Class I (100,000 and above)	Class II (50,000–99,999)	Class III (20,000–49,999)	Class IV (10,000–19,999)	Class V (5,000–9,999)	Class VI (<5,000)	All Class
Population per town (million)							
1991	38.0	6.8	3.0	1.5	0.7	0.3	4.7
2001	40.4	7.0	3.0	1.4	0.8	0.3	5.5
Change	2.4	0.2	–	0.1	0.1	–	0.8
Density per square kilometre							
1991	5,633	3,766	2,040	1,343	1,101	785	2,445
2001	6,337	3,153	2,034	1,381	1,075	813	2,466
Change	704	–613	–6	38	–26	28	21

Source: Census of India (2001), Cities and Town Agglomerations, A 4 Table-2001, Registrar General and Census Commissioner, Government of India, New Delhi.
Note: The analysis over the selected parameters is confined to the 1991–2001 census period, since similar comprehensive as well as compatible data on Cities and Town Agglomerations (A 4 Tables) for Census 2011 and 2021 have not been made available officially.

process has seen an addition of 546 cities and towns of different class sizes. Second, and significantly, except for Class VI towns, all the other sizes of cities and towns have naturally increased in numbers, which is an indication of the people's preference during the two censuses. Like in the past, it may not be wrong to say that Class I cities have continued to be the centres of urbanization (Mohan 1985), as a result of the concentration of decent public and private services and better educational and employment opportunities for skilled and unskilled labour force. In fact, being the most preferred urban places for human settlement in India, Class I cities have increased their number from 331 in 1991 census to 441 in 2001 census—an increase of 119 cities. Similarly, Class III and Class IV urban areas have also registered a phenomenal increase in their numbers, respectively, from 1,161 to 1,387 and from 1,451 to 1,564 between the periods. The net additions have been in the order of 226 and 113 towns, respectively. Further, Class II and Class V towns have registered almost a natural and similar pattern of growth in their numbers at 75 and 71, with the increase from 421 to 496 and 971 to 1,042, respectively. Third, however, much against the established increasing trend, Class VI towns, which are the last category of all sizes, have decimated their numbers and recorded a net decline of 58 towns during the review period. It goes without saying that the declining trend is on account of the lack of socio-economic opportunities in these towns in general, and the same would have prompted upper mobility of the people to other urban centres that have registered better growth prospects. Conclusively, apart from the number of towns and cities, Class I urban areas have posted the highest growth of 36.96 per cent in relative terms, followed by Class III (19.47%), Class II (17.81%), Class IV (7.79%) and Class V (7.31%). Finally, against this positive trend, Class VI towns have recorded a negative growth of 20.07 per cent during the period for the reasons stated already.

Undoubtedly, the census has been capturing and bringing out the critical details of urban expansion, which facilitates and authorizes the government and the urban authorities to redefine the urban areas geographically time to time. Accordingly, the Census 2001 revealed that the urban areas of the country have expanded geographically by 14,364 sq. km, having increased from 63,836 to 78,200 sq. km, owing to the mobility of people towards urban areas for settlement. This geographical increase is worked out at 22.5 per cent in the first instance, although the change varies across different class sizes. Class I cities have alone accounted for 44.51 per cent in the net increase, which is almost twofold more than the national average. Interestingly, no other size class towns have recorded a similar but phenomenal increase. This was followed by Class III cities at 21.62 per cent, Class II cities at 17.55 per cent, Class IV towns at 8.94 per cent and Class V towns at 5.34 per cent. However, Class VI towns—commonly known as very small towns—have lost 277 sq. km in favour of the other towns for reasons stated already. Lack of investment on the part of the private sector in manufacturing activities, lack of promotion of public entrepreneurships by the government and growing unemployment could be other reasons.

Demographically, urban areas have not been lagging behind from adding population to their folds. From the natural population growth as well as from migration, urban areas have together attracted a population of over 70.3 million additionally into their domain. Having attracted over 70 million net population, the total urban population had increased to 286.1 million in 2001, as against 215.8 million in 1991, which is a 32 per cent increase. But the most disheartening fact is that the increasing population in urban areas has not been evenly spread across all sizes of cities and towns. Instead, the increase is more concentrated in the vibrant urban areas. It is evident that Class I cities have attracted as much as 55.9 million or 80 per cent of the net additional population and have become the most sought-after urban areas in the country. Further, of the total population, Class I cities have been housing 178.2 million urban population (62%), with an average of over 40 million. As a result of the biased urbanization, all other sizes of towns had experienced an erosion of the population roughly from 43 per cent in 1991 to 38 per cent in 2001, as is evident from Table 2.1. With regard to population density, India's urbanization process has added 21 persons more for every square kilometre, although the trend is not universal across all sizes of cities/towns. Further, the density of population in Class I cities continued to be the highest in the country, with 6,337 per square kilometres—a net addition of 704 over the 1991 position. This is 2.5-fold more than the national average. In the case of other cities (Classes IV and VI), the increase in density was marginal but still above the average. However, the drop in the density of population in Class II cities was more conspicuous, which could be largely due to the close proximity to Class I cities and increasing interface between them.

GROWTH IN HOUSEHOLDS

A household is defined

> as a group of persons who normally live together and take their meals from a common kitchen unless the exigencies of work prevents any of them from doing so. The persons in a household may be related or unrelated or a mix of both. If a group of unrelated persons live in a census house but do not take their meals from the common kitchen, they are not considered a part of a common household. Each such person is treated as a separate household. (Census of India 2011)

Therefore, the most important consideration in determining a household is the kitchen and meals. The size of a household can vary depending upon the number of person(s), which could range from one—the lowest—to more than nine or even more—the highest. The understanding of a household is further ratified by the National Sample Survey Office (NSSO) that guests and visitors are excluded from the ambit of household, if they stay less than six months within the household, but at the same time, if a person(s) stays away from the household for less than six months, they are included (NSSO 2009). A household as a very significant social institution is a critical unit of consideration in the public sphere, especially in public policymaking and in its implementation to achieve socio-economic well-being of the people. Moreover, in the political economy framework and in making provisions for the supply of goods and services by public authorities, a household and its size play a pivotal role. It applies invariably to the planning and development of a housing facility for homeless people/families and different sections of the population in rural or urban societies. An understanding of the change in the pattern of growth in the number of households is extremely important, as it constitutes significant dynamics in the assessment of housing need and housing supply by the development authorities and agencies.

At the outset, it must be noted that an upward increasing trend in the number of households has been continuing in urban India in particular and the country in general. A net increase of 54.7 million households has been added, which is a little over 28 per cent compared to 192 million in 2001. The total number of households has increased to 246.7 million in 2011 in India, and the same is presented in Table 2.2. It is important to observe a significant change in the households' composition between rural and urban areas and conspicuously in the latter, as heralded during the period. Undoubtedly, households in general and the newly formed ones have been showing the tendency to move towards their nearby urban areas for want of better living conditions coupled with employment opportunities, higher wages, better working environment, etc. While doing so, such households would not have attached any importance to the settlement or resettlement challenges like housing and other living conditions in urban areas. The number of urban households has increased to 78.6 million in 2011, as against 53.7 million in 2001—a net addition of 25.2 million households in the decade. It has increased the share of urban households to 32 per cent from 27.97 per cent at the same time. In other words, of the total number of households increased during the period, urban areas accounted for 46 per cent, which indicates the preferences of the new households. Both push and pull factors could be attributed for the change in the composition of households, especially the newly formed ones. On the one hand, the lack of a decent living environment, adequate employment opportunities and adequate educational and health services could be attributed as push factors from rural areas; on the other hand, a wide range of employment opportunities, high income earnings, availability of social and economic opportunities (if not in abundance) and good educational and health services could be attributed as pull factors in urban areas. Consequently, although rural households increased from 138.3 million in 2001 to 167.8 million in 2011, with a net addition of 30.0 million, the share of rural households has visibly dropped from 72 per cent to 68 per cent. It can be said that households as part of their traits in rural areas have been unwillingly compromising on deprivations of both economic opportunities and social services. In addition, these households are neither prepared to leave behind all their belongings

Table 2.2 *Growth of Households in India by Size and Number of Rooms: 2001–2011*

Households by Size and Room	*2001*			*2011*			*Change*		
	Rural	*Urban*	*Total*	*Rural*	*Urban*	*Total*	*Rural*	*Urban*	*Total*
Total	138.272 (72.03)	53.692 (27.97)	191.964	167.827 (68.03)	78.866 (31.97)	246.693	29.955 (54.00)	25.174 (46.00)	54.729 (28.51)
Single	0.348	0.375	0.355	0.369	0.361	0.367	0.021	–0.014	0.012
Double	0.817	0.824	0.819	0.980	0.955	0.972	0.163	0.131	0.153
Three	1.045	1.272	1.108	1.258	1.592	1.365	0.213	0.320	0.257
Four	1.771	2.242	1.903	2.096	2.637	2.269	0.325	0.395	0.366
Five	1.848	1.923	1.869	1.887	1.850	1.875	0.039	–0.073	–0.006
Six–eight	2.956	2.439	2.811	2.690	2.061	2.489	–0.266	–0.378	–0.322
Nine+	1.215	0.925	1.135	0.720	0.544	0.663	–0.495	–0.381	–0.591
Number of rooms									
One	3.978	3.511	3.847	3.942	3.213	3.709	–0.036	–0.298	–0.138
Two	3.017	2.953	2.999	3.217	3.061	3.167	0.200	0.108	0.168
Three	1.328	1.709	1.435	1.270	1.838	1.451	–0.058	0.129	0.016
Four	0.712	0.867	0.748	0.660	0.926	0.745	–0.052	0.059	–0.003
Five	0.276	0.327	0.290	0.229	0.324	0.259	–0.047	–0.003	–0.031
Six and above	0.359	0.400	0.370	0.252	0.331	0.278	–0.107	–0.069	–0.092
No rooms	0.330	0.233	0.311	0.430	3.07	0.391	0.100	0.074	0.080

Source: Census of India (2001), Tables on Houses, Household Amenities and Assets, Series 1, Registrar General and Census Commissioner, Government of India, New Delhi; Census of India (2011), Tables on Houses, Household Amenities and Assets, Series 1, Registrar General and Census Commissioner, Government of India, New Delhi.

Note: Figures in million and %.

and migrate for better prospects nor willing to face new settlement challenges in urban areas.

The size of the household is generally determined by the members in addition to the external factors, although there exists no hard and fast rule or definition. Usually, a household consists of parents, spouse and children, and the number varies from time to time, ranging from one to nine or even more, as categorized by the census. By using this logic, the size of the household in the country falls in the bracket of six to eight persons, which continues to constitute a majority at one-fourth of the total, although this category has experienced a drop in the share from 28 per cent in 2001. This change has simultaneously taken place in urban areas and rest of the country, though the incidence is a bit large in urban areas. The respective households have had a negative growth to the extent of –3.78 per cent in urban areas, which is more than the national or overall average of –3.22 per cent. The other households that have followed suit rather aggressively are the households in the bracket of nine+ persons, whose growth behaviour is even more conspicuously dismantling. The share of these households, which was at over 11 per cent in 2001, has declined to less than 7 per cent in 2011—a net erosion of 6 per cent in the country, largely in rural areas. A growing orientation towards nuclear families coupled with mobility, quality, freedom, etc., could be attributed for the changing scenario in the household composition. However, despite a dropping trend, households that have maintained a constant growth are the five-person households and one-person households. These households have remained at 19 per cent and 4 per cent, respectively, during the period of assessment, except for a marginal decline of –0.06 per cent in the case of five-person households and a marginal increase by 0.12 per cent in the case of one-person households. Against these two dramatic scenarios, households that have posted a positive growth are the two-person (possibly married/unmarried couple), three-person (possibly couple with a child or a relative or a guest) and four-person (couple with two children or two parents or a child and a parent) households. These households have registered a normal growth rate, respectively, at 9.72, 13.65 and 22.69 per cents in 2011 as against 8.19, 11.08 and 19.03 per cents, respectively, in 2001. The net growth of these households is 1.53, 2.57 and 3.66 per cents, respectively. At this juncture, two very important observations can be made. First, the importance of two-person, three-person and four-person' households has rather scaled up to the extent noted over the years. Second, the net loss in the growth of the six to eight-person and nine+-person households at –9.13 per cent has been compensated to a large extent by a net gain in households put together at 7.76 per cent in the two-person, three-person, and four-person household bracket.

Before an analysis of households' distribution across rooms is attempted, it is indeed necessary to note that all households have sheltered themselves irrespective of the type and accommodation. Adequate space and accommodation have their place in the quality of housing, and it is generally understood that a separate space for various needs would go a long way in achieving the quality of living. Capturing such analysis for a definite period of time not only brings to the fore the changes that have occurred but also reflects on the social compulsions and economic conditions of the people. Keeping this in view, the present pattern of distribution of the households in the country by rooms encompasses three very important traits. First, the households tend to change towards better living conditions with comforts in living space, given the economic prospects. This is true in the case of single-room households that are in majority in the total composition, more so in urban areas. Improved economic conditions have bettered these households. The incidence of single-room households is in the order of 37.09 per cent in 2011 at the all-India level, which has marginally reduced from 38.47 per cent in 2001. By and large, urban India has also replicated this scenario with 32.13 per cent in 2011 from 35.11 per cent in 2001. About 13 per cent of the households with rooms numbering four, five and six and above have also fallen into this category, though the volume of transformation is negligible in the case of households with four and five rooms; however, it is significant in the case of households with rooms numbering six and above, particularly in rural India. In other words, the households (one + four + five and six + room) that have bettered their conditions were at around 50 per cent. Second, the households with constant economic conditions tended to adjust to their given situation, even with additional households/members and have increased from 44.34 per cent in 2001to 46.18 per cent in 2011. Finally, still a good number of households (about 4%) have hardly had any option with regard to rooms but to live in a dormitory-like accommodation. However, a significant aspect is that households with no consideration or regard for the rooms are equally spread across rural and urban areas.

GROWTH IN HOUSING STOCK

Housing stock can be referred to as buildings that are constructed for residential purposes by families/households by using various building materials available within their surroundings, which are either modern (burnt brick, sand, cement, steel, etc.) or traditional (mud, stone, slabs, tiles, etc.) for walls, roof and floor. Based on the nature of the building structure, the total housing stock of the country has been classified into three categories as pucca (standard/good), semi-pucca (substandard/liveable) and kutcha (dilapidated) purely on the basis of the materials used for the construction of walls and roof. A standard/good (pucca) house is one that is constructed with predominant materials such as burnt bricks, galvanized iron (GI) sheets or other metal sheets, stone cement, concrete, etc., for walls and tiles; slate; corrugated iron, zinc or other metal sheets; asbestos cement sheets; burnt bricks; lime; stone; reinforced brick concrete/reinforced cement concrete (RBC/RCC), etc., for the roof. Substandard/liveable (semi-pucca) houses are those with either walls or roof made of pucca materials but not both. A dilapidated (kutcha) house is the one where the walls are made of mud or thatch and roof made of thatch or grass, leaves, reeds, etc. (Rao 1988). Kutcha houses have been further divided into serviceable (solid mud walls but thatched roof) and non-serviceable (walls and roof are made of flimsy materials). These units need to be rebuilt at regular short intervals, as they may not last long and may not withstand climatic changes over a year. With regard to the acceptance of dwelling, it is not that all the three categories are accepted to be inhabitable, but standard/good and substandard/liveable stocks are considered to conform to the living standards. But dilapidated household stock is not considered suitable, as these households can collapse at any time and are not secured for the dwellers. Subsequently, by and large, on similar lines and rationale, housing stock has been classified as permanent and semi-permanent, temporary and serviceable temporary and finally, non-serviceable temporary houses for both urban and rural areas. It may not be inappropriate to say that these three types of houses are being constructed by the needy people depending upon their economic status. Undoubtedly economically well-of people (rich/high income) and upper middle income, urban salaried class with financial assistance constructs good/standard housing units. Against this, economically weaker sections and poorer sections construct serviceable stock initially and keep attending to housing repairs frequently, as and when the necessity arises. Such units become dilapidated if they are not repaired at frequent intervals. Repair or reconstruction is an important intervention in the life of the housing stock, especially the kutcha houses, to upkeep their dwelling suitability. Otherwise, even the good ones can become liveable, liveable can become dilapidated and the dilapidated building can collapse.

The growth in the housing stock of the country portrays a positive scenario in the census period. The total housing stock has increased from 187.063 million in 2001 to 236.063 million in 2011 and has added a net increase of 49 million or 26.13 per cent increase, which is 2.38 per cent less than the growth of households itself (Table 2.3). Three very interesting observations can be noted in the growth of housing stock. First, there is a narrowing down of the growth difference between rural and urban areas, as the volume of growth in the housing stock is almost the same at 50.77 per cent and 49.23 per cent, respectively. Second, there is a declining share of the housing stock in rural areas from 72.20 per cent in 2001 to 67.75 in 2011—a net decline of 4.45 per cent for the reasons already noted. Finally, there is a proportionate increase in the share of housing stock in urban areas from 27.80 per cent to 32.25 per cent during this period. Further, a very significant aspect is the change in the composition of the housing stock in the country. Standard housing units have increased their share in the total stock from 50.21 per cent in 2001 to 53.43 per cent in 2011—a net increase of 3.22 per cent, which is a good development. This change towards building up the standard units is on account of increasing consciousness of the people to ensure decent dwelling, secured housing as well as to withstand all the environmental threats. But the main concern is that the change in composition is highly lopsided or biased towards the urban areas largely due to the availability

Table 2.3 *Changing Housing Characteristics in India: 2001–2011*

Housing Characteristics	*2001*			*2011*			*Change*		
	Rural	*Urban*	*Total*	*Rural*	*Urban*	*Total*	*Rural*	*Urban*	*Total*
Total stock	135.051	52.012	187.063	159.929	76.134	236.063	24.878	24.122	49.000
Good	4.489	6.403	5.021	4.614	6.875	5.343	0.125	0.472	0.322
Liveable	4.888	3.233	4.428	4.729	2.837	4.119	–0.159	–0.396	–0.309
Dilapidated	0.623	0.364	0.551	0.657	0.288	0.538	0.034	–0.076	–0.013
Tenure status									
Owned	9.425	6.895	8.631	9.473	6.916	8.656	0.048	0.021	0.025
Rented	0.363	2.945	1.181	0.336	2.755	1.109	–0.027	–0.190	–0.072
Other	0.212	0.160	0.188	0.191	0.330	0.235	–0.021	0.170	0.047
Building materials for roof									
Grass/thatch/wood	2.773	0.697	2.192	1.995	0.461	1.505	–0.778	–0.236	–0.687
Plastic/polythene	0.037	0.077	0.048	0.063	0.064	0.063	0.026	–0.013	0.015
Tiles	3.756	1.969	3.256	2.873	1.322	2.377	–0.883	–0.647	–0.879
Burnt brick	0.556	0.561	0.557	0.722	0.541	0.660	0.166	–0.020	0.103
Stone/slate	0.732	0.782	0.746	0.885	0.795	0.856	0.153	0.013	0.110
Asbestos sheets	0.984	1.612	1.160	1.593	1.590	1.594	0.609	–0.018	0.434
Concrete	1.099	4.245	2.535	1.832	5.187	2.907	0.733	0.942	0.372
Others	0.063	0.057	0.062	0.037	0.040	0.038	–0.026	–0.017	–0.024

Building materials for walls									
Grass/thatch/wood	1.265	0.392	1.020	1.190	0.270	0.896	–0.075	–0.122	–0.124
Plastic/polythene	0.026	0.035	0.029	0.033	0.033	0.033	0.007	–0.002	0.004
Mud/unburnt brick	3.972	1.278	3.219	3.046	0.928	2.369	–0.926	–0.350	–0.850
Wood	0.093	0.088	0.092	0.075	0.052	0.068	–0.018	–0.036	–0.024
Stone	1.046	0.673	0.941	1.368	1.500	1.411	0.322	0.827	0.470
Asbestos sheets	0.037	0.135	0.065	0.046	0.085	0.058	0.009	–0.050	–0.007
Burnt brick	3.421	6.802	4.367	4.004	6.348	4.755	0.583	–0.454	0.388
Concrete	0.117	0.574	0.244	0.174	0.725	0.349	0.057	0.151	0.105
Others	0.023	0.023	0.023	0.064	0.056	0.061	0.041	0.033	0.038
Building materials for floor									
Mud	7.225	1.746	5.711	6.264	1.223	4.652	–0.961	–0.523	–1.059
Wood/bamboo	0.077	0.040	0.067	0.075	0.036	0.062	–0.002	–0.004	–0.005
Brick	0.202	0.301	0.230	0.225	0.242	0.231	0.023	–0.059	0.001
Stone	0.445	0.910	0.575	0.615	1.225	0.810	0.170	0.315	0.235
Cement	1.809	4.831	2.651	2.424	4.583	3.114	0.615	–0.248	0.463
Mosaic/floor tiles	0.218	2.048	0.730	0.373	2.594	1.083	0.155	0.546	0.353
Others	0.024	0.069	0.036	0.024	0.097	0.048	0.00	0.028	0.012

Source: Census of India (2001), Tables on Houses, Household Amenities and Assets, Series 1, Registrar General and Census Commissioner, Government of India, New Delhi; Census of India (2011), Tables on Houses, Household Amenities and Assets, Series 1, Registrar General and Census Commissioner, Government of India, New Delhi.

Note: Figures in million and %.

of affordable housing finances (AHF). The change in the share of standard housing units has increased by 4.72 per cent in urban areas than 1.25 per cent in rural areas, which is more than the national average. Corresponding to the increasing stock in the standard stream, liveable stock's share has declined by 3.09 per cent, from 44.28 per cent to 41.19 per cent in both rural and urban areas. This only indicates that apart from new construction, an improvement in the liveable housing stock has also contributed to this positive change. However, the positive impact in the standard housing stock and the corresponding erosion of the liveable housing stock have hardly had any impact on the volume and share of the dilapidated housing stock, which is generally the housing option of the poorer sections. These houses would have become dilapidated either for want of major repairs or requiring total replacement, which could not have been afforded by the poor dwellers. Consequently, the dilapidated housing stocks (also known as distress housing and life-threatening stock), which constituted at 5.51 per cent in 2001, have remained at 5.38 per cent in 2011, with only a marginal reduction of 0.13 per cent in the total. While the incidence of dilapidated housing units is pegged at 0.34 per cent in rural areas (from 6.23% to 6.57%), the same has registered improvement to the extent of 0.76 per cent for reasons stated already.

The tenure status of the housing stock by and large indicates a standstill position in the country, almost without any noticeable change between the owner and the rental segments. However, the 'other segment' that largely includes the community housing stock has performed somewhat better. The owner-occupied housing stock continues to hold the nerve at 87 per cent, and similarly, the rental housing stock has maintained itself at a little more than 11 per cent in total; however, the other stock has grown to more than 2 per cent. Table 2.3 further indicates that the ownership stock has marginally increased in both rural and urban areas, as against the declining trend in the rental stock, which is again a positive trend that rental dwellers are becoming homeowners, which may be for better economics. But with regard to other stocks, rural and urban areas have registered divergent positions, in the sense that the stocks have eroded in rural areas but swollen in urban areas. The net increase in the other stock segment in urban areas is in the order of 1.70 per cent as against the overall average of 0.47 per cent. This indicates an active participation of community organizations in urban areas in the creation of housing wealth, which is a positive development.

The quality/standard of the residential building is generally guided by the building materials used for the construction of walls, roof and floor. By using standard building materials, the dwelling-related insecurities can be eliminated for a very long period, apart from ensuring that the residential building withstands all the threats, including earthquakes, jolts, and climatic variations. Also, more importantly, living standard and social standing are ensured with the use of standard residential materials to construct houses, especially in rural areas, besides ensuring higher longevity of the building.

In other words, use of the standard building material ensures quality residential buildings and if the standard materials are sacrificed either for walls or for roof, then the buildings would certainly be substandard. If standard materials are not used, the construction would amount to sacrificing quality. In the Indian situation, three models of construction or housing pattern can be observed: first, using standard building materials for the entire building (walls, roof and floor); second, using standard building materials either for walls or for roof and not for both; and, finally, using customized or local materials for building/structure construction. It goes without mentioning that if the first and second options are obviously the choices of high-income groups (HIGs) and MIG, the third option is generally the choice of the poor because of the cost factors of construction. One of the notable factors in the last decade is the changing face of the housing sector and the gradual realization of the importance of using standard building materials in the construction of residential houses in the country, including the countryside. As a result, there has been a gradual shift towards using standard materials as well as minimizing the dependence on local building materials and thereby becoming more conscious about the quality of residential houses that provides safety to the dwellers throughout the year. It can be observed in Table 2.3 that burnt bricks are being used in large scale for the construction of walls of the residential buildings, more so in rural areas, which is followed by stones and concrete. This has resulted in a declining trend in the use of mud, unburnt bricks, grass, thatch/wood and even asbestos sheets. Similarly, for the roof of residential buildings, standard materials such as concrete, asbestos sheets and slates are being used by a large number of home builders.

Buildings with concrete roofs have increased to around 30 per cent in the country, with over 18 per cent in rural areas and around 52 per cent in urban areas. The stock with asbestos sheet buildings is prevalent on the same scale at about 16 per cent in both rural and urban areas, and buildings with slates increased to around 9 per cent. Proportionately, the use of local building materials for the roof of buildings has eroded during the same period. However, for the floor in residential buildings, the success is far from satisfaction in the sense that mud flooring continues to constitute the majority, despite the increasing use of standard building materials for walls and roof. Buildings with mud flooring, which stood at over 57 per cent in 2001, have declined to about 47 per cent in 2011. The net decline in residential buildings with mud flooring is in the order of over 10 per cent, and, importantly, this change has taken place across the country, apart from being more pertinent in rural areas than in urban areas. Further, in addition to the dominant feature of mud flooring, the growing use of other materials for flooring, particularly cement, has been increasing, which is evident from Table 2.3. Residential buildings with cement flooring have increased to over 31 per cent in 2011 as against 26.51 per cent in 2001. Similarly, the use of mosaic/tiles has increased from 7.30 per cent to 10.83 per cent, and stone flooring has increased from around 6 per cent to over 8 per cent. Although rural areas have increasingly conformed to the changing national trend in the use of cement and mosaic/tiles for flooring, the urban trend appears to be quite different. The use of cement for flooring in residential buildings has reduced, and the preference is towards the use of mosaic/tiles and even other materials that generally include granites. However, and interestingly, the use of wood, bamboo and bricks for flooring is still in practice for reasons known to the users. It can be said that the incidence of using such materials for flooring has been intact without any change, especially in rural areas. At the same time, the use of wood, bamboo and bricks for flooring is reduced in urban areas if not drastically.

PART II
DEPRIVATION OF AMENITIES

Good housing, apart from being constructed with standard building materials, also encompasses provision of drinking water, lighting, sanitation, drainage connectivity, proper fuel for cooking and many other facilities (UN Habitat 1996). Housing stock with these facilities always leads to hassle-free living conditions and thereby promotes good health for the dwellers. The importance and development of these facilities within the housing unit or within the housing premises do not need to be emphasized, as each of the facility is a critical requirement of the family members. But what is critically needed is the convergence of capital investment of the amenities and the cost of house construction both by the needy people and the state that implements social housing schemes for the poor and disadvantaged sections of society. Only then can equity in the attainment of fulfilling the housing amenities can be achieved. By tradition, urban India accesses drinking water—a lifeline requirement of the people—by two means: (a) traditionally depending on wells, tanks, ponds, rivers, springs and canals and (b) development intervention of government (state/municipalities/local self-government) by public investment through pipes/taps/hand pumps/tube wells, etc. The first source is the community-based method that has been in vogue for centuries out of necessity or compulsion with least or no cost, although these sources have been catering only to a statistically insignificant number of families in urban areas. The other reality is that these sources have been hardly found in urban environment, whereas, in its counterpart, these sources are the lifeline although they are subjected to contamination and pollution. It goes without saying that the lack of development in remote places is the obvious reason for depending on the traditional source. The other method has been adopted by the state, as one of its responsibilities in order to meet the basic needs and to achieve a higher standard of living in both rural and urban areas. A striking feature is that over the years, the dependence on the first source altogether has declined from 22.08 per cent to 14.50 per cent, largely on account of wells that have dried up owing to an increasing number of tube wells and hand pumps in the country (Table 2.4). The declining pace of the wells as a source of drinking water is more conspicuous in rural areas, though the source is almost intact in urban areas. This

Table 2.4 *Household Access to Amenities in India: 2001–2011*

Households by Size and Room	2001			2011			Change		
	Rural	Urban	Total	Rural	Urban	Total	Rural	Urban	Total
Drinking water by source									
Tap*	24.28	68.66	36.70	30.81	70.63	43.54	6.53	1.97	6.84
Well**	22.23	7.71	18.17	13.31	6.15	11.02	–8.92	–1.56	–7.15
Hand pump	43.20	16.24	35.66	43.64	11.86	33.48	0.43	–4.38	–2.18
Tube well	5.74	5.11	5.56	8.28	8.90	8.48	2.54	3.79	2.92
Spring	0.93	0.25	0.74	0.71	0.16	0.53	–0.22	–0.09	–0.21
River/canal	1.33	0.19	1.01	0.84	0.17	0.63	–0.49	–0.02	–0.38
Tank/pond	1.28	0.31	1.01	1.06	0.38	0.84	–0.22	0.07	–0.17
Other	1.01	1.53	1.15	1.35	1.75	1.48	0.34	0.22	0.33
Toilet facility									
Water closet	7.11	46.12	18.03	19.43	72.57	36.42	12.32	26.45	18.39
Pit latrine	10.30	14.60	11.50	10.54	7.10	9.45	0.24	–7.50	–2.05
Other latrine	4.51	13.00	6.88	0.76	1.68	1.05	–3.75	–11.32	–5.83
No latrine	78.08	26.28	63.59	69.27	18.65	53.08	–8.81	–7.63	–10.51
Drainage connectivity									
Closed	3.91	34.50	12.46	5.75	44.50	18.14	1.84	10.00	5.68
Open	30.27	43.36	33.93	31.01	37.26	33.01	0.74	–6.10	–0.92
No drainage	65.82	22.14	53.61	63.24	18.24	48.85	–2.58	–3.90	–4.76

Source of lighting									
Electricity	43.52	87.59	55.85	55.30	92.67	67.25	11.78	5.08	11.40
Kerosene	55.61	11.61	43.30	43.16	6.48	31.43	–12.45	–5.13	–11.87
Solar energy	0.28	0.24	0.27	0.55	0.22	0.44	0.27	–0.02	0.17
Other oil	0.11	0.07	0.10	0.24	0.12	0.21	0.13	0.05	0.11
Any other	0.16	0.15	0.16	0.22	0.17	0.20	0.06	0.02	0.04
No lighting	0.32	0.34	0.32	0.53	0.34	0.47	0.21	0.00	0.15
Cooking fuel by source									
Fire wood	64.10	22.74	52.53	62.50	20.01	48.98	–0.16	–2.73	–3.55
Crop residue	13.10	2.12	10.03	12.33	1.45	8.85	–0.77	–0.67	–1.18
Cow dung	12.80	1.98	9.77	10.88	1.72	7.95	–1.92	–0.26	–1.82
Charcoal	1.07	4.58	2.05	0.77	2.89	1.45	–0.30	–1.69	–0.60
Kerosene	1.62	19.16	6.53	0.73	7.53	2.90	–0.89	–11.63	–3.63
LPG	5.67	47.96	17.50	11.40	65.03	28.55	5.73	17.07	11.05
Electricity	0.13	0.31	0.17	0.07	0.15	0.10	–0.06	-0.16	–0.07
Biogas	0.47	0.37	0.44	0.41	0.41	0.41	–0.06	0.04	–0.03
Others	0.83	0.18	0.64	0.62	0.20	0.48	–0.21	0.02	–0.16
No cooking	0.23	0.60	0.34	0.29	0.51	0.33	0.06	–0.54	–0.01

Source: Census of India (2001), Tables on Houses, Household Amenities and Assets, Series 1, Registrar General and Census Commissioner, Government of India, New Delhi; Census of India (2011), Tables on Houses, Household Amenities and Assets, Series 1, Registrar General and Census Commissioner, Government of India, New Delhi.

Notes: * includes treated as well as untreated sources; ** includes covered and uncovered sources; figures in %.

shift has resulted positively in terms of the increasing scale of coverage of the people under the second method from 77.92 per cent to 85.50 per cent, though it is still far away in terms of total coverage. The achievement is significant with regard to drinking water supplied through taps, which is a principal strategy of government intervention in the entire country. Incidentally, taps have come to be known as a status symbol of rural households, as their access is within the premises and have been preferred over other sources like hand pump and tube wells, which are located outside the housing premises. The household connection to the taps has increased from 37 per cent to about 44 per cent in the country, and the rural access of the households to the taps has jumped from 24 per cent to 31 per cent in rural areas. However, the disappointing reality is that the gaps in the coverage of households by taps between the rural and urban areas are quite conspicuous. The same can be further reflected as compared to only a quarter in urban areas, over two-thirds of the households in rural areas have been deprived of tap water supply and heavily depend on hand pumps (44%), followed by open wells (13%) and tube wells (over 8%).

India is one of the countries with the dubious distinction of not developing a proper method for the disposal of human excreta. Historically and alternatively, open defecation has been in vogue for centuries, especially in rural areas, due to lack of access to decent provision (household latrine). The situation has not improved entirely in urban areas, but open defecation is also prevailing near open drainages, storm drainages and other areas, although the incidence varies. The development efforts of household toilets by the governments and local bodies have brought some respite to the incidence of open defecation from the 1990s. These efforts have not only kindled the mindset to change but have also facilitated transformation towards the development of household toilets through various methods in both rural and urban areas. As a result, three methods (water closet, soil pit and others) of household latrines have been in vogue with varying scales of success in society. Between the three methods, water closet is found to be officially the most preferred one because of its convenience, hygiene, and availability within homes. The number of households having access to water closet method of household toilet has doubled from 18 per cent in 2001 to 36 per cent in 2011.

Interestingly, the achievement in rural areas has been eye-catching, as around 20 per cent of the households have attained having water closet toilets, which is more than 2.5-fold at 7 per cent in 2001 and over the national average. The urban areas have also significantly enhanced their access to water closet toilets to over two-thirds of the households (72%) over the years. The second most preferred method is soil pits, which is considered simple, cost-effective and easily accessible. Because households have now moved towards water closets, the significance of the household soil pits has been eroding in the country and more conspicuously in urban areas. But much against this trend, the soil pit method with home connectivity continues to be an important means for defecation. But what is significant to note is that the other form of latrine method (possibly community) is drastically disappearing throughout the country; this may be largely owing to the problem of accountability, maintenance, distance from home, security of women, etc. Despite the three practices, the problem of open defecation is prevalent across the country, as the development interventions are not adequate enough to cover the entire population. It is disheartening to say that over half of the households or population have been deprived of a decent defecation facility, which calls for a mission-oriented and time-bound public intervention towards the total coverage, although the incidence is declining.

Household connection to drainage is as important as availability of water within homes and any other facilities, given the associated environmental challenges. Drainage connectivity always ensures easy flow of household wastewater, which would otherwise result in waterlogging around the residential premises that further leads to the development of pits, potholes, filthy environment, etc. To ensure a free flow of household wastewater, public interventions over the years have resorted to two methods of development: (a) open drainage system and (b) closed drainage system. Together, the country has so far achieved covering a little more than half of the total households—33 per cent with open drainage and 18 per cent with closed drainage connection systems. This leaves a greater challenge to the development efforts of the state. Between the period of analysis, it is significant to note that there seems to be development slackness in the entire country, as the households' drainage connectivity is very tardy at less than 5 per cent.

Especially, rural India achieved only a negligible scale of progress with a net coverage of only 3 per cent as the household drainage connectivity increased from 34 per cent to 37 per cent. That apart, public efforts for the transformation of open drainage into closed drainage in the countryside are altogether far from satisfactory with only 2 per cent achievement. However, in urban areas, there has not only been a marked change in the coverage of households with drainage connection from 78 per cent to 82 per cent during the period, but a significant change has also occurred in the development of a closed drainage system from 35 per cent to 45 per cent, with a corresponding decline in the open drainage system from 43 per cent to 37 per cent. Finally, the deprivation of drainage facility to the households is a matter of concern in the country, given the non-coverage of the households. The deprivation, which was in the order of 54 per cent in 2001, was marginally reduced by around 5 percentage point at 49 per cent, with a varied scale in rural and urban areas. In rural areas, the net reduction in deprivation was around 2.58 percentage points (from 66% to 63%), and the same was around 4 percentage points in urban areas (from 22% to 18%).

Access to housing amenities for slum households is as important as other urban settlements from the viewpoints of equity, promotion of good health, and eliminating deprivation. Slums being the settlements of largely poor people and labour class, they have been starving for the development of socio-economic infrastructure. The various scales of development achievements, as detailed in the preceding section, clearly indicate that there have been a series of endeavours to marginalize the development gaps between the urban slums and the rest of the urban areas. The marginalization of the development gaps is achieved in a few cases, as shown by the official data. The first and foremost parameter is the housing stock, which can be categorized into three types—permanent (standard), semi-permanent (substandard) and temporary (dilapidated). Between the slums and other urban areas, there has been a difference of 8 per cent in the composition of permanent stock. The former has 78 per cent of permanent housing stock, as against 87 per cent in the latter. The present order of permanent stock in slums has been on account of construction of standard housing units, on the one hand, under public-assisted interventions, and upgrading of the existing substandard units, on the other hand.

The argument with regard to the increment in the standard housing units can be further substantiated by the National Sample Survey data (65th round) that because of over 9 per cent increase (from 47.50% to 57%), the total substandard and dilapidated housing stocks have declined by 6 per cent and 3.50 per cent, respectively. Similarly, the incidence of the substandard and dilapidated stock in the slums together constitute to around 22 per cent over the rest of urban areas, which is at 13 per cent. Semi-permanent housing units, which constitute 35 per cent, have scaled down to 29 per cent and temporary units from 17.5 to 14 per cent. Second, the situation with regard to access to drinking water is very encouraging for about 65 per cent of slums and urban households, as they have been covered with treated water (Table 2.5). Interestingly, the other quarter of the households has been depending on the supply of untreated water through unprotected sources. Water from hand pumps, bore wells and other sources cover a good number of households, but in reality, it can be considered as untreated. There is a considerable coverage of slum dwellers with drinking water supply through sources such as taps, hand pumps and tube wells (85%) as compared to 82 per cent in other urban areas. The rest have no alternative but to depend on untreated water sources like open wells and other sources, whose quality is always questionable. Third, being economically good in nature and given its contribution to domestic economic activities, the necessity of household connection to energy hardly needs any emphasis. Electricity being the main source of energy, its access by urban and slum households has been commendable (i.e., over 90%). At the same time, the other sources of energy have also continued to cater to the need of those, particularly who have no access to electricity. It is important to note that kerosene, as the second most accessible energy in an urban set-up, has been the source of lighting of over 6 per cent of urban households and 8 per cent of slum dwellers. Although the rest have resorted to other sources of energy, households without any means of lighting accounted for less than 1 per cent. It goes without saying that these households could not have had access to electricity largely on account of unaffordable installation and consumption charges. However, an amazing reality of the slums has been that most of the deprived households have resorted to unauthorized electricity connections from street lights.

Table 2.5 *Development Gaps in the Housing Amenities between the Urban Areas and Urban Slums: 2011 (%)*

S. No.	*Development of Housing Amenities*	*Urban Areas*	*Urban Slums*	*Difference (+ or –)*
A	Access to drinking water			
1	Treated tap water	61.3	65.3	04.0
2	Untreated water	08.3	08.7	00.4
3	Covered well	01.8	00.8	–01.0
4	Uncovered well	05.0	02.3	–02.7
5	Hand pump	11.7	12.7	01.0
6	Bore well	09.2	07.6	–01.6
7	Others	02.4	02.7	00.3
B	Access to energy			
1	Electricity	93.1	90.5	–02.6
2	Kerosene	06.1	08.2	02.1
3	Solar energy	00.2	00.3	00.1
4	Other oil	00.1	00.2	00.1
5	Any other	00.2	00.2	00.0
6	No lighting	00.3	00.5	00.2
C	Access to kitchen and fuel			
1	Has kitchen	82.0	67.3	–14.7
2	Does not have kitchen	17.5	32.1	14.6
3	No cooking	00.5	00.5	00.0
4	LPG	67.9	51.3	–16.6
5	Kerosene	06.2	14.0	07.8
6	Others	24.7	33.3	08.6
D	Access to sanitation			
1	Flush latrine	75.7	57.7	–18.0
2	Pit latrine	07.3	06.2	–01.1
3	Night soil to open drain	01.1	01.6	00.5
4	Service latrine	00.5	00.6	00.1
5	Public latrine	04.1	15.1	11.0
6	Open defecation	11.3	18.9	07.6

S. No.	*Development of Housing Amenities*	*Urban Areas*	*Urban Slums*	*Difference (+ or –)*
E	Access to bathing			
1	Bathroom	79.8	66.6	–13.2
2	Bathroom without roof	08.4	14.5	06.1
3	No bathroom	11.8	19.0	–08.8
F	Access to drainage			
1	Closed drainage	46.1	36.9	–09.2
2	Open drainage	35.8	44.3	08.5
3	No drainage	18.8	18.8	00.0

Source: Census of India (2011), Housing Stock, Amenities and Assets in Slums, India Series 1. Registrar and Census Commissioner, India.

Fourth, access to kitchen is as important as any other housing amenities in urban areas because kitchen facilitates cooking at home, eating together, socialization at the household level, etc. It is astonishing to note that one-fourth of the slum households do not have this important space in their residential houses, which is twice the deprivation level of the rest of the urban areas. It is not only the kitchen that is important, but the type of fuel one uses cooking also matters. Although liquefied petroleum gas (LPG) has made the life of 51 per cent of the slum households easier, which is about 17 per cent lesser than the other households, kerosene use for cooking in slums is higher comparatively. This also means that next to LPG and kerosene, other fuels have also been playing an important role in meeting the cooking requirements of the urbanites. Fifth, the other important concern in which slums as well as non-slum urban areas have been facing a pitiable situation is with regard to sanitation (latrine) facility. A harsh reality has been that open defecation still prevails in varied degrees as access to a decent latrine system is deprived to many urbanites and slum dwellers, in particular. Over 11 per cent of urbanites have been by and large deprived of a decent latrine system, and they have resorted to open defecation. In this regard, slum dwellers can be classified into two types: one with access to latrine, irrespective of the source, and the other with no access to latrine, which has left these dwellers with no other choice but to embrace open defecation. What is officially evident is that slum dwellers with access to latrine facility have increased from 66 per cent to 80 per cent, and as a result, the incidence of open defecation due to non-availability of latrine facility has reduced from 34 per cent to 20 per cent, which is a phenomenal achievement. The community source has covered more than half of the slum dwellers, against 37 per cent in 2002. The 'other' sources (possibly pay-and-use initiative) have covered additionally 12 per cent of the slum dwellers, upscaling to over 16 per cent from 4 per cent. Finally, sharing (between households) latrine arrangement has declined significantly from 12.5 per cent to 8.7 per cent.

Sixth, a separate corner for shower (bathroom) is always a comfort for the low-income households and more so for the slum households. It is not only an indicator of decent dwelling in urban areas but also a matter of dignity, especially for women. In this regard, it is heartening to note that around 80 per cent of urban households and about two-thirds of slum households have attained this important comfort with bathroom, though some of them have been facing discomfort on account of the facility being open to sky or having no roof. However, as compared to the level of deprivation (i.e., roughly 12%) in urban areas, the incidence of deprivation of bathroom in slums is 19 per cent, which is far greater than that in urban areas. Further, slums and unfavourable environmental conditions are synonymous in the Indian context and are interchangeably used. In fact, slums have the dubious distinction of being the centres of degraded environmental conditions. Public initiatives to improve the conditions though have brought some respite in slums, but much is yet to be achieved. One such environmental issue is that connectivity needs to be developed between bathrooms and the drainage system, which has a direct bearing on the degraded environmental situation. The development performance in slums has been very low as compared to that in the rest of urban areas. In both closed and open drainage systems, slums have lagged far behind the other urban areas by more than 10 percentage point difference. But the startling reality is that roughly 19 per cent of the households have been totally deprived with no drainage connectivity at all in urban areas, including slums.

3

Housing Finance System and Major Development Contours

This chapter portrays the major developments which have taken place in the development history of housing of the country. It identifies and presents four major contours which have contributed to the housing development of the urban areas. It can also be said that, but for these contours, urban India could not have experienced the present level of housing development. Incidentally, urban areas being the first experimental place as compared to their counterpart, most of these contours have commenced their functioning and to a larger extent focussed on business prospects. Housing finance being the first critical input for housing development, this chapter attempts to discuss housing finance in greater detail in the backdrop of the practices prevailing elsewhere, including India's housing finance mechanisms under the aegis of NHB. The finance system was founded after independence in the late 1980s, with a Parliament legislation in 1987 to be precise. This legislation not only gave birth to the NHB but also led to the development of a financing system for housing in the country. The NHB has been striving hard to rope in several players from public and private sectors to supply affordable finance for housing activities. Therefore, the role of the NHB cannot be undermined since it has occupied a pivotal place in the success achieved to date in housing development. Before understanding the holistic development scenario, it is necessary to note that the finance system has undoubtedly played a catalytic role in promoting urban housing development. In addition, an attempt is also made to recount the genesis, growth and contribution of the century-old people-led cooperative movement with its resource base. The movement was founded after passing the Cooperative Act of 1912 and has a history of over a century. The movement, which is a publicly promoted institutional mechanism, has played a significant role by supplying housing development inputs to its members. Undoubtedly, having taken birth during the British rule, the cooperative housing movement was the only ray of hope to realize owning a house in the absence of the Indian government and institutional interventions. Especially, the PHSs have taken the lead to meet the housing needs of the homeless members in the absence of any apex institutions. Subsequently, ASs were added to the movement after the independence and were assigned major responsibility to govern and facilitate the cooperative housing activities. The other major contour is the establishment of the NHB itself during the watershed period to develop the institutional mechanisms to supply housing finance to all. Its refinancing strategies have facilitated the promotion of affordable housing for all income class, including the low, middle, EWSs and poor. Finally, changes brought into the urban walks of life by the national government have also been discussed as the milestones. SCM, PPPMAH, RERA and PMAY-HA have been categorically presented.

PART I
HOUSING FINANCE SYSTEM

The debate on the development of an HFS, although initiated during the early 1980s, holds good even to date for the developing countries of the world. The argument is all about promoting a feasible HFS to cater to all the needy households, with an eye on low-income households in particular. The debate entrusts a challenging responsibility to the government to organize a housing credit market with dual strategies, which would be discussed in the ensuing paragraphs. Before the discussion on how the government can fulfil its responsibility, it is indeed necessary to understand the nature of housing finance and credit market and the manner in which it differs from other segments. Housing finance is a specialized form of financial service in the overall capital market that plays a critical role in housing production. Housing finance helps the consumers to construct their own dwelling units besides helping them to purchase land, which is the other principal input. Housing finance is a market-based system, which is peculiar in its nature and distinguishes itself from other forms of financing social goods such as education and healthcare. Housing finance is generally a long-term credit made against a secured/tangible asset. It is advanced to those who own the title. The loan component is always less than the final cost of the housing unit, and the loan sum is a multiple of borrowers' annual income. The repayment is on a periodic basis and consists of principal and interest amount. The investible funds are unlikely to be raised from a public source, except for a limited extent of annual investment for housing the target citizens by governments. In other words, a large part of the capital is raised either from the capital market on commercial terms or/and from private savings. On the basis of this, the rate of interest on housing loans is usually on the higher side. Housing credit also involves costs other than the contractual fee or interest. The costs include debt servicing, administrative fee, establishment fees, etc. To avail housing financial service, a regular guaranteed income is one of the preconditions. Thus, chances of availing housing credit by low-income/resourceless families are very limited or altogether absent. This is because the mode of operations followed by the housing credit market is not compatible with the economic and financial needs of low-income households. More specifically, it is argued that since low-income families lack verifiable income and collateral, they cannot afford high transaction costs of housing loans. What is worse, housing finance agencies are non-existent in low-income areas. Also, it is believed that the poor will not repay (UN Habitat 1996). This does not mean that resourceless families are altogether left in lurch. Although much needs to be done, governments have created specialized lending institutions with an initial capital and low-cost funds to provide credit for housing activities at subsidized interest rates.

Considering the incredible needs of the consumers, including low-income households for housing credit, the literature on housing finance suggests two solutions. First, the government should encourage financial innovation by evolving the housing credit market to provide/boost residential investment on a viable basis. It need not be specified again that such a market would meet housing financial needs of the households/people who can afford the services, including the cost. Second, there is a good case for credit to the low-income households through subsidy-mixed specific housing programmes. Therefore, attaining the second objective is entirely the responsibility of the government, as low-income households cannot get access to formal housing credit (World Bank 1984). To accomplish these goals, it is suggested that a Central government body be established to bring about coordination between housing sector policies and housing finance policies and to supervise various financial institutions. The proposed body is expected to organize the housing credit market and to promote household savings besides broad-based financial benefits to housing consumers, including low-income households. Besides, the proposed apex institution should also clearly spell out the role it could play in the housing sector development, types of project financing and its geographical distribution, methods of curbing the informal market and promoting financial deepening through cooperative agreement with other financial institutions like regional and commercial banks. Emphasis is laid on mobilization of household savings since it is an important means of capital for housing investment. The added advantage with household savings is that the converted capital is less costly. Also, people can be motivated easily by the savings mobilizing agency, as home ownership is a powerful incentive for households to save. Similarly, it would be a futile attempt if the housing credit market loses sight of the common man's needs. Especially, in the context of attaining equality and welfare goals, meeting the financial needs for housing of low-income households assumes greater significance. Further, it is not a viable or justifiable proposition to organize the housing credit market for the benefit of the small segment (affordable sections) leaving behind the interest of the huge masses of disadvantaged sections.

Establishment of a central body, promotion of household savings and broad-based services by themselves do not ensure effective functioning of the HFS. There are other issues, which need to be considered carefully by governments. One of which is minimization of conflicting measures. No doubt, preferential measures would increase the supply of finance to low-income households, but such measures should not affect the other priority sectors' investments. This implies that additional resources have to be generated for these purposes without diluting the financial plans of other sectors. But at this juncture, how do we generate additional resources? The answer would be to encourage middle-class savings at a moderate rate of interest if the housing credit is to be supplied at an affordable rate. The same could be ensured through financial institutions, especially by the commercial and regional banks. Further, affordable mortgages to low-income households would go a long way if the opportunity cost of capital is borne by them. Second, these goals could be accomplished by establishing a deep and broad-based financial commitment for housing within the capital market or the banking sector as they have an advantage of huge and low-cost savings. Financial commitment based on savings thus ensures flow of funds for housing at an affordable cost. Moreover, increasing investment on housing activities does not greatly affect or cut short the investment on the other sectors. It is further argued that deep and broad-based financial commitment ensures effective management of scarce resource besides avoiding capital fragmentation. The argument is not for creating a new set of specialized HFIs but to broad base the application of capital of the existing capital market, including the banking sector. Setting up of new financial institutions for housing finance would only mean proliferation. Although multipurpose financial institutions provide long-term finance, such an approach would not only contrast the existing financial setup but also promote dualism in financial services. Moreover, the added disadvantage is that the specialized HFIs operate on a higher scale (higher rate of interest on deposits/lending, cost on loans, etc.) and cater only to the higher income class and not to low-income households.

FINANCING MECHANISMS

The response to the ongoing debate for evolving a housing credit market with deep and broad-based financing services for housing has been overwhelming in those countries that have considered housing as a merit good and have exhibited political commitment for the same. Removal of constraints, development of mortgages, insurance for investment and broad-based residential investment (for land acquisition, construction, redevelopment, etc.) are the principal strategies employed for alleviating homelessness. However, in most of the developing countries, the efforts of an evolving HFS are mediocre or ad hoc largely owing to not have considered housing a priority sector. The literature has identified three distinct housing finance mechanisms generally evolved according to the needs and capacities of various countries. Market facilitation and government financing, being the first and second approaches, exist predominantly in the most advanced Western and Western European countries, respectively. The other form of financing is the mixed approach in which case both governments and market cater to each of their own clientele, but none of them would have successfully met the total financial needs of the people. Indeed, it is necessary to say that each of the first two approaches has achieved a fair degree of success in supplying finance for housing and in alleviating housing deprivation across different income consumers. While in the case of the other, huge financial needs, resource crunch and lack of investment promotion measures have inhibited housing activities. This section analyses in greater detail the three different financing mechanisms for housing with their own instruments of functioning.

Market Finances

Under the changing economic circumstances, market facilitation for the production of various social and economic goods and services has gained momentum. Besides, in the most advanced and industrial countries, the market has increased its share of investment in the economic sphere, but slowly in developing countries. Mismatch between the public financial services and increasing demand for goods and services by a variety of consumers together with a shrinking role of the government have increased the pace of market facilitation in these countries. Housing being a social and merit good, its production is largely dominated by the private sector in both the developed and developing regions. The government, due to the huge requirement of funds to meet the total housing needs and resource shortage at its disposal, has increasingly facilitated various players (production agents) in the housing market with a facilitating environment. This facilitating environment has enhanced opportunities for both production and consumption of housing benefits by different income consumers. On an uninterrupted basis, finance, which is one of the principal housing inputs, is being supplied to consumers on an affordable price by different financial institutions. Similarly, a large number of private developers have been encouraged to take up land development as well as house construction activities. These positive measures have resulted in alleviating housing deprivation, and in some cases, they have brought about housing surplus. Governments, on the other hand, have redefined their commitment to only the persons of dire need. Housing subsidies and other incentives as the instruments of government interventions have continued to be the hopes of the most vulnerable groups notwithstanding their inadequacy and untimeliness.

The ideology of these measures has been neither total privatization nor wholesale participation of the government in the production and distribution of housing benefits to various income groups. The objective of the mixed economy approach as pointed out is 'to contain and reduce the role of the government in social welfare and to encourage non-governmental organizations (NGOs) and agencies, which in turn reduces the pressure on government financing, less bureaucracy, more decentralization, more community involvement and greater participation' (Mishra 1990). Correspondingly, the production of housing units privately by the individuals as well as by the institutional builders has been very well supported financially and encouraged fiscally over the years. In fact, the long-term objective is to ensure dwelling of a decent standard to all needy at prices they can afford; this has been sought to achieve through grants and loans to developers and consumers. Again, the overall purpose of such continuous support of the government to the housing production industry and to the market is only to ensure healthy flow of funds for residential buildings and production of adequate number of homes. The market financing system has four different pillars as discussed in the following paragraph.

The first and foremost pillar of the market financing is a host of financial institutions with private capital. They encompass commercial banks, insurance companies, trusts and mortgage loan companies. Each of these institutions with a definite resource constituency is closely regularized and monitored by the government at all levels. Commercial banks raise short-term deposits and insurance, while trust companies sell insurance bonds and manage trust and pension funds. These institutions with specific investment avenues enjoy the freedom in determining the volume of funds to be made available for mortgage lending. These institutions control a huge part of the mortgage loans for housing. Second, mortgage insurance for the housing loans is one of the major breakthroughs in securitizing the assets/investment, which has given a greater confidence to private investors over the years and has ensured uninterrupted supply of finances. The facility of mortgage insurance has been extended to the acquisition of apartments and purchase of existing buildings besides the newly constructed units. A significant development in this regard is the level-payment mortgage (high loan to value ratio), which could be paid in 25–30 years of time. The insurance premium ranges from 0.5 per cent to around 4 per cent of the loan amount. Mortgage loan insurance is generally made available to all homebuyers through centrally approved financial institutions. Homebuyers have the freedom to reduce mortgage cost and its payment. Third, since competition is the inherent characteristic feature of market finance, a huge inflow of financial institutions into the housing finance segment would bring about reduction in the rate of interest on housing loans. This would prompt a higher demand for housing loans by homebuyers. There are instances where the mortgage loans are made available at fairly cheaper rate. For example, Canada is one such country to have supplied mortgage loans for housing at a lower rate to facilitate housing activities on a large scale across different income groups (Mahadeva 2002a). Similar to lower interest rate, an increasing tendency to survive in the market together with accumulation of financial resources would bring about a higher loan ratio or lower down payment of the housing cost. It has been argued that lower down payment on housing loans always influences the housing-related decisions of the families in the sense that it propels to own housing and vice versa (Lawrence 1974). The final but important segment of market finance is the role of the government itself. Although market-led housing finance is sumptuously sufficient, governments also have retained fewer responsibilities. One such responsibility is the supply of subsidies for owners and rental housing units. Families with dire need are being allowed to dwell in government-owned buildings on subsidized rent, which is less than the mortgage and operating costs of the buildings.

Families are also allowed to rent the units of non-profit organizations or privately owned units. Insured loans on lower interest rate have been made available to non-profit organizations. Grants for first-time owners of housing and improvement assistance are also made available. The purpose of improvement assistance has been to enhance the health of the building as well as to ensure safe dwelling.

Public Financing

Financing housing activities by governments has been the second most common method from time immemorial, which is totally in contrast to market financing that exists in almost all countries, irrespective of whether they are rich or poor. Government credit provision for housing prevails for two reasons. The first reason is that organized housing credit markets would have remained undeveloped and would not have broad based their financial services at interest of affordable rates to meet the housing financial needs of different income groups. The government's role has been emphasized to meet the housing financial needs of low-income families. It has been advocated that the government credit programmes are the only solution for housing the vulnerable sections, especially in the absence of any organized financial services. The second reason is to bring about equity and justice in the distribution of resources through transfers, as the market financing system is insensitive and irresponsive to the needs of vulnerable sections. Housing credit programmes of the government are the effective methods to spread the benefits and to transfer resources towards low-income groups (UN Habitat 1996). But for the government financing programmes, low-income families would not have had opportunities to house themselves, although such interventions are often considered incompatible and inefficient. Therefore, government financing for housing should be seen more as opportunities for low-income families than as a burden to the government. Government finances for housing are the investment capital that encompasses both subsidies and loans targeted mainly to those whose financial needs for housing are not met by the market. At the same time, it is also not uncommon that wherever housing has been considered as a merit good, governments have been financing all the needy. In countries wherever governments are the principal source of housing finance, subsidies are the important form of financial transfers.

In the government-led HFS, the overall focus has been to increase housing stock in both owner and rental sectors. To accomplish this goal, governments have intervened in three forms: first, as a regulator; second, as a provider of subsidies; and, third, as a direct investor (Papa 1992). As a regulator, governments regulate the housing market, especially the financing of rental and owner sectors. As a provider, governments fix the housing price, which is below the cost. This instrument is used to boost supply and demand for housing for producers and consumers, respectively. Finally, as a developer, governments invest in the production of housing units for rental and selling purposes. Subsidy is the difference between the cost price and the actual paid-out cost and is a very important instrument in overall financing; it is a non-compensated payment by the government to private parties/or institutions made available from the public exchequer. Subsidy is made available for three different purposes: for construction or rehabilitation of dwellings, for acquisition of and improvement of house sites and for occupants of dwellings. Loans and mortgages are the other instruments for house construction and rehabilitation purposes, which are extended on the basis of family income. Especially, loans are extended at the below market rate.

Mixed Financing

Mixed financing typically refers to the coexistence of all major forms of housing finance mechanisms with an edge over informal source of financing, which is largely found in developing countries around the world for reasons discussed later. This is because this part of the world has neither attempted to organize a full-fledged HFM with an investment-friendly environment as it used to be market-driven economies nor governments have the resource capacity to meet the total housing financial needs. At the same time, it should not be mistaken that the market does not exist and the government shoulders no responsibility. The market finances those who fulfil the loan conditions for housing activities like regular and guaranteed income earners, while governments finance the social housing commitments meant for the vulnerable sections. But unfortunately, none of the major sources have been able to meet the total financial needs of their target groups let alone all housing consumers. To be precise, neither has the market fully met the housing financial needs of all sections nor have governments covered vulnerable sections fully. It is these structural inefficiencies that have laid the foundation for the existence of informal sources of financing for housing activities. An informal source, being non-institutional in nature, plays a very dominant role in meeting the needs. The informal financial market, for all practical purposes, is referred to as any market for cash finance; it is not regulated by government and is loosely monitored. This source includes moneylenders, friends, relatives and family savings, which is estimated to have met up to 80 per cent of the housing finance in developing countries in general and South Asian countries in particular (Okhpala 1994).

HOUSING FINANCE SYSTEM IN INDIA

Before discussing the HFS in the Indian context, it is indeed necessary to note two very important developments that have occurred in the early 1990s, which have laid the foundation for the expansion of the housing sector and for evolving the HFM. First, considering the housing sector as one of the core and priority sectors for investment purposes, emphasis was laid on mobilization of additional resources to the sector. During the period, the changes that affected the housing sector coincided with the new economic policies. The government has tried to address the hitherto unattended structural and operational bottlenecks in order to increase the supply of housing. More emphasis was laid on private sector participation and community involvement besides the government taking upon itself the responsibility to attend to the needs of the weaker sections' housing. The second change was the realization of the role of the fiscal incentives in housing production in the early 1990s, though such realization has come belatedly. The commitment of the government to increase housing stock in the owners' segment was exhibited through a number of concessions from the payments under income and property taxes. These concessions are being offered to both individuals and the corporate sector. Under section 88 of the Income Tax Act, concessions were offered to individuals to deduct interest paid towards the housing loans. This was initially raised from ₹1,000 to ₹5,000, then to ₹15,000, to ₹30,000, to ₹75,000 and later up to ₹1,50,000 from the financial year 1999–2000. These concessions were offered in addition to 20 per cent deduction of principal loan repayment. Carry forward facility of losses of housing property against future income of individuals was extended for eight years since 1998. This apart, tax holiday under section 80-1A was extended for a built-up area up to 1,500 square feet of dwelling units of approved projects in urban areas other than Mumbai and Delhi to encourage high-income housing activities for people who could borrow more than ₹500,000. Further, from 1993 to 1994, the value of one residential house, or part thereof, was exempted from the levy of property tax. These concessions notwithstanding, their revenue loss to the exchequer played a promotional role of housing activities. Similarly, to boost the housing activities in the corporate or business sectors, many concessions were shown to them. The focus was to ensure housing security to the employees working in these sectors. Prominent incentives include tax holiday to the tune of 100 per cent for the first five years for housing projects and 30 per cent for another five years, and 50 per cent exemption of profits of the companies engaged in housing projects. Especially for the HFCs, concessions were also shown by increasing depreciation rate from the present 20 per cent to 40 per cent on new dwelling units. In addition, it was pronounced to calculate interest on loans on an actual basis rather than on accrual basis from 1999 to 2000 onwards.

For centuries, housing development was expected to take place without a financing market and fiscal incentives. But from the beginning of the 20th century, attempts were made to organize CHSs, with an Act of Parliament, to supply housing credit to their members. In fact, cooperatives were the only source of financing for housing till similar attempts were made to organize a housing credit market. Nationalization of the insurance sector and subsequently the commercial banks has further paved the way for the implementation of various social housing schemes by the governments and increasing volume of finances for housing activities in the country. The Life Insurance Corporation (LIC) was mandated to invest 25 per cent of its controlled funds in socially oriented schemes, including housing development activities through the government. Similarly, the General Insurance Corporation (GIC) was statutorily guided to invest 35 per cent of its investment funds through state governments for housing and for loans, bonds, debentures and preference shares of Housing and Urban Development Corporation (HUDCO; RBI 1978). Employees Provident Fund has been another important source of financing as non-refundable advance provision facilitated its subscribers for house-building activities, including acquisition of residential sites. From the early 1970s, commercial banks were also encouraged to finance housing activities. Currently, commercial banks have been earmarked to invest 3 per cent of their incremental deposit ratio. The United Nations' declaration of 1987 as the International Year of Shelter for the Homeless has not only sensitized the Indian government towards the housing sector but has also prompted to establish NHB as a subsidiary of Reserve Bank of India. The NHB was expected to organize a housing credit market to provide long-term finance and to develop housing savings by the households. Commercial banks, insurance companies and other private companies were also allowed to set up their own subsidiaries to supply housing finance. Despite these attempts, a noteworthy feature of the Indian HFS is the existence of informal moneylenders for centuries, who cater to vulnerable sections on a very large scale. There have been hardly any attempts to scale down the role of informal moneylenders in both rural and urban areas. This section analyses four distinctly different financing methods for housing activities in India (Table 3A.1), which have emerged as critical sources, namely (a) informal financing, (b) cooperative housing finance, (c) subsidized financing and (d) market financing.

Informal source of financing housing in India is as old as any financing system. Generally, it can be defined as a financial source that is independently sustaining with private capital, and its terms and conditions are framed according to the convenience of the lenders. In other words, these financial services are purely non-institutional and non-governed in nature. Their operations are not guided by any regulations of the central bank or government on the matters of investment, interest structure, period, social responsibilities, etc. In a lighter way, it can also be said that informal financial services are dominated by independent moneylenders with their own private capital that generally comes from their own savings, ancestral transfers, liquidation of assets, and borrowings of friends and relatives. Informal financing services in general and for the housing sector in particular exist and sustain mainly for three reasons. Because of the lack of a well-structured financing system, housing development was expected to take place without the financial support or services. In the absence of any such system, housing activities were confined to the public servants, with the help of government loans and other services. Eventually, the housing activities of other segments of the population, until recently, were left to themselves. Thanks to the efforts of evolving a HFS in the late 1980s, the newly evolved system has not yet overturned the situation as far as meeting the financial requirements of all segments of the population is concerned. The HFS is highly biased towards the white-collared jobholders and towards the urban areas, and it has not reached out and geared to meet the total housing financial needs (World Bank 1984). Moreover, the financial services are not broad based to meet the needs of all segments of residential activities. Since the HFS has hardly had any impact on the vulnerable groups, which in itself paved the way for the sustenance of informal financial services. Finally, there is a positive relationship between the informal sector and poverty, and the informal sector is dominated by individuals with low income and poor housing conditions (Pugh 1990). India, with more than one-third of her population below the poverty line, hardly fulfils the lending criteria of the institutional source and is thus forced to resort to informal sources to raise finances to improve dwelling conditions.

As mentioned already, financial services for housing in the informal segment are provided by individual moneylenders at a very high rate of interest. Being exploitative of the local conditions, moneylenders provide their services at the doorstep of the borrowers, especially in rural areas. One of the greatest advantages of the informal system is that financial services are provided against no collateral or non-mortgage of the house. Instead, financial services are provided on an oral agreement or against the preparation of a pro-note in favour of the lenders. In the eventuality of death of the principal borrower, the burden of repayment will be shifted to the immediate heir. However, confiscation of assets owing to non-repayment of loans is very rare. Yet another advantage is that the borrower can raise the loans up to the full cost of the housing project, and therefore, the question of borrowers' contribution in the total project does not arise at all.

The modes/tools against which finances are obtained from the informal sector differ from rural to urban areas. Oral understanding between the lenders and the borrowers predominates over the other methods in rural areas. However, pledging of immovable assets (land) and commercial crops (cotton, groundnut, sunflower, etc.) cannot be ruled out. Further, though bondage labour is legally abolished, instances of child bondage labour for informal financial services continue to exist. However, in urban areas, finances from informal sources are obtained mostly against pledging of ornaments. Further, liquidation of the additional residential assets is a common practice. Of late, acquisition of the residential site for speculation purposes and disposal of the same to finance the margin money component of the housing project is an emerging trend. In a number of cases, financial assistance from friends and relatives also forms an important source although such arrangements take place without any guarantee or pledging of any securities (NIUA 1992).

In the absence of a strong database, it is difficult to quantify the role of the informal sector in housing finance. However, despite the increased access to institutional sources in the late 1990s, informal sources continue to play a significant role. It is argued that housing finance made available by budgetary allocations and net financial assistance from GIC, LIC, Unit Trust of India (UTI), banks, provident fund and all HFIs is not more than 16 per cent, and the remaining 84 per cent of housing finance requirements are met by the informal sector (Raj 1994). Further, it is evident that out of the total investment in rural housing, only 5.18 per cent has come from institutional sources and the rest from the informal sector that includes savings (42.57%); borrowings from friends and relatives (9.36%); liquidation of assets (22.03%); and professional moneylenders, landlords, traders and others (20.86%; Government of India [GoI] 1993–1994). Although, over the years, the institutional source has increased its share in rural housing activity, an enormous amount comes from the informal segment. The share of the institutional source in the gross capital expenditure on purchase and improvement of plots and residential buildings was in the order of 9.67 per cent, and thus, the remaining investment comes from different sources of the informal segment (NSSO 1998). The informal source continues to have a strong hold even in urban areas in meeting the residential investment, although the situation is not as poor as that in rural areas. The gross capital residential expenditure of the institutional source in urban areas is about 21.26 per cent, and the rest comes from the informal segment.

Notwithstanding the beginning of the cooperative movement in housing in the first decade of the 20th century, the cooperative movement took a definite shape only with the establishment of state-level bodies as the spokesman during the 1950s. Today, cooperative housing has two tiers—ASs at the state level mobilize funds and channelize the same through primary societies and primaries at the grassroots level that play a very critical role in the construction of houses of their members. Although there exists no uniform structure in primary societies, the Working Group on Housing Cooperatives (GoI 1964) has broadly classified them as all-the-way cooperatives, co-venture cooperatives and flat ownership cooperatives on the basis of their functioning. Some function as purely financing societies, some construct houses on behalf of their members, some construct houses and own them jointly, and some own houses and let their members to live on rental basis. CHSs have spread to all the nooks and corners of the country and have grown to strength organizationally. The number of societies and their memberships has increased sevenfold during the period between 1965 and 1966 and between 1995 and 1996, and there has been around 58-fold increase in the working capital. Similarly, the loans for the members have also increased by over 53 times to construct a total number of over 1.728 million units. A noteworthy feature is the increasing emphasis on owners' segment in the independent category during the 1990s. However, the disappointing part of the CHSs is the low level of use of the working capital, which clearly shows that loans as a percentage of the working capital are lower at a little above 10 per cent. This means that a substantial part of the working capital has not been put to the construction of houses for their members but would have been invested elsewhere or on securities. Considering the huge scale of resources in the form of working capital, housing societies could have easily doubled the construction of houses and could have increased the coverage of members as well as number of houses per society. Unfortunately, the coverage of members was only just below one-third, and the average number of houses per society was a little more than one-fifth.

India has a tradition of having a number of social housing schemes meant for poorer sections ever since her independence. Although these schemes were directly financed by national and state governments during the first two decades of their implementation, this practice was discontinued with the establishment of a central body, that is, HUDCO, in the early 1980s. HUDCO was constituted to implement the government commitments on housing the weaker sections, namely low- and middle-income households, and to promote housing activities by supporting state governments and their agencies. In addition to the national body, a number of state governments have set up rural housing finance corporations with their own financial resources, for example, Gujarat Rural Housing Finance Corporation (GRHFC) and Rajiv Gandhi Rural Housing Corporation (RGRHC) in Karnataka. These bodies aim at financing new house construction as well as replacing the unsafe housing units in rural areas. It goes without saying that vulnerable groups are the targets of these institutions. HUDCO, ever since its establishment, has been in the forefront in financing social housing schemes in urban and rural areas. Under housing programmes for industrial workers, low- and middle-income families, slum dwellers, and low-paid government employees, HUDCO has assisted in the construction of over 2.9 million housing units in different urban areas of the country by the turn of 1996. Also, it has facilitated public authorities to acquire over 2.8 million hectares of land for residential purposes. In rural areas, over 14.2 million housing units have been constructed for the occupation of the landless and agricultural labourers, socially deprived sections, ex-bonded labourers and other poor families.

Ever since the late 1980s, one of the major changes in the Indian housing sector is the constant effort to organize a financing system with an edge over market financing. These efforts have not only paved the way for the entry of new financial institutions from the commercial, insurance and private segments but also have made the availability of funds for housing activity at fairly affordable rates. These institutions have infused a great deal of competition in their functions and have brought in what is called 'interest war', mainly to thrive and sustain in the HFM. Commercial banks, besides directly financing housing activities of their customers, have also promoted their own subsidiaries in the market. Similarly, the insurance sector, apart from fulfilling its mandatory roles, also has subsidiary outlets to cater to housing financial needs of the common public. The exposure of the market to the private sector has also come in a big way with the presence of Industrial Credit and Investment Corporation of India (ICICI) Bank, Housing Development Finance Corporation (HDFC) and others. However, the presence of the commercial banks in the market with cheap and huge resource base has been taken with serious caution by other HFIs, as these institutions are operating in the market with high-cost borrowed capital. As a result, consumers in general not only have options of housing finance but are also at gains as the financial services are available at affordable rates of interest.

There are two conspicuous developments in the market segment of housing finance. First and foremost is the availability of housing finance at the convenience of the consumers. Barring a few, almost all the HFIs have made their financial services available for a minimum of three periods, that is, up to 5 years, above 5 years and below 10 years, and above 10 years and below 15 years (Table 3A.2).

Although interests are charged on the reduced balance of principal in both cases, floating rates are cheaper than fixed rates in most cases. The difference ranges anywhere from 0.25 per cent to 1 per cent in all slabs of loans. However, there are instances of fixed loans being cheaper than floating rates, and to facilitate the consumers with more financial requirements, loan periods are being stretched up to 20 years or even more. This facility is made available by a few HFIs irrespective of their segment—commercial, subsidiary or private. For example, Corporation Bank is offering housing financial services in five streams, spreading over the loan period from a minimum of 5 years to a maximum of 25 years. Similarly, Canara Bank, IDBI Bank and HDFC go up to 20 years. Second, historically, housing loans were carrying higher rates, which were unaffordable, ranging from a minimum of 12 per cent to a maximum of 19 per cent in the early 1990s. In fact, it was during this period that people were reluctant to avail housing loans, especially people with low and moderate income. Then the period of the late 1990s was marked with increasing number of HFIs from all corners and supply of loans for housing with a drop in interest rates. Since interest rate influences the demand for housing loans, there has been a spurt in housing activities, thanks to the low interest regime.

Housing loans have been made available to the consumers by a large number of HFIs in the market in two different schemes of interest—floating and fixed—which cannot be interchanged even once during the term. Floating rate refers to a facility in which the consumers have the benefit of paying interest over their loans according to the changes that occur from time to time in the market. For example, if the rate of interest on housing loans is reduced, the consumers will pay according to the reduced rates and vice versa. In the case of a fixed regime, the interest rates are fixed at the time of availing for the entire term of housing loans. In other words, the consumer loan repayment chart will not be altered even if there are any changes in the market. Although interests are charged on the reduced balance of principal in both cases, floating rates are cheaper than fixed rates in most cases. The difference ranges anywhere from 0.25 per cent to 1 per cent in all slabs of the loans. However, there are instances of fixed loans being cheaper than floating rates or having no difference at all—for example, Can Fin Homes and HDFC products, respectively. Further, ever since the emergence as a segment of capital market, non-existence of a uniform rate is the characteristic feature of the Indian HFS. Cost of fund, charge on capital, cost of operation, regulatory provisioning and margin of profit are some of the important considerations for fixing of interest rates. RBI, being the apex body of the monetary system, fixes the interest structure for the loans advanced by commercial banks, housing financial subsidiaries and cooperative societies. Other private financial institutions charge an interest rate over and above the prevailing interest rate in the market. It is needless to say that the difference in interest rates across various institutions is over 1–1.5 per cent.

PART II
COOPERATIVE HOUSING MOVEMENT

Cooperative housing movement has been a people initiative in the country with institutional network, that is, housing societies. The movement led by housing societies has been a prominent player in the housing market, which has contributed in its own way in realizing the dream of homeless families. These societies have been realizing housing dreams both in ownership and rental streams. Having begun the operations from the first decade of the 20th century, the cooperative housing movement has spread over its activities throughout the country. Especially in major and medium urban centres, these societies have earned distinction as a third sector in the housing market, next to the government and the private sector. In fact, cooperatives are the largest institutional network today in the housing sector of the country. Although it is difficult to precisely ascertain the share of cooperative societies in the total housing production, they do play a significant role in supplying critical inputs like developed residential sites and long-term credit for housing activity, apart from supplying constructed houses for owning and rental purposes. Over the years, cooperatives have also supplemented the action of housing production along with other financial institutions such as commercial banks, insurance sector, and financial subsidiaries. With the increasing emphasis on social development and considering housing as a social infrastructure, demand for housing inputs like land and finance on a sustainable basis has increased tremendously. The development strategies have mooted a multi-agency approach to supply residential plots as well as housing finance to meet the gigantic needs of the people of various income brackets. It is at this juncture that cooperatives have come to be a cost-effective agency for supplying housing inputs. However, notwithstanding their institutional network and their strength, the housing cooperatives are caught between market lending rigidities and low financial base. Overdue and bad/doubtful debts have hampered the financial viability of the movement.

Under the changed development strategies and the new economic policy since the late 1980s, which have together paved way for large-scale participation of the private sector, cooperatives have been expected to play a reinvigorated role and to prove their utility in meeting the housing needs of weaker sections in particular and the homeless in general. With the new expectation, the cooperatives may have to acquire a new status as alternative non-profit agencies to the market system to supply housing benefits at a fairly cheaper rate in the years to come. The existing cooperative setup and its weak performance should not come in the way of better opportunities and relegate the importance of housing cooperatives into the background. There is a great need to reorient the actions of CHSs to make them an alternative way in the changing economic circumstance and to meet the affordable housing needs of the people in general, and their members in particular. There are a number of issues concerning CHSs, with regard to their organizational structure, financial performance, quantum of housing benefits, working performance, etc. It is also necessary to discuss about the evolution and structure of CHSs as it is seen today; the financial performance of CHSs with respect to their resource base; levels of borrowings; portfolio performance beside the house construction performance; working results, including functional operations over the years; and the alternative methods available for CHSs in order to enhance their share in the housing stock.

EVOLUTION AND SPREAD

The beginning of the cooperative movement in the housing sector dates back to the first decade of the 20th century, although it did not spread its activities to every nook and corner of the country. Rather, its operation was confined and limited to a few major cities, especially to a few Presidency States. The first CHS was set up in the year 1909 in the erstwhile Mysore State (Khurana 1986). This was followed by the Bombay Cooperative Housing Association in 1913 by the Bombay State, and the Madras State then organized CHS in 1914 (Naik 1971). The first two Presidency States were the pioneers in the efforts of organizing people to form housing cooperatives and were the centres of the cooperative housing activities in the entire country. It would be inappropriate not to mention that housing societies had the moral and financial support of the respective state governments during this crucial period. Bombay State was the first to grant assistance of state loans on easy terms at a low rate of interest to housing societies. Similarly, during 1934–1935, the Government of Mysore granted a soft loan at 5 per cent interest to the Bangalore Housing Society, which was a premier cooperative housing institution in the state that was responsible for the formation of a cooperative colony. In this regard, Madras State went one step ahead with the formulation of housing schemes for cooperatives besides extending financial assistance (RBI 1950). The Madras Central House Mortgage Society was organized as an apex cooperative housing finance society, together with House Mortgage Banks. The objectives of these bodies were to advance loans to the PHSs for the construction and renovation of houses on a mortgage basis.

However, in the states other than Bombay, Mysore and Madras, the progress of housing societies was either comparatively limited or was altogether lacking. The cooperative housing activities were confined to registration of one or two societies in other states, but other than that, they could not show any stability for lack of financial support and peoples' mobilization. There was a slight spurt of activity in some states with financial support. There were 10 house-building societies in Punjab; 2 in Orissa 9 each in Uttar Pradesh, Ajmer and Delhi; and 12 in West Bengal in addition to three presidencies. But by and large, the cooperative housing movement underwent a period of hardships between 1927–1928 and 1948–1949, and it was marked by two important world events, namely the Great Depression and the Second World War. Each of these affected the cooperative housing movement negatively. On account of a lull in trade and industry during depression, rents were slashed down, and flats of housing societies were vacated in large numbers; these had an adverse effect on co-partnership societies. About this time, in some places, stopping of loan assistance to housing societies, compulsory payment of property tax and other conditions have further worsened the situation. Similarly, the Second World War left behind devastation of an unparalleled nature, not only in countries, which were actual theatres of war but also throughout the world.

The position of India was also not good. Very few buildings were constructed for civilian occupation as all building materials were diverted to war purposes. Rigid controls over the production of building materials hampered the housing activities. Existing dwellings deteriorated considerably owing to lack of proper maintenance and repairs (GoI 1946). Further, the partition of India in 1947 led to burning or destroying of many houses, and several millions of people were uprooted from their houses. When this was the housing situation, the position of housing societies was beyond imagination in the sense that they were unable to undertake any large-scale building construction for dwelling purposes of their members. Then came the period of revival during which housing societies were organized on a large scale throughout the country, and the support of the state governments was made available. Housing societies were allowed to borrow up to 75 per cent of the value of land and building, with a repayment period of 35 years (RBI 1956). As a result of the financial support from state governments, there was a steep rise in the activities of cooperative housing in the country, especially in the organizational front.

The CHSs took a definite shape with the establishment of apex CHSs at the state level and National Cooperative Housing Federation of India (NCHFI). These two apex-level organizations were expected to be the spokespersons of PHSs and to lead and guide the activities of the cooperative housing movement. With the constitution of the ASs, the movement itself got the organizational structure with mainly two tiers. At the grassroots level, primary societies were formed by people who were in need of housing facility and were expected to affiliate to the ASs at the state level, which in turn was affiliated to the NCHFI set up in 1969. This national federation has a number of laudable objectives such as raising of funds through borrowings, granting loans to its members and procuring and supplying raw materials to its members. The other objectives are to deal with technical, financial and practical problems and to organize and guide the functioning of member organizations and primaries in general. Given these objectives, it is indeed necessary to mention that the role of the national federation should be confined more to the second set of the objectives as they involve coordination with the government at different levels to create a facilitating environment for the cooperative housing system. Moreover, there are state-level ASs to raise funds from different sources and grant loans to the member societies and members. In fact, the objectives of the national federation are overlapping with those of state-level societies. Yet the reality is that the national federation failed to live up to its own objectives of raising funds and granting loans, as there has not been a single case of having raised the funds and loans granted by the national apex body. Over the years, NCHFI has only become analogous to some of the credit federations such as the National Federation of State Cooperative Banks and the National Federation of Land Development Banks, which either functioned as effective spokesman of the cooperative banking system or discharged the responsibilities of coordination. It has been further observed that 'A major weakness of the cooperative system has been the neglect of the base level institutions and the tendency of the higher-level institutions to look after their own interests, often at the cost of primaries' (RBI 1988).

Next to the national federation, the immediate higher bodies in the cooperative housing structure are the ASs at the state level, which are crucial. The objectives of these societies are (a) to promote house-building activities in the cooperative sector of the state; (b) to supervise, coordinate and guide the housing programmes of PHSs; and (c) to mobilize the necessary capital through its borrowing activity and in turn channelize the same for promoting the housing activities of PHSs in the state. After independence, there has been a spurt in the organisation of state-level ASs to fulfil the above-stated aspirations. The recommendation for setting up of an AS in each state, where more than 100 housing cooperatives are functioning, has further strengthened the cooperative housing structure (GoI 1964). Majority of the Indian states have passed acts to establish state-level ASs, except for a few states and UTs. Despite this positive action, the ASs have failed to cover the entire population of PHSs and strengthen the movement, which will be discussed in greater details in the forthcoming paragraphs.

The most vital part of the cooperative housing structure is the lower tier, namely primary societies. These societies directly cater to the housing needs of their members. For different reasons, there is no uniform structure in primary societies throughout the country. It can be noted that over the year, various types of societies have come into existence. The Working Group on Housing Cooperatives

(GoI 1964) broadly classified the PHSs into three groups, namely all-the-way cooperatives, co-venture cooperatives and flat ownership cooperatives, on the basis of their functions in the centres of cooperative societies like Madras and Bombay (GoI 1964). Some function as purely financing societies, some construct houses on behalf of their members, some construct houses and own them jointly along with members and some own houses and let their members occupy them on a rental basis. In some states such as Delhi, Gujarat, Karnataka and Rajasthan, plot holders' cooperative societies can also be seen in addition to the aforementioned categories. By and large, all the forms of societies coexist in the rest of the states and UTs.

With the advocacy of increased housing production at fair and affordable price, the number of PHSs at the grassroots level has increased in every nook and corner of the country, if not on the same scale and magnitude. Some of the states have taken a major lead in organizing the cooperative housing movement, some have made a beginning in proportion to the initiative of the people, and many have not bothered to have a third option in the production and distribution of housing benefits to the needy. Maharashtra has been in the forefront in the first category of states and has accounted to over half of the PHSs in the country. This is followed by Gujarat, Andhra Pradesh (Undivided), Bihar, West Bengal, Madhya Pradesh, Uttar Pradesh, Delhi, Karnataka, Haryana and Rajasthan, in which the registration of the PHSs as an alternative institutional mechanism to address the housing problem has been quite visible and prominent. In other words, the people of these states have invested their faith and founded PHSs as an alternative means for realizing the dreams of housing; more than 7,000 societies are now functioning on an average in each state. The second group of the states has been led by the state of Punjab with around 35 per cent of the PHSs, and the other states that have followed suit are Goa, Kerala, Assam, Himachal Pradesh and Tamil Nadu, with an average of a little over 300 societies in each state. A very thin presence of the CHSs is functioning in the other seven states, namely Orissa, Jammu and Kashmir, Meghalaya, Mizoram, Manipur, Tripura and Arunachal Pradesh. The housing cooperative movement has suffered with its total absence in four states such as Chhattisgarh, Nagaland,

Sikkim and Uttaranchal without a single registered society. Further, except for Lakshadweep, all the other UTs have made a significant effort to organize housing cooperative movement.

Setting up of a three-tier structure at the national, state and primary levels in the cooperative housing movement does not mean anything to the housing societies, as the movement has suffered on account of lack of deep compartmentalization and a proper integrated network. Limited services of the ASs are the prime reason for the limited coverage of PHSs. Most of the ASs are engaged mainly in supplying housing finance of a limited number of PHSs, which have come into operation for financing purposes. This limited concern has naturally discouraged those PHSs established to acquire, develop and distribute the residential plots for their members from becoming the affiliated members of ASs. At the same time, ASs have also hardly coordinated and represented the cause of PHSs with regard to their land requirement with land development agencies. Similar is the case with most of the employees' housing societies (EHSs) whose numbers have increased manifold in recent years. The principal objectives of EHSs are to acquire land in bulk for residential purposes with the savings of their members and to facilitate their members to acquire finances for house construction. Above all, the changing market conditions have further discouraged such PHSs from becoming members of ASs. The emerging HFM is broad based (meeting financial needs of all segments of residential houses such as land purchase, construction and renovation), consumer friendly and highly competitive (rate of interest, repayment period, low processing charges, etc.). Especially, the market is more responsive to the organized residential activities of cooperatives, as the latter are public interest institutions (PIIs).

Like in the case of difference in the number of PHSs, there is also a widespread variation in the coverage/non-coverage of PHSs by the ASs as their affiliated members across states/UTs. At this juncture, it can be said that 'lesser the number of PHSs, larger the affiliated members of the ASs and vice versa'. Precisely, the incidence of non-coverage of PHSs by ASs is more in such states/UTs, which have more number of primary societies. The extent of exclusion/non-coverage of PHSs by ASs is more than the national average in two regions (Delhi and

Andaman and Nicobar) of the five UTs and in four (West Bengal, Bihar, Maharashtra and Madhya Pradesh) of the 23 states. In five other states, the exclusion of PHSs is still at an alarming level although the same is below the average. In view of the small coverage and large exclusion of PHSs by ASs, the question that obviously arises is whether PHSs are organized on viable lines for effective management in terms of a definite size of membership per society. Although yet to be considered by the apex bodies (national and state levels) and the union government, the Government of Karnataka has fixed the number of membership for each primary society, keeping in view viability and better management (Government of Karnataka [GoK] 1985). In the case of house-building cooperative societies, the size of the membership is restricted to only 500, and it is 400 for employee's house-building societies. Provision is also made to register an additional society with slight distinction in the name of the society in case there is a large number of eligible employees of the same organization. From this point of view, PHSs in most of the states (excluding Tamil Nadu, Orissa, Pondicherry, Kerala and Karnataka) are unviable as their average membership per society is even less in a large number of states, which ranges from 15 (minimum) to 53 (maximum). Besides, the scenario is by and large the same in the case of states, which have registered a large number of primary societies. This issue needs greater consideration at the state and national level to make these societies more viable. Otherwise, the strength of PIIs would be reduced to the level of the family affairs of vested interests as it happened already in some parts of the country (Mahadeva 1992). If this trend is unchecked, the question that invariably arises is—should there be an institution for a small group of people? Can there be cost-effectiveness in their operations and business? How are these institutions going to sustain?

PERFORMANCE OF THE MOVEMENT

Resource Base

Understanding the performance of the CHSs with regard to their resource base is as important as its movement, keeping the sustainability in view. This is because the resource base determines the success of the movement itself. The resources can be classified into two types: internal and external sources. Internal sources refer to own resources that include own capital, paid-up capital and deposits of the members, whereas external source includes mainly borrowings from various sources. It goes without saying that these two sources constitute the working capital, which is used to carry out their designated day-to-day functions. In this regard, it must be mentioned that 'promotion of thrift' among the members is one of the principles of cooperation to facilitate the cooperatives to meet the internal sources by inculcating savings habit among the members, apart from accepting deposits from the general public. But in reality, the housing societies have not lived up to this very important principle, which would have supplied easy capital for their business. Similarly, in the absence of any evidence, it is difficult to accept that CHSs are engaged in mobilizing deposits of various types by their members/households and thereby promoting thrift among the members of societies. Incidentally, it is found from a case study of 30 PHSs (all types including employees' societies) that none of them have mobilized any form of deposits from their members, which could have strengthened not only the internal financial capacity but also would have been an important constituent of the working funds of the CHSs. Also, such savings from the members would have easily qualified them to avail housing finance either for new construction or for renovations of the existing housing units. Leaving behind this important and cost-effective source, the CHSs have heavily depended on their own funds, which are limited in nature, and market borrowings on commercial terms. But at the same time, the working funds of CHSs (both apex and primaries) have increased tremendously over the years, notwithstanding the savings from the members. In the case of the ASs, the total working funds have increased from a mere ₹273.6 million in 1965–1966 to ₹15,985 million in 1995–1996. Over 57 times increase in 30 years has, however, exhibited a disappointing reality of the erosion in the growth in real terms between the decades. Between 1965 and 1966 and 1975 and 1976, the working funds increased over eight times, but in the subsequent decade, this tempo could not be sustained, let alone increasing the same. During 1975–1976 to 1985–1986 and 1985–1986 to 1995–1996, the growth in working funds dropped to a little over three times and two times, respectively. The same arguments hold good even in the case of PHSs. Although the volume of working funds of PHSs was more in absolute terms as compared to ASs, the growth in real terms was far less than the latter. It has grown only at around 22-fold, which was over 2.5 times less than that of ASs. The growth was unimpressive between the decades. The real-term growth has continuously dropped from 3.83 times during 1965–1966 to 1975–1976 to 2.45 times during 1985–1986 to 1995–1996. However, in absolute terms, the working funds of PHSs have increased from ₹1,133.5 million to ₹24,564.9 million during the period.

Own funds are the second important constituent of working funds, and their share has increased in absolute terms; however, in relative terms, the same has declined and is constant in the case of PHSs and ASs, respectively, during the period of analysis. It has grown from a mere ₹31.9 million in 1965–1966 to ₹1,885.4 million in 1995–1996 for ASs; similarly PHSs have grown from ₹262.3 million to ₹4,742.8 million. But as in the case of total working funds, the growths in real terms of own funds of PHSs were unimpressive as compared to ASs. The former registered a growth at only 17 times as against more than 58 times of the latter. This means that growth of own funds of PHSs was less than one-third of the ASs. The other interesting dimension is own funds of ASs have constantly contributed (i.e., at around 12%) to the working funds over the years, except for a little more (i.e., at around 14.50%) during the period 1975–1976 and 1985–1986. However, the share of own funds in the working capital of PHSs has dropped significantly from 23.14 per cent in 1965–1966 to 13.70 per cent in 1985–1986. By the end of 1995–1996, the share of own funds of PHSs, however, improved to 19.31 per cent. It must be understood that own funds of the CHSs (like any other cooperatives) accumulate from two sources: first is the paid-up share capital, and the second is the reserve and other funds. The share capital contribution grows in relation with members' enrolment and number of borrowings, and similarly, the reserve funds grow in accordance with the working results of CHSs. Each individual admitted as a member of PHSs is required to purchase at least one share, and members are also required to purchase shares in proportion to their total borrowings from society. In the case of ASs, each primary society admitted as a member requires to purchase shares. Between the two segments of own capital, the volume of the share capital is generally more than the reserves. Before we analyse these figures, it is important to note that the total share capital and reserve held by a society are determinants of its borrowing power from different sources. The paid-up capital of ASs and PHSs has increased from ₹27.4 million to ₹1,326.9 million and from ₹208.1 million to ₹2,495.7 million, respectively, from 1965–1966 to 1995–1996. Although the increase appears to be phenomenal in the case of PHSs, in real terms, it lags behind as compared to ASs. It has grown at only around 11 times as against 48 times of ASs. Similar is the situation with reserve funds. It has increased by over 123-fold for ASs against only 40-fold increase for PHSs. It is also significant to note that during the 1990s, the share capital and reserve funds have, by and large, equally contributed to the working funds of PHSs. The growth was fabulous in the case of reserve funds as the net increase was ₹1,928.9 million (or over six times) as against just ₹318.2 million in 1985–1986, whereas during the same period, the net increase of share capital was ₹1,440.5 million (or 1.36 times). This trend indicates only a drop in the enrolment of individual members and borrowings from primary societies. Further, despite the increase in the volume over the years, paid-up share capital per society and per member was at lower levels. The increase in paid-up share capital per society was only ₹17,684 during 1965–1966, while the same increased to ₹30,467 in 1995–1996; consequently, the average member share capital increased from ₹275 to ₹462. Certainly, for the institutions of public interest with main thrust on providing housing benefits to common man and especially for employees of various concerns, the current volume of share capital and individual contribution are unviable. This has prompted the housing societies to depend excessively on external borrowings to meet the housing needs of their members. This raises an important question: what should be the minimum share capital contribution for individual members, which could strengthen the internal financial base of the cooperatives and increase the share of their own resources in the working funds? Though this question has not yet been addressed in the larger context, the Government of Karnataka has made an attempt towards that direction. Accordingly, the minimum share capital to be subscribed by each member of employees/(in particular) societies shall be ₹1,000, and if necessary, share capital could be paid in instalments (GoK 1985).

Borrowings are the other major segment of the working funds of CHSs, importantly, for two reasons: first, CHSs themselves are not in a position to promote housing activities with their own resources for reasons already discussed, and second, to meet the increasing demand from primary societies followed by their members for housing activities. Before the volume and sources of borrowings of CHSs are discussed, it is important to note a major positive development. Over the years, the cooperatives have broad based their borrowings, as there are a growing number of participatory institutions. Along with central financing agencies (CFA) and the government functioning as traditional supporting institutions, the 1970s, 1980s and 1990s have been marked with entry of public sector institutions like LIC, HUDCO and NHB, respectively, as borrowing sources. This has resulted in a drastic reduction in the scale of government source of borrowing by CHSs as has been an increasing volume of borrowing from the new sources. The share of borrowings in the working capital has been constant at over 88 per cent in the case of ASs and has increased from around 77 per cent in 1965–1966 to 81 per cent in 1995–1996 in the case of PHSs. This only indicates the extent of dependence on borrowings. However, there is a wide gap in the growth of borrowings between ASs and PHSs. The total borrowings of ASs have gone up from ₹241.7 million in 1965–1966 to ₹14,099.6 million in 1995–1996. ASs have borrowed funds from CFA, LIC, HUDCO, NHB, SCHFS, government and others. Similarly, PHSs borrowings have also gone up from ₹871.2 million to ₹19,822.1 million. PHSs, in addition to all the other institutions, have also borrowed from their affiliated body of ASs. If LIC was the principal source of borrowings for ASs, SCHFSs are the real financing agencies of PHSs. LIC, which began to finance ASs from the 1970s, continues to be the main source of borrowings although its share had dropped from 85 per cent initially to around 77 per cent in the 1990s. HUDCO's share, which was only around 3.5 per cent in the 1980s, has further dropped to a little over 2 per cent in the 1990s. This is a cause of concern, as ASs have not fully exploited the potentialities of HUDCOs, which finance on a soft-term basis. Interestingly, the borrowings from CFAs have increased enormously from 0.5 per cent to over 14 per cent. The same is not the case with PHSs. On account of their affiliation, borrowings from ASs form the major source of PHSs. The total borrowings have gone up from over 48 per cent to 62 per cent in the 1990s. Similarly, HUDCO and LIC have increased their share from 1.75 per cent and 0.79 per cent to over 9 per cent and 5 per cent, respectively, during the same period, whereas the borrowings from CFAs have drastically dropped to 3.77 per cent from 20.73 per cent. As mentioned earlier, the government, which was one of the important sources of borrowings of CHSs, has not retained its position in the 1990s. The borrowings of ASs and PHSs were in the order of 15.68 per cent and 24.55 per cent, respectively, from the government in 1965–1966. But in 1995–1996, it has dropped to only 0.20 per cent and 2.60 per cent, respectively. The NHB has made a beginning in the 1990s with around 4 per cent and 0.77 per cent share, respectively, with ASs and PHSs. Refinancing rigidities of the NHB have been a stumbling block for CHSs, especially for PHSs as they cannot fulfil most of the conditions (Mahadeva 1993).

Notwithstanding progressive borrowings of ASs and PHSs over time from different sources, CHSs have not lived up to their own potential. Generally, CHSs can borrow 10 times (even more) of their own funds (paid-up share capital + reserve and building funds – accumulated loss). But in reality, CHSs have borrowed far below their capacity, especially the PHSs. Accordingly, although the actual borrowings of ASs in absolute terms have increased, it is below their capacity in real terms. Moreover, it has significantly dropped from 67.32 per cent in the 1960s to 58.79 per cent in the 1990s. Precisely, it had borrowed only ₹241.7 million against ₹359 million in the 1960s and ₹14,059.6 million as against ₹23,984.0 million. The decreased was only 6.73 and 5.88 times, respectively. The point to be noted is that with more borrowings, ASs could have financed far more number of housing projects. Similarly, the situation is more disturbing in the case of primaries. The borrowing gaps of PHSs are exceedingly more, that is, over 89 per cent. They borrowed only ₹19,822.1 million (10.89%) against ₹182,082.0 million in the 1990s. If PHSs had lived up to their own capacities, they could have increased the cooperative housing stock by another eight times the present stock. This gap may be due to a lack of motivation or persuasion from ASs to PHSs and ultimately to members to take up housing activities on a large scale.

Lending Operations

CHSs provide long-term loans for periods of 15 years (and even above) to their members for purposes of house purchase, construction, extension, renovation, etc., on mortgage basis. The ASs provide loans to its affiliated primaries and, primaries, in turn, to their members. Primaries can also raise loans from any other agency (e.g., commercial banks, financial subsidiaries, private bodies, etc.) on behalf of their members for house construction. The amount of loans advanced by both ASs and PHSs since 1965–1966 is presented in Table 3.1, which clearly shows that there has been a substantial increase in the same. The CHSs have started modestly lending from ₹152.4 million in 1965–1966, and the same has drastically increased to ₹17,110 million in 2003–2004, which is 13-fold in four decades. Further, lending as a percentage of borrowings shows an increase to roughly one-fourth from a mere 15 per cent during the same period. With this, it can be said that the societies have not fully lived up to their financial potential in availing the financial services, owing to either their members' inhibitions in terms of the demand or due to lack of motivational initiatives or supply constraints. But what is impressive is that the loan outstanding that has increased manifold from a mere ₹620 million to ₹91,070 million, which is 145-fold in the period of assessment. Undoubtedly, the outstanding loan is the accumulated asset value, which is based on the past performance, which reflects on the contribution of societies to the housing asset creation for the members.

The financial relation between the PHSs and ASs is as interesting as the functional relationship. The loans advanced by PHSs, which was marginally over ₹101.5 million in 1965–1966 has increased by many folds to ₹6,710 million in 1995–1996. Interestingly, the borrowings of the PHSs from the ASs were only ₹50.9 million or 52 per cent in 1965–1966, and this has increased to ₹1,440 million or 22 per cent

Table 3.1 *Functioning of Cooperative Housing Societies in India (1965–1966 to 2010–2011)*

Particulars of the Societies	*1965–1966*	*1975–1976*	*1985–1986*	*1995–1996*	*2003–2004*
Number of societies	11,778	27,646	51,580	81,930	100,000
Membership (million)	0.762	1.743	3.587	5.313	700,000
Working capital (million)	1,410	9,430	24,580	81,310	1,253,480
Loans advanced (million) (%)	152.4 (10.83)	799.7 (8.48)	4,609.2 (18.75)	8,149.9 (10.02)	17,113.8 (14.71)
Loans as % of borrowings	13.69	14.82	31.08	24.02	33.13
Loans outstanding (million)	620.1	3,284.0	11,338.5	44,337.9	91,071.3
Total number of houses	65,574	379,367	875,728	1,727,934	2,402,000
Independent houses	17,087	142,682	459,513	964,725	1,458,800
By societies	6,666	71,459	154,413	NA	NA
By members	10,421	71,223	305,100	NA	NA
Tenements	48,487	236,684	416,215	763,209	943,200
Coverage of members (%)	8.62	21.77	24.42	32.52	34.12
Average houses per society	5.57	13.72	16.98	21.10	31.11

Source: NABARD, Statistical Statements Relating to Cooperative Movement in India, Part: II – Non-Credit Societies, Mumbai, and Various Issues.
Note: Publication of data pertaining to the cooperative housing movement is available up to the period of 2003–2004, as per the official notification of the NABARD website. Thereafter, the data are not made available. Also, these comprehensive data are not being published by any other agencies of the country, including the National Cooperative Housing Federation of India (NCHFI).

in 1995–1996. This trend offers a number of justifications, including minimizing borrowing dependence over the ASs to make the loans cheaper by eliminating intermediaries, administrative delays, and putting own funds into the use. Above all, the availability of financial services directly from the financial institutions, owing policy innovations and changes, has been a facilitating factor. At the same time, interaction with the authorities of the societies pointed that the volume of lending could not grow during the 1990s like the earlier period, due to indifferent attitude. It was reported that a number of housing societies did not use the borrowed funds for the purpose of housing benefits of the members and maintained the funds for non-designated reasons. Especially, if working funds, including the borrowings of CHSs, are presumed to be meant for the investment of housing production, then it is very disappointing to note that a large part of these borrowing funds has not been invested for the purpose. The incidence is reported higher in the case of the ASs that have experienced a declining trend in the 1990s as against the level of the 1960s. Further queries about the remaining working funds and more so of borrowings and overestimation of demand for housing loans and thus more borrowing have not been answered. These questions also cannot be answered owing to paucity of information and structured data. Therefore, the existing gap between the borrowings and the loans of the cooperative housing structure needs further examination.

House Construction

Construction of house or facilitating housing activities among the members is the ultimate goal of CHSs. They facilitate construction of two types of housing units—independent units and tenements. The former are constructed both by the members and societies with financial support. The members hold the ownership of the houses on a mortgage basis. The second category of houses is promoted and owned largely by societies as a source of revenue. It should not be misunderstood that ASs finance the housing activities of members directly; instead, they finance through the primaries. There has been a continuous increase in the number of housing units financed by PHSs. The housing units have increased by more than 36-fold from

65,574 units in 1965–1966 to 2,402,000 units in 2003–2004. It can be observed that over the years, there is an increasing emphasis on the construction of ownership units by the cooperatives. It is clear from Table 3.1 that the average share of independent ownership housing constitutes to be 60 per cent. Correspondingly, the share of tenements has been maintained at around 40 per cent currently although their share has dropped from 74 per cent in the 1960s. Between societies and members under independent houses, the latter's contribution overrides the former as the houses constructed by members have increased by around 13-fold as compared to around 10 times of societies. Further, as a result of the increase in the number of housing units, the average number of housing units per society has also increased from 6 in the 1960s to 21 in the 1990s, which is more than threefold. This apart, the coverage of members of CHSs for housing benefits has also posted a similar performance over the years. The total coverage of members for housing benefits was in the order of around 9 per cent in 1965–1966, which has been enhanced to around 34 per cent in 2003–2004. With the increasing own and financial services, especially from the mid-1980s, the CHSs could have covered more members for housing benefits. But that did not happen for reasons stated elsewhere. Fortunately, the movement has recovered in the mid-1980s, and from then, over 1.5 million housing units have been added to the cooperative fold. About 965,000 units have been added in the ownership segment alone. Another interesting dimension is that the state-level ASs could have led the cooperative housing movement better by contributing on a larger scale in the total number of housing units. But that did not happen, as there exists a minimum organizational and functional linkage between ASs and PHSs. Since PHSs have been largely left to themselves in the cooperative housing structure, it is the need of the hour that ASs need to prove their existence.

PART III
NATIONAL HOUSING BANK

The NHB was established in 1988, as envisaged under the National Housing Bank Act, 1987 and is wholly owned by the RBI. The NHB is an apex body established to promote a sound and stable HFS in the country. It caters to provide financial services to housing activities by promoting HFIs. It has committed itself to the development of market-based solutions to meet the financial needs of low- and moderate-income housing segments by building an institutional framework and by developing confidence among various stakeholders (NHB 2014). The NHB has four broad objectives:

1. Promotion and development of market infrastructure: Registration of HFIs for conducting housing finance business, onsite and off-site supervision, consumer interface, protection and coordination with other regulators, integrating housing financial services with broader financial sector and capital market.
2. Refinancing and direct financing housing activities: These have been the major responsibilities of the NHB since its inception. It has four different refinancing products separately for SCBs, HFCs, cooperatives and RRBs.
3. Expansion of scope for financing low- and moderate-income housing: Apart from the promotional and financing activities, promoting inclusive expansion with stability in the HFM to serve the housing needs of all segments of the population with focus on the low- and moderate-income housing.
4. Supervision of HFIs: It has been one of the responsibilities of the NHB as per the act. Of the total number of registered 59 HFCs, 18 have been permitted to accept public deposits (6 of them require written permission from the NHB before accepting public deposits), and the remaining 41 HFCs have given certificates of registration without permission to accept public deposits. Keeping the public interest in view, the NHB regulates the HFCs in order to prevent them from engaging in any detrimental business activities of the public deposits. As part of the regulation, the NHB issues directions and guidelines related to the asset liability management, anti-money laundering, fair practice codes and know your customers, including complaints redressal cell and onsite/off-site surveillance.

The NHB has its own strategy of resource mobilization to meet its objective of meeting financial needs of people for housing purposes.

By composition, it is clear that NHB has five sources of funds (a) bonds and debentures; (b) deposits from public and HFCs; (c) loans against deposits; and (d) borrowings (domestic—RBI/term loans and foreign source). In addition to these basic sources, the NHB has been the guardian/resource application authority of the two very important specific funds: (a) rural housing fund (RHF) and (b) urban housing fund (UHF). If the fund base of the first four sources works out to 54 per cent, the specific fund source was in the order of 46 per cent. Further, if borrowings, term loans and bonds/debentures have been the major sources for the NHB, RHF has been playing its own part in face-lifting the NHB itself and in promoting inclusive housing finance in rural areas. The RHF was introduced in 2008–2009 to enable primary lending institutions to finance the targeted groups housing financial needs in rural areas. The corpus under the RHF has increased progressively to ₹190,000 million currently, but it is imperative that HFCs play a significant role than any other institution in taking the benefits of the funds to rural areas. HFCs have been responsible for over 61 per cent in total investment of the RHF, whereas the SCBs with huge institutional network in rural areas have been accounted to 20 per cent of the fund. This would not only question the very real presence of the bank branches in rural areas but also indicate the reluctance and rigidity in the business attitude of the SCBs. Cumulatively, SCBs and HFCs have been playing a pivotal role in the refinancing services with around 54 per cent and 43 per cent, respectively in total. The other two institutions (cooperatives and RRBs) have had a limited role of 3 per cent. The NHB has increased refinancing activity from ₹42,350 million in 1999–2000 to ₹1,204,850 million in 2013–2014. Between the urban and rural areas, the total refinance was in the order of 57 per cent and 43 per cent, respectively. Especially, RHF and Golden Jubilee Rural Housing Finance Scheme (GJRHFS) have been instrumental in garnering the finance for rural areas. Similarly, under direct financing, the NHB has approved 445 projects with a cost of ₹81,890 million for low-income housing for the poor through public housing agencies, microfinance institutions (MFIs), NGOs and private partnership projects. A detailed account of the refinance schemes, purposes, eligibility criteria, tenure, type of interest and the remarks is presented in the affordable housing section in the following paragraphs.

PART IV
RECENT POLICY INITIATIVES

One of the major changes that has taken place in the urban housing development history is to develop a responsive mechanism to bring in a new look to urban areas as well as to achieve inclusive urbanization. This section highlights a few major changes brough into the development administration.

SMART CITY MISSION (SCM)

SCM is one of the major initiatives of the GoI in 2015 for the face-lifting development of 100 cities selected among several cities in the country. This facelift measure is imminent considering the urban lifestyle, such as congestion, degraded environment, acute shortage of water, sanitation deficiencies, pathetic housing conditions of the poor people and others. The SCM earmarked a total expenditure of ₹1 trillion, at ₹10,000 million a city (approximately) to be incurred in a span of a five-year programme (2017–2022). The union cabinet has approved a capital expenditure of ₹980 billion for the 99 cities under the mission nominated and finalized by the state governments. The states and UTs have been given immense responsibilities to nominate at least one city under the mission for the facelift activities. It is also the responsibility of the state to create an SPV for each city of the mission with an exclusive chief executive office establishment for implementation purposes. Central and state governments equally share the financial expenditure of ₹10 billion per city, at ₹5 billion each. Although a few states have not participated in the mission, the SCM has finalized 99 cities (see Table 3A.2) to implement the development package in the country (GoI Website 2018).

Capturing the progress of the SCM and its impact assessment have yet not been possible, as the mission itself is under the initial stage of implementation and in the teething process. Moreover, while the selection of the cities, as proposed by the states and UTs, has just finalized (see Table 3A.3), it is very difficult to capture the impact on various urban factors such as congestion, housing deficits, water and sanitation, and slums. However, a stronger focus in terms of the expenditure incurred among the top 60 cities under the mission clearly indicates that housing accounts for only 12.7 per cent of the total. It is not only grossly inadequate in view of the precarious housing situation in urban areas, like dilapidated and crowded housing stock among the poor and unaffordable sections, but it is also difficult to give a major facelift, which is an un-avowed objective of the SCM. Out of these inadequate resources, it is the real estate activities that have garnered half of the housing expenditure, and as a result, the other major segments have been less prioritized in the mission. Housing the EWS and slum development have had limited expenditure. Even more disappointing is the rental housing and night shelters, which would have facilitated the employment-related floating population and would have discouraged pavement dwelling, have been grossly neglected. Similarly, hostels with resident services that could benefit the career pursuant have also suffered in the priority. Thus, needless to mention that prioritizing the ugly concerns of the urban life would have been better reflected of the urban life. At the same time, it would have been an opt intervention for the temporary migrants, marginalized and neglected sections.

PUBLIC–PRIVATE PARTNERSHIP MODELS FOR AFFORDABLE HOUSING

Affordable housing is an ideal situation for countries like India, where housing units are made available at an affordable cost to the consumers/needy. It is also a better and effective mechanism to solve the problem of housing that the country is facing. This strategy of supplying affordable housing units would certainly prompt the demand for housing, especially by the middle-income, low-income and the poor homeless families to realize their dreams. Unlike the housing development interventions hitherto, the development of affordable housing is a new concept. In other words, the key housing suppliers like the government and the market used to supply either at low cost but without the housing amenities or at high/unaffordable cost with all comfort and luxury to the buyers. The other dichotomies have been that public supply used to provide always very limited number of units that were far behind the market needs, and the others used to supply more than the required needs and sometimes in excess that have led to the situation of housing vacancies or housing glut. It is high time that the affordability dimension itself has been thought of to ensure effective housing supply. As far as the design of the initiative goes, affordable housing units are necessarily developed in public–private partnership (PPP) by sharing all the input costs such as land, capital and risks. The strategy is a win-win situation for the public and private sectors in the sense that the burden of housing production is jointly shared between the producers (public and private) and the consumers after aligning the land availability, pooling of the financial investment and other costs.

The consumers at the end achieve their lifetime housing dream at an affordable price. Having experienced the benefits of other PPP models, the housing governance has realized its importance in order to increase the availability of affordable housing. The other intension could be to put in place the public intention to achieve housing equilibrium, matching the supply to the demand and supply of the housing needy, if not housing surplus. The strategy (GoI 2017) envisages four very important dimensions of challenges and the strategic choices: (a) enhancing access to low-cost land; (b) cost reduction through the construction and operations; (c) access to finance and capital markets; and (d) housing risk mitigation strategies. With regard to the first, the policy suggests five different options as follows:

- portion of land for affordable housing against permission or approval of the government for intensive utilization of land or land incentives;
- cross subsidy transfers from high-end housing buyers to the low-end consumers against the permission to build high-end housing;
- unlocking unutilized/underutilized government-owned lands to private sector to build houses;
- redevelopment of underutilized urban areas and makeshift temporary structures, ramshackle single-storey tenements and GI sheet roofs mostly in urban slums; and
- change of land use of agricultural lands on self-propelled basis for affordable housing with a low or no dependence for subsidies or cross-subsidies. Such initiatives shall provide trunk infrastructure consisting of roads, water, sewage, electricity, etc., to be structured as PPP and public sector projects.

Regarding the cost reduction, the policy suggests strongly to use technology, better management and construction practices in order to achieve cost-efficiency in the PPP housing projects. One-time delivery and lower cost would add to the increasing supply of affordable housing. It expects to achieve economies of scale by undertaking large projects and large number of private partners. Third, the private sector is expected to bring in private investment for a fair return from it for affordable housing, necessarily to meet the land and construction cost, in addition to the government subsidies and incentives. Upon successful delivery of the houses to the allotters, the investment is recoverable. Rental and leased units being part of affordable housing could be a good source of recovering maintenance cost. In doing so, the private sector can act as financial intermediary and facilitate bringing the affordable housing customers into the debt market, besides being the microfinance lenders. Finally, given the risks in the affordable housing projects at the pre-construction, construction, allocation and at the operation–maintenance phases, the policy suggests for a flexible environment of the regulatory requirements, especially in the matters of floor area ratio, land-use conversion and approvals from the regulatory authorities.

REAL ESTATE REGULATORY AUTHORITY

RERA was passed in both the houses of the Parliament of India in 2016 and came into force in the entire country with twin objectives: first, to protect homebuyers, and second, to boost investment in the real estate industry. The act provides for the establishment of RERA in all the states to regulate the real estate sector and to adjudicate the disputes arising among the stakeholders. The act provides for security, transparency, fairness, quality and authorization in the real estate activities (GoI 2016a). It prohibits using unaccounted money in the sector, and 70 per cent of buyers/investors' money of each project shall be kept in a separate bank account and be used for the land and construction purposes. The money thus collected by the buyers shall not be diverted or used in any other project. The promoters shall not demand more than 10 per cent of the project cost towards the advance payment by the buyers before the sale agreement and protect them from paying a large amount. Builders must submit the original documents of the projects, and no changes to the plans are allowed without the consent of the buyers. The promoters shall charge only for the carpet area (total area of the floor within the walls of the apartment) of the building than for the super built-up area, including open terrace, shafts, balconies, etc., and is mandatory for the builders to disclose the carpet area. The promoters are not supposed to inflate carpet areas to increase the prices. The builder must rectify any issue faced by the buyers within five years of purchase and within 30 days of a complaint. The developers shall not advertise, sell, build, invest or book a plot without registration and project-wise unique registration number obtained from RERA. In this regard, the Act made it mandatory to register for launching commercial and residential projects with land over 500 square metres, or eight apartments, to ensure transparency in project execution and marketing. Failing to register attracts 10 per cent penalty of the project cost or a three-year imprisonment for the promoters/developers. In the case of delayed completion of the project by the promoters and delayed payments of the buyers, both have to equally pay the same amount of interest to each other. Finally, the promoter is liable to pay full compensation to the buyers in case the property has a defect in the title. Complaints from the promoters and the buyers can be filed with the Appellate Tribunal, as provided by the Act.

Undoubtedly, RERA has been a very significant intervention in the urban housing administration and governance. This is because such a mechanism was imminent, given the spurt in sky-rise option in urban areas, owing to a limited scope for horizontal expansion. It must also be noted that RERA is a timely intervention, given the onset trend for urban settlement, especially in the mega- and metropolitan cities due to the innumerable advantages. Commensurately, RERA infused greater accountability on the part of the promoters/builders in the urban areas in terms of their goals/commitments and, as a result, prompted only professional builders in the market and wiped out weeds besides promoting healthy competition. The other points are the financial discipline and transparency in all the transactions of the project. However, as is already noted that the Act has failed to suggest a mechanism for corrective action over the discriminatory urbanization trend, as evident from the official information. In the process, urban settlements are exponentially preferred in major cities due to the opportunities and quality than the other urban tiers. As a corrective measure, what is needed apparently is the incentive-based penetration of real estate activities in the other urban tiers. This would certainly ensure a balanced urban expansion coupled with economic opportunities in the long run.

PRADHAN MANTRI AWAS YOJANA-HOUSING FOR ALL

PMAY-HA aims at ensuring housing for all by 2022 by constructing 20 million houses in rural and urban areas (GoI 2016b). The subsidy-linked credit is being offered to the EWSs, LIGs and MIGs and with a family income ceiling of up to ₹300,000, ₹600,000 and ₹1.8 million, respectively. These beneficiaries are entitled for the interest subsidy of ₹600,000 and ₹1.2 million respectively, to construct 3 square, 6 square and 16–20 square carpet area. Subsidy is also made available for the extension of room, kitchen, toilet, etc., in the existing house. PMAY was introduced to boost the increased supply of affordable houses and also as a counter-strategy for the real estate sector. Central and state governments share funding responsibility at 60:40 ratio. The then Indira Awas Yojana (IAY) has been merged with PMAY in 2016, retaining all the features. It mainly provides financial assistance to the homeless and households living in dilapidated houses to construct standard houses in entire rural India, except in Delhi and Chandigarh. Beneficiaries includes Scheduled Castes (SCs) and Scheduled Tribes (STs), freed bonded labourers, Non-SC/ST and minorities under Below Poverty Line, kin and widows of paramilitary forces, ex-servicemen and individuals killed in action. The beneficiaries are selected by the *gram sabhas* of the village panchayats. Unlike rural areas, the urban PMAY has broader canvass on a mission mode basis considering the pathetic situation of urban housing. It is being implemented in four components (a) in situ slum redevelopment—with a grant of ₹100,000 per house after taking land as a resource and by private participation; (b) subsidy of beneficiary-led individual house construction—for individuals of EWS categories with state to prepare separate projects; (c) affordable housing through credit-linked subsidy—for EWSs and LIGs' new house or incremental housing; and (d) affordable housing through credit-linked subsidy for MIGs—with PPP. The beneficiaries include EWSs with an annual income cap of up to ₹300,000, LIGs (₹300,000–600,000) and MIGs (>₹600,000 to 1.8 million). The last category of beneficiaries are covered under credit-linked subsidy scheme.

APPENDIX A

Table 3A.1 *An Overview of the Housing Finance System in India*

Type	*Name of the Institution*	*Source of Funds*	*Target People/Clientele*
Informal source/ doorstep lending	Moneylenders, chits, relatives and friends	Ancestral capital, own savings and other capital	Individuals of all income groups, people in need of money, people unable to mobilize margin money and others
Cooperative finance	Credit societies and housing societies	Deposits of the members, working capital and borrowings	Members of societies
Subsidized financing	Housing and Urban Development Corporation (HUDCO)	Borrowings from LIC, GIC, international agencies and sale of debentures	Development authorities, housing boards and cooperative Housing societies
	Rural Housing Finance Corporations	Budgetary allocations of state governments	Vulnerable sections and poorer Sections
	House Building Advances of GoI	Budgetary allocations	All categories of the employees
	Employees Provident Fund	Contributions/subscriptions of employees and employers	The contributors and subscribers
Market/commercial financing	Scheduled commercial banks	Deposits and business income	Depositors, salaried employees business class
	Life and General Insurance Corporations (LIC and GIC) of India	Premium income and income from investments	Central government, HUDCO, state governments, employees housing societies and builders
	Subsidiaries of public–Private sector banks, companies and others	Public deposits, NHB refinance, borrowings from parent banks, companies, market and UTI	Employees, individuals, builders and societies
	Housing Development Finance Corporation	-Do-	-Do-

Source: Compiled from the respective company profiles and annual reports.

Table 3A.2 *Selected Functional Parameters of Housing Financial Institutions*

Name of the Financing Institution	*Terms and Repayment Period*	*Rate of Interest*	
		Floating	*Fixed*
I. Commercial banks			
(a) Canara Bank	Up to 5 years, 10 years, 15 years and 20 years	8.50 and 9.25 to 9.50	8.75 and 9.75 to 10.00
(b) Corporation Bank	Up to 5 Years, 10 years, 15 years, 20 years and 25 years	8.00, 8.75, 9.00–9.25	8.25 and 9.00
(c) Central Bank of India	Up to 5 years, 10 years and above 10 years	8.5, 9.00 and 9.50	8.75, 9.25 and 10.0
(d) Bank of Baroda	Up to 5 years, 10 years and over 10 years	9.0, 9.5 and 10.0	
(e) Indian Bank	Up to 5 years, 10 years and above 10 years	8.5, 9.0 and 9.5	9.0, 9.5 and 10.0
(f) Indian Overseas Bank		9.75	9.5–10.25
(g) State Bank of India	Up to 5 years, 10 years and above 10 years	8.00, 8.75 and 9.25	8.25, 9.00 and 9.50
(h) State Bank of Mysore	Up to 5 years, 10 years and above 10 years	7.75, 8.75 and 9.25	9.25, 9.75 and 10.50
(i) State Bank of Travancore	Up to 5 years, 10 years and above 10 years	8.50, 9.25 and 9.50	
(j) Syndicate Bank	Up to 5 years, 10 years and 20 years	8.25, 9.00 and 9.25 to 9.50	8.25, 9.00 and 9.25 to 9.50
(k) Vijaya Bank	Up to 5 years, 10 years and above 10 years	7.50, 8.50 and 9.00	
II. Subsidiaries			
(a) Can Fin Homes	Up to 5 years, 10 years, 15 years and 20 years	8.25, 9.00, 9.25 and 9.75	8.25, 8.50, 8.75 and 9.00
(b) BOB Housing Finance	Up to 10 years and above 10 years	9.25 and 9.75	9.00, 5 years
(c) GIC Housing Finance	Up to 10 years and above 10 years	9.50 and 9.75	9.75 and 10.0

(d) LIC Housing Finance	Up to 6 years,12 years, 16 years and 20 years	8.75, 9.00 9.75 and 9.75	9.75, 10.75, 11 and 11.50
III. Private companies/banks/trusts			
(a) Housing Development Finance Corporation (HDFC)	Up to 5 years, 10 years, 15 years and 20 years	9.00, 9.25, 9.75 and 9.75	9.00, 9.25, 9.75 and 9.75
(b) Industrial Credit and Investment Corporation of India (ICICI)	Up to 5 Years, 10 years, 20 years and 30 years	8.25, 8.75 and 9.25	8.75, 9.25, 9.75 and 10.25
(c) Industrial Development Bank of India (IDBI)	Up to 5 years, 10 years, 15 years and 20 years	8.25, 8.50, 8.75 and 9.00	
(d) Standard Chartered Bank	Up to 5 years, 10 years and 15 years	8.25, 8.50 and 8.75	9.0, 8.75 and 9.00
(e) HSBC Bank	Up to 5 years	7.75	
(f) Sundaram Home Finance	Up to 5 years, 10 years and above 10 years		8.75, 9.25 and 9.25
(g) Weizmann Homes	Up to 20 years	10.50.	
(h) Birla Home Finance	Up to 5 years, 13 years and 20 years	8.75, 9.50 and 9.75	9.0, 9.75 and 10.0
(i) Citi Bank	Up to 3 years, 5 years, 10 years and 15 years	7.99, 8.75, 9.25 and 9.75	
(j) Dewans Housing Finance	Up to 5 years, 10 years and 20 years	10.00 for all loans	9.25, 9.75 and 10.25
(k) Orient Bank of Commerce	Up to 5 years, 10 years and above 10 years	8.50, 9.25 and 9.75	
(l) National Trust Housing Finance	5–15 Years	9.5–10.5	
(m) Karnataka Bank Ltd.	Up to 5 years, 10 years and above 10 years	10.5, 11.0 and 13.00	

Source: Compiled by the author from information provided in Real Estate Association brochure titled 'A Guide to Home Loans', Volume 2 Issue 1 (2003).

Table 3A.3 *Smart City Mission of India: Selection and Distribution*

S. No.	State and Union Territory (Cities)	Selection of Cities in Phase					Remarks, if Any
		1	2	3	4	5	
1	Andhra Pradesh (4)	Vishakhapatnam Kakinada		Tirupati			In the first round, 98 cities were shortlisted (selected) in Jan 2016 under the mission In the second round, Bengal Government withdrew from the Smart City Mission and rejected the financial offer under the mission In the third round, state capital cities Patna, Trichy (Thiruvananthapuram), Bengaluru, Amaravati, Itanagar, Gangtok, Shimla and Naya Raipur were selected beyond the quota allotted to the state
2	Gujarat (7)	Surat Ahmedabad		Vadodara	Rajkot Gandhinagar Dahod		
3	Madhya Pradesh (7)	Jabalpur Indore Bhopal		Ujjain Gwalior	Sagar Satna		
4	Tamil Nadu (11)	Coimbatore Chennai		Vellore Madurai Thanjavur Salem	Thoothukudi Thiruchirapalli Tirunelveli Tiruppur	Erode	
5	Karnataka (7)	Davanagere Belagavi		Mangalore Tumakuru Shivamogga Hubli–Dharwad	Bangalore		
6	Kerala (2)	Kochi			Trichy		
7	Telangana (2)		Warangal		Karimnagar		

8	Maharashtra (9)	Pune Solapur		Kalyan Nagpur Thane Nashik Aurangabad	Amravati Pimply-Chinchwad		In contravention of the rules, Srinagar and Jammu, and Rae Bareli and Meerut were selected from Jammu and Kashmir and Uttar Pradesh, respectively
9	Uttar Pradesh (10)		Lucknow	Agra, Kanpur Varanasi	Jhansi Allahabad Aligarh	Saharanpur Moradabad Bareilly	
10	Rajasthan (4)	Jaipur Udaipur		Kota, Ajmer			Meghalaya has not nominated one of its mission quota
11	Punjab (3)	Ludhiana		Amritsar Jalandhar			
12	Bihar (4)		Bhagalpur		Patna Muzaffarpur	Bihar Sharif	
13	Haryana (2)		Faridabad		Karnal		
14	Assam (1)	Guwahati					
15	Odisha (2)	Bhubaneshwar		Rourkela			
16	Himachal Pradesh (1)		Dharamshala		Shimla		
17	Uttarakhand (1)				Dehradun		
18	Jharkhand (1)		Ranchi				
19	Sikkim (1)			Namchi	Gangtok		
20	Manipur (1)		Imphal				

(Table 3A.3 Continued)

(Table 3A.3 Continued)

S. No.	State and Union Territory (Cities)	Selection of Cities in Phase					Remarks, if Any
		1	2	3	4	5	
21	Andaman and Nicobar (1)		Port Blair				In the fifth round, 99 cities were finalized out of the 100 in the mission. Finally, nine more cities—Erode, Saharanpur, Moradabad, Bareilly, Itanagar, Silvassa, Diu, Kavaratti and Bihar Sharif—were included
22	Arunachal Pradesh (1)				Pasighat	Itanagar	
23	Chandigarh (1)		Chandigarh				
24	Chhattisgarh (3)		Raipur	Naya Raipur	Bilaspur		
25	Dadra and Nagar Haveli (1)					Silvassa	
26	Daman and Diu (1)					Diu	
27	Delhi (1)	New Delhi					
28	Goa (1)		Panaji				
29	Lakshadweep (1)1					Kavaratti	
30	Mizoram (1)				Aizawl		
31	Nagaland (1)			Kohima			
32	Puducherry (1)				Puducherry		
33	Tripura (1)		Agartala				
34	Jammu and Kashmir (2)				Srinagar Jammu		
		20	13	27	30	09	

Source: https://en.wikipedia.org/wiki/Smart_Cities_Mission

Development of Housing Policies for the Urban Poor

4

Evolving the pan-India policy for housing development of the country has been indeed a dream of independent India, which has become a reality after the lapse of 70 years. In fact, the process of pan-India policymaking was commenced from the late 1980s with watersheds in the housing sector. However, it should not be misconstrued that the country never had the development commitment towards the housing sector for seven long decades. The ad hoc interventions were adopted during the period, although their nature and impacts were insignificant, as the public commitments were only in response to the emergent housing crisis rather than to completely mitigate the housing problem. If this was the overall situation immediately after the independence, it would be next to impossible to imagine the position of the housing sector during the pre-independence era. It is obvious that in the absence of an effective and responsive public policy and institutional financial support, the housing activities were by and large left to the whims of the private initiatives of those who could afford to construct by themselves. It should also be noted that even if there were development attempts prior to the launch of the national development plan, they were characterized as lopsided, marginal role of the government and lack of legislative support. Owing to these constraints, the housing position of the poorer sections has suffered even after independence of the country and after adopting the development planning process. These sections have continued to be the development laggards, excluded from the mainstream institutional purview, and have been the permanent dole seekers from government as the only source. It has not been a surprising reality that the poorer sections have been facing the problem of overcrowded and deficient dwelling, which are the two critical components of housing poverty in the country. Although the situation has had some impetus on a very limited scale from the First Five-Year Plan onwards, the position of housing the poor is very challenging even today. This chapter deals with an overview of the public housing policymaking in the country, especially affecting the poorer section's housing in urban areas. The policy changes are discussed in two time periods, that is, the period of ad hoc approaches and the watershed period from the Eighth Five-Year Plan, including the present focus of development of affordable housing in the country.

PERIOD OF AD HOC APPROACHES (1950–1991)

Housing responsibility of the houseless in general and the poor in particular has been colossal, and the financial implications have been enormous. Meeting such Herculean tasks under the absence of an appropriate financial system was even more difficult. Therefore, state and Central governments were expected to meet the bulk of the expenditure on housing, especially in urban areas (Table 4.1). Three important initiatives need to be highlighted during the first decade of development planning. First, the Planning Commission accepted in principle that a large measure of responsibility has to be borne by the Central government in meeting the housing demand in the country through its national housing programmes. In addition, the Planning Commission also recommended for setting up of SHBs at the regional level to administer the housing fund and to implement the housing programmes in the country. Second, industrial workers and private employees were allowed subsidy as well as long-term loan facilities, respectively, during the First Plan period, through housing boards and cooperatives, although a large part of the activities had to be taken up by private enterprises. In this regard, the Planning Commission observed that even though housing secured a nominal place in the First Plan, in the future, the major share of the building programmes will have to be undertaken by private enterprises themselves (Planning Commission 1951). Nevertheless, a beginning was made in the First Plan, but the state played only a limited role in providing housing facilities to the people. Third, slum clearance and rehabilitation were considered a part of the housing activity and municipalities, and local

Table 4.1 *Housing Investment during the Plan Period (₹ in Million)*

			Allocation for Housing			
Five-Year Plan	*Period of the Plan*	*Total Allocation of the Plan*	*Total (%) in the Total Allocation*	*Public*	*Private*	*Share of Urban Housing in the Total*
First	1951–1956	33,600	11,500 (34.22)	2,500	9,000	NA
Second	1956–1960	67,500	13,000 (19.26)	3,000	10,000	992.3
Third	1961–1965	104,000	15,500 (14.90)	4,250	11,250	991.6
Fourth	1969–1973	226,350	28,000 (12.37)	6,250	21,750	999.3
Fifth	1974–1979	475,610	46,800 (09.84)	10,440	36,360	976.9
Sixth	1981–1985	722,010	129,910 (17.99)	14,910	115,000	972.8
Seventh	1986–1991	3,491,480	314,580 (09.01)	24,580	290,000	981.7

Source: Calculated from the various plan documents of the Planning Commission, Government of India.
Note: The figures of the annual plans during 1965–1969 and 1979–1981 could not be calculated for the lack of the data.

authorities were given sufficient powers to arrest the problem of slums in urban and semi-urban areas during the Second Plan (Planning Commission 1956). Little attention was also given to land acquisition and development in urban and semi-urban areas. In this regard, the Planning Commission recommended assistance from the Central and state governments and from state and local authorities for developing sites for sale to persons who had low incomes and wished to build houses for their own use.

Although the government confined its role to house the weaker sections in urban areas, during the first decade of planning, in order to facilitate the earlier actions, emphasis was laid on land acquisition and its development during the Third Plan. A land acquisition scheme was introduced to enable the state governments to acquire and develop lands in selected places and allot plots on a priority basis for slum clearance, industrial housing, and low- and middle-income housing. In addition, a high-level advisory committee on slum clearance was set up. The committee estimated that 1.55 million urban slum houses were totally unfit for human occupation (Planning Commission 1960). The committee also suggested that, as an immediate measure, minimum amenities such as good approach to road, paved streets and proper lighting, sanitary latrines, proper drainage and potable water supply should be provided. The Third Plan also envisaged the distribution of free sites in villages situated in the neighbourhood of industrial towns, villages with a large proportion of backward class population and with poor living conditions on account of poverty and inadequate building sites. For this purpose, the emphasis was laid on acquisition of land and its development for the improvement of housing and development of community facilities.

Despite these efforts on the part of the government, it was not possible for public operations to touch even the fringe of the problem due to constraints in resources. The Working Group on Housing for the Fourth Plan pointed out that the overall rate of construction in both urban and rural areas was only about two houses against the recommended norm of the expert body of United Nations (UN) of 10 houses per year per 1,000 population (Hudli 1975). Public financing was the main source of finance to the public operations in the field of housing in the country, but such allocations were too often inadequate when compared with the extent of the housing problem. To improve the situation of under-financing, the Fourth Plan envisaged to create a proper institutional mechanism for housing finance with the establishment of HUDCO as a government-owned company to assist and finance the state governments and housing boards to undertake housing activities in their respective states. Apart from this, the government also sponsored LIC to provide financial assistance to the housing sector on the guarantee of the state government.

One of the major lacunae of the housing policies hitherto has been lack of proper attention to renovate the existing housing stock in the country, under the pretext that the housing problem was only on account of supply shortage. To fill this gap, the Fifth Plan emphasized the need for the preservation and improvement of the existing housing stock in addition to the extensive provision of housing sites to the landless labourers to the tune of 19 per cent of the total investment in the housing sector. Emphasis was also laid to continue the schemes to provide houses on a subsidized basis and to support HUDCO and housing boards to subserve their objectives in this regard. The other significant impediment in the way of increased housing activity was the non-availability of land at reasonable prices, as the government has not formulated a well-defined land policy. Moreover, of all the government efforts in the housing sector, it was only the urban section that has benefitted the most than the entire country, which is evident from Table 4.1. In this regard, the Revised Draft Sixth Plan (1978–1983) observed that the government approach to this problem had been limited and was almost exclusively devoted to the urban areas till the end of the Fourth Plan. It is only from 1973 that attempts to deal with the rural housing problems have been made, mainly through the provision of land sites to landless labourers (Planning Commission 1978). As is evident, rural housing has been neglected throughout the plan period under reference, and the average investment for the purpose has been only 1.45 per cent.

During the Seventh Plan, the government, instead of leaving the housing activity to follow the past pattern of unsystematic and slow growth, rather tried to attack the housing problem in a more meaningful way. The emphasis was on providing massive financial assistance to housing development, assistance for house construction for those who already own a site and developing low-cost technology to suit the paying capacity of the targeted groups such as the EWSs, LIGs and MIGs. Based on this strategy, a concerted effort from the government, public, private, corporate, cooperative and household sectors was called for the problem of housing during the plan. While doing so, the role of the public sector was clearly spelt out. First, a significant development during the Seventh Five-Year Plan towards housing was the formulation of the full-fledged National Housing Policy (NHP). The objectives of the policy were to encourage investment in the housing sector, to help the homeless population for afford a better shelter, to create a better environment of human settlements, to promote repairs and preservation of the present housing stock and to encourage the production of building materials with special emphasis on local-based materials. The policy was claimed to be innovative in its nature and approach to provide housing for all in general and weaker sections in particular. Another development contemplated was to initiate steps to mobilize resources for the housing sector on an adequate scale, as it was deemed that the lack of funds inhibited the construction of houses on a large scale. For this purpose, the NHB was established in 1987. The main concern of the bank was to mobilize the resources from the capital market and the household sector, particularly from those seeking to build houses. The other concern was to continue the efforts to provide subsidized financial assistance for housing to segments of rural poor, economically weaker sections and slum dwellers in urban areas. For other sections, finance was expected from a network of HFIs with an apex bank for refinance (i.e., NHB). The plan also suggested the government to develop the necessary delivery system in the form of an HFM and to take steps for easy accessibility to the developed land at reasonable prices. Further, it was also felt that as far as possible, the public sector should not assume direct house construction, except in the case of the weaker sections of society.

Although the government has formulated various housing schemes to mitigate the housing problem for various sections, much could not be achieved during the plan period. The interventions of the government have been ineffective due to the non-development of a sound housing financial system to cater to the needs of people and due to non-availability of developed land at reasonable and affordable prices. A large section of the population is still out of the reach of the general finance system, and housing finance is not yet available and unaffordable even if available to this population. Major inadequacies of the system have been institutional and operational. The practices and norms effectively disqualify a large portion of potential borrowers. The disqualifications are linked to one or more of the several criteria that form the basis for a housing loan appraisal. The operational inadequacies pertain to the marginal money contribution of the borrowers, the loan to home value ratio, high cost of loan servicing, complex terms/conditions, specific period of amortization, etc. People can and do build the bulk of the housing units themselves, but what they cannot do is to obtain land, assemble it in large sizes and arrange the basic infrastructure such as water supply, sanitation, roads and lighting. The Urban Land (Ceiling and Regulation) Act, 1976, instead of easing the situation, has rather added problems to the distribution of land. The operation of this Act in the present form is stated to have frozen the land market, pushed up land prices, generated corruption and, in fact, not achieved the social purpose for which it was enacted. Although the NHP of 1988 has been a bold step in the housing sector, there are many serious omissions from the policy point of view. Prominently, the negligence of the private sector is conspicuous even though private investment in housing has increased tremendously from 78 per cent during the First Plan to 90 per cent in the Eighth Plan. The expected role that could be played by the private sector in the years to come has not been spelt out clearly. Similarly, the NHP also failed in giving the status of industry to the housing sector, despite its contributions to capital formation, forward–backward linkages, and employment generation for skilled and unskilled labourers. It was estimated that an investment of ₹10 million at the 1990 price would generate 670 man-years of employment. Similarly, housing contributed 16.72 per cent to the gross domestic capital in 1984–1985.

As these policies focus during the pre-watershed period (from the First to Seventh Five-Year Plans), the investment pattern and its analysis clearly highlight three very interesting concerns for housing administration, as depicted in Table 4.1. First, importance was given to the development of housing for the homeless people in the country. The allocation for housing was in the order of ₹11.50 billion, which was over 34 per cent in the total allocation in the First Plan. Unfortunately, this trend could not be sustained in the subsequent plans, and as a result, the allocation for housing dwindled substantially to a single-digit level, although the absolute earmarking increased by manifold. The total allocation for housing during the Seventh Five-Year Plan, which was the last development strategy before the housing watershed, was only 9 per cent, which was more than a 3.5-fold drop from that in the First Plan. Second, the strategy during the plan period under assessment was to give a major thrust to the private sector investment in housing, while the public sector investment also increased. The private sector investment was a major constituent in the total plan allocation that increased from 78.26 per cent in the First Plan to 92.19 per cent in the Seventh Plan period. At the same time, though public sector investment increased absolutely, in relative terms, it declined from 22 per cent to just 8 per cent during the same period. This only makes it clear that the housing development activities were by and large in the hands of the private sector. It also points to the fact on how concerns for housing the poor homeless households has been sustaining and continuing even to date, owing to the crumbling role of the state. Third and interestingly, the housing investment was almost entirely skewed towards the urban areas during the period under analysis. As is evident that except for a very negligible portion, more than 98 per cent of the allocations were garnered or invested in urban areas for housing development, which is obviously due to the source of funding the plan finances. Thus, if the rural housing problem prevails conspicuously, it is due to the lack of investment, particularly from the public sources.

THE NATIONAL HOUSING AND HABITAT POLICY, 1998

The declaration of the year 1987 as the International Year of Shelter for the Homeless by the UN Assembly has its own impact on its member countries over the years. Especially, the Indian government responded positively by designing its NHP for the first time in 1992 and made available for public opinion and comments. This policy was approved by the Parliament in 1994 (GoI 1992). It is needless to note that until 1994, the housing development strategies/programmes for different income groups were by and large ad hoc (as discussed earlier) and without a proper framework, which could have given the needed direction to the government and other players for taking up housing development activities in the entire country (GoI 1994). However, this policy was subjected to a number of criticisms from the academia and people from other walks of life, on the ground that the policy has not emphasized to create a true facilitating environment, especially in delivering the critical housing inputs such as finance, land and building materials. Subsequently, the successive governments have also not attempted to plug the loopholes in the policy, especially in promoting a sound financing system, user-friendly land market and consumer-preferred building materials. The policy was also further criticized on the ground that it lacked household-based resource mobilization strategies and network for refinancing activities of housing in the country. It was believed that the Indian Parliament, while approving it in 1994, could attempt to address the loopholes of the NHP, and that this policy could give a direction to different players of housing development, especially in the context of new economic policies initiated in the country from 1992 onwards. But that did not happen, and many of the issues were unresolved, which paved the way for fresh thinking of the housing sector. Subsequently, the Indian government brought out another policy by adding habitat dimensions for human settlements, namely NHHP in 1998 (GoI 1998).

The NHHP had a three-pronged focus: (a) to motivate the homeless population to adequately house themselves; (b) to encourage investment in the housing sector; and (c) to eliminate the constraints in maximizing the housing efforts. Its other far-reaching objectives are discussed subsequently. Although this policy did attempt to influence the government to create a facilitating environment, especially in encouraging the entry of the private sector, by and large, the efforts towards that direction remained more or less half-hearted. The measures that were initiated during the early 1990s were mostly in increasing the housing stocks in the owner-occupation sector by giving fiscal concessions and other benefits to the individual house builders. Well-defined attempts to organize a sound housing financial system to cater to the needs of the common man (EWSs, LIGs, etc.) of the country were still missing, despite having the National Housing Bank Act, 1987. It is with this backdrop that the NHHP of 1998 was prepared and adopted by the National Development Alliance (NDA) government headed by the Bharatiya Janata Party.

The NHHP is said to be a broader framework with change in focus and approach, aiming to achieve housing and related environment development in the country. This policy has claimed to have encouraged a housing revolution to minimize human deprivations in housing and housing services. It has rightly pointed out the multidimensional causes for the increasing housing shortage (Census of India 1991), such as the formation of new families, migration to urban areas and institutional failures to deliver the needed infrastructure and critical inputs for housing development. At the same time, it has also been argued that inadequate financial resources have marred housing development. Therefore, it has directed the government to create a facilitating environment needed for the sector rather than shouldering a heavy responsibility by itself by assuming directly in delivering the housing benefits. It directed to rope in partners from private and cooperative sectors to solve the resource inadequacy problem and recommended that fiscal concessions and other incentives should be made available to the different players in the field of housing development. While it is needless to mention that the government intervention in this effort is imperative, at least as far as the socially and economically deprived sections of society are concerned, the policy had also taken note of the investment requirements to the tune of ₹1,510 billion for housing development during the Ninth Five-Year Plan period and has rightly projected the fact that 75 per cent of the finance has to come from the informal and household sectors. This only gives us an indication that the present resource mobilization strategy of the HFS has to be remodelled with a view to integrate the practices of the informal sector with the formal one. This policy has a clear direction of evoking massive participation of the private sector not only in housing production but also in its distribution. The policy also underlines the fact that the housing development should not only be seen solely as a measure to ensure shelter for different income groups but also as an important means to generate employment activities for skilled and unskilled labourers of the country. Finally, the policy has made a strong case for augmenting the network of PPP for mitigating housing and habitat deprivations. It is needless to mention that the private sector, as an important partner, would be encouraged in the developmental and distributional areas with fiscal concessions and regulatory reforms in the legal framework by the government.

THE OBJECTIVES

The NHHP has a number of broader objectives intended to bring changes in the sector, aimed at elimination of homelessness and creation of a conducive neighbourhood. Among many others, the following are the main objectives of the policy:

- create surplus in the housing stock with shelter options to the citizens, especially for the vulnerable groups including the poor;
- boost housing activities to generate more employment for skilled and unskilled persons in rural and urban areas;
- ensure basic sanitation facilities and water to all the dwelling units;
- remove barriers in legal, financial and administrative processes for an easy access to land, finance and other housing inputs;
- ensure a progressive shift from a subsidy-based housing activity to cost-sharing and from the target group approach to the demand-driven approach;
- empower Panchayati Raj Institutions (PRIs) and cooperatives to mobilize resources to increase the housing stock with basic amenities in rural areas, meeting the housing needs of social groups such as SCs/STs, disabled, freed bonded labourers and slum dwellers and the special needs of single women and working women households.

GOVERNMENT: APPROPRIATE ROLES

Given the three-tier government structure in India (national–sub-national–grassroots or Central–state–local self), the NHHP has directed the governments to shoulder different responsibilities at different levels in order to achieve its stated objectives. This has been done with a specific intention to give a definite role to meet the multifarious challenges of housing of the country. At the national level, the union government is expected to:

- take steps to bring in reforms in legal aspects to ensure easy flow of resources for housing and habitat purposes (including the creation of secondary mortgage facilities) and
- provide fiscal concessions and evolve strategies to protect the environment for better human settlements.

Similarly, the state governments at the middle level are expected to:

- play a complementary and dominant role, since housing is a state subject in the federal setup of India;
- liberalize the legal and regulatory framework to promote a large-scale private initiative and cooperative activity;
- define the specific role of public and private sectors to boost housing activities in rural and urban areas; and
- empower the local bodies to take full advantage of the 73rd and 74th Constitutional Amendments to discharge their development functions.

Finally, as the last tier of governance, the local authorities (village panchayat and municipality) have been entrusted with another set of responsibilities:

- to identify housing shortage in their areas of jurisdiction;
- prepare housing action plan; and
- devise strategies to meet the housing shortage (particularly to supply land for housing).

This has been done with a view to promote sustainable development of human settlement across rural and urban areas and to ensure a balanced growth between them. Public agencies such as housing boards, development authorities and corporations have been asked to be more responsive in meeting the housing needs of poor and vulnerable groups, especially to revamp their method of working and to redefine their role for facilitating the availability of housing inputs. In this regard, these agencies are asked to restructure their organizations to eliminate dependence on the government for budgetary support by devising their own strategies for sustenance. It was also expected by the policy that these institutions should go hand in hand with the private and cooperative housing activities. On the other hand, private, cooperative and other corporate bodies have been given a lead role in organizing the land and other related services, besides enhancing the housing stock in the ownership and rental sectors. Another important responsibility entrusted to these bodies is to provide housing for their employees, especially the cooperative sector needs to be provided with all encouragement to fulfil the needs of their members in general and the vulnerable groups in particular.

LAND AND FINANCE: CRITICAL INPUTS

Apart from classifying the responsibilities for the governments at different levels for the promotion of housing development, the policy has also indicated certain specific action plans with regard to the supply of land and finance, since these two are the critical inputs for housing development. At this juncture, it is needless to mention that the framers of the policy believed that land and finance will have direct bearings on the level of housing development. The special emphasis of the policy with regard to land has been:

- to evolve statutory support to the public and private sectors to take up procurement of the land and develop the same to increase the availability of land for housing activities, especially in urban peripheries on a large scale;
- to bring in an amendment to town and country planning legislations to pave the way for higher density use of the land;
- to provide land at affordable rates for housing purposes to those who provide essential services;
- to repeal the Urban Land (Ceiling and Regulation) Act, 1976 to enhance the supply of land for housing purposes in urban areas; and
- to give homestead right to landless category, especially persons belonging to SC/ST communities by providing them land in rural areas.

Similarly, with regard to housing finance, the policy rightly perceived the need to develop a debt market for housing and infrastructure development, as part of the overall financial market. Provision for securitization of assets and development of secondary mortgage to provide refinancing housing activities has been the other step in this direction. In this regard:

- the NHB, HUDCO and other leading financial institutions have been asked to act as leading support to fulfil the above-mentioned objectives;
- in view of the concessions and exemptions that are available elsewhere for housing activities, the policy suggested to extend similar benefits to individuals, HFIs, mutual funds, companies, trusts, etc., to encourage investments on a large scale in both the ownership and rental sectors;
- HFIs and companies have also been directed to mobilize resources from the PF, IF and MF in general and to develop innovative approaches to mobilize domestic saving in particular;
- fiscal incentives and concessions should be extended for resource mobilization activities for funding the housing for the weaker sections, rental housing activities of LIGs and disaster rehabilitation housing activities; and
- finally, governments have also been encouraged to motivate the non-resident Indians (NRIs) and overseas corporate bodies and invite foreign direct investment (FDI) in housing, real estate and infrastructure development activities keeping in view the national interest.

One of the significant steps proposed for this purpose is to institute a 'national shelter fund' and 'risk fund' to meet the funding requirements of the poor and to extend underwriting facilities in financing the rural and urban poor housing activities, especially under exigencies. These funds could be built up from the resources from the corporate sector and by contributions of the HFIs by surrendering a part of their profits. Commercial banks have also been asked to step up the quantum of funds released under the priority sector for housing, especially to the extent of 1.5 per cent of incremental deposits for housing. With regard to the role of the government in meeting housing finance, it is necessary to underline here that they have been asked to allocate resources/assistance according to the action plan prepared on the basis of the local governments' demand survey.

The legal and regulatory frameworks that exist in India have been characterized as cumbersome and complex. This has over the years marred the housing activities in the country instead of becoming a critical backbone of housing development. It has been argued in this regard that governments (union and state) have hardly attempted either to replace them totally or to bring about suitable amendments, especially to the archaic legislations to make them suitable to the changing needs of the sector. As a result, private, cooperative and other sectors have not only failed to make a significant dent but also experienced undue delay, corrupt practices, frustration and anger, resulting either in postponement or abandonment of housing projects. It is in this context that the policy has given a direction to bring about the needed change in the regulatory domain. While doing so, governments are asked to create a facilitating environment, especially in the building plan approvals. Chartered registered architects would be empowered to sanction building plans. State governments and local authorities are advised to lay down suitable norms and enforce accountability with respect to the approval of plans. The policy has also called for framing of a national rent control legislation to address the difficulties faced by various state governments. In order to encourage the investment in the rental sector, it has empowered the governments to exclude new constructions from the ambit of rent control. This has been done since the rental sector is found to be a viable shelter option for LIGs in large and medium cities. Similarly, the National Housing Bank Act, the Insurance Act and the Transfer of Property Act have been indicated to take up amendment on a priority basis to expedite the foreclosure procedures and to facilitate mortgage insurance. Further, states have also been advised to bring about an amendment to the laws related to housing cooperative societies, to simplify the registration procedures and to bring down and rationalize the stamp duty to about 2–3 per cent, especially in the case of housing cooperatives. It is further indicated to add a special chapter in the states' cooperative legislation enshrining a definite and leading role to housing cooperative societies with financial autonomy. States have also been asked to enact apartment ownership legislation besides bringing an amendment to the municipal by-laws.

Technology plays an important role generally in improving the quality of life of the people and specially in empowering the homeless households to manage affordable housing by developing cost-effective technology and building materials. It has been argued that, by developing common man-friendly technology, affordable shelter could be offered to the people. For that purpose, technological devices need to be developed to increase the life of the locally available material used to construct economical housing, and benefits of such devices should be put into use for the common man. It is in this context that the policy emphasizes to take up research activities in designing housing units at an affordable price. It has been further emphasized to promote large-scale use of building materials and components from industrial and agricultural waste. Devices need to be worked out to minimize energy consumption (lighting, ventilation, heating, cooling, etc.) in everyday life. It has also been suggested to devise techniques for low energy-consuming construction. States have particularly been asked to develop wood-substituting material for house construction.

With regard to the issue of sustainability, the policy direction includes development of settlements in such a manner that minimizes energy consumption, transportation, water supply and other services. It lays down norms for the development of urban sprawls and settlement townships to reduce the strain on services and decongestion measures to ease the strain on metro and megacities. Further, it is also suggested to implement poverty alleviation and employment-generating programmes on a large scale to bring about a healthy human settlement. Since building and construction sectors are employment-oriented, especially for unskilled workers, it is suggested that the training programmes aimed at upgrading skills for the workers should be taken up in order to bring about higher income in their hands. This training will further keep them abreast of the technological advancement taking place in this sector. Since the building industry is the biggest employer of women workers and perhaps the biggest wage provider, preferences to women workers in upgrading skills should be given. Second, slum improvement/reconstruction should be taken up on a large scale to bring about a better environment with cross-subsidization. Other partners such as CBOs, NGOs and SHGs are involved in such activities. It is suggested to the government to take up income-generating activities in slums to improve quality of life and monitor land and shelter activities strictly to ensure non-transfer of the assets given to the dwellers. SC and ST families are given a fair share in the allotment of houses or sites in rural and urban areas developed by state agencies, including the private sector. It is also suggested to the government to set up an independent rating agency for housing agencies to infuse public confidence in their activities. A similar body is suggested to be instituted to undertake demand assessment, surveys and independent assessments of projects relating to land and housing activities. The industry should be provided with fiscal concessions, which should include housing cost of their employees in their industrial projects, and such housing should be planned in the close vicinity of their place of work. Finally, in rural areas, it is suggested to follow an integrated approach for the construction of houses with provision for drinking water, latrines and smokeless *chulhas* to bring about housing development at par with urban areas.

To sum up, the NHHP of 1998 is the first of its kind in the history of the development administration and definitely a guiding force in housing development activities in the country (Mahadeva 1994, 1997). As a big transformation over all the other ad hoc approaches adopted hitherto, it has committed itself to achieve a number of workable objectives, which have taken a major shift in the context of changing economic scenario. It has drawn to itself the needed inspiration from the Istanbul understanding in the Habitat-II meet, which has designed a workable and feasible 'Global Shelter Strategy' by entrusting a definite role to different players (government, market, private sector, people, etc.) for housing development. The NHHP has taken a major shift in setting its objectives. The housing development approaches existed hitherto have given a pivotal role to the government in the supply of (a) critical housing inputs; (b) assistance for upgrading unserviceable or badly structured houses; and (c) basic services and amenities in order to face the grim situation of homelessness. But, the NHHP attempted a huge departure to bring about housing surplus in coordination with other major players of housing production. Further, envisaging appropriate roles for governments at different tiers along with other public agencies is a direction. Second, it attempted to promote a balanced growth in housing development between rural and urban areas, breaking the tradition of concentration of housing units in urban areas and neglect of rural housing activities, as it happened during the first three decades of planning. In addition, empowerment of the cooperatives and PRIs in credit mobilization for housing activities would definitely go a long way in bringing about a balanced growth. Similarly, it is a welcome change to make the local municipalities and other statutory bodies involved in the assessment of housing shortage, preparation of action plan and execution for housing production in their respective jurisdiction, as has been practised in most of the West European countries. Third, the policy indicated to empower the hitherto neglected institutions such as Panchayat Raj, village cooperatives and housing cooperatives. With these changes, the government would place itself as a facilitator by removing all the legal hurdles coming in the way of different agencies in the housing development market. At this juncture, it is needless to say that the government continues to provide housing benefits to the economically weak, socially deprived and vulnerable groups.

With regard to the financing of housing, it is noteworthy to develop a full-fledged debt market with secondary mortgage facility, asset securitization and other incentives, which would empower the HFIs to be more responsive in meeting the financial needs of the LIGs and other affordable sections. Similarly, call up to the development of innovative mechanisms to mobilize domestic savings for housing activities would not only bring about attractive financial services but also strengthen the resource base of the financial institutions as capital market borrowings are always costlier and sometimes unaffordable to certain categories of people. Further, the establishment of 'national shelter fund' and 'risk fund' would definitely minimize the risk involved in housing finance, if the HFIs are motivated to contribute to the fund, and its accessibility and management are properly addressed. FDI in home financing would pave the way for increasing the resource investment. As mentioned already, the creation of a legal-friendly environment is one of the preconditions for hassle-free housing development and to ensure that the same policy is called for immediate amendment of the housing-related legal and regulatory framework, which is the need of the hour. A decentralization approach for the building plan approval and evolving national rent control legislation would eliminate corruption and improve tenant–landlord relationship (MRCL 1992). The new Rent Control Act aims to rationalize provision of rents, including the amicable settlement of rent-related disputes. It is a timely intervention on the part of the policymakers to direct the states to give homestead rights to the landless, SC/ST persons and rural poor, and equally important is the decision to allot house sites/houses to SC/ST communities according to their size of population.

One should hope that the technological support for housing development will go a long way in providing affordable shelters to the rural poor. It is a challenging task to change the minds of people as they are used to employ traditional materials for house construction for various reasons. Any technological innovation, which is intended to replace the traditional material like wood, should be available at an affordable price and in abundant quantity. Unless this is ensured, technological support in minimizing the usage of natural materials would hardly have any impact. But at the same time, it is an appropriate strategy to develop techniques to economize energy consumption. There is a need to make all these innovations available at a reasonable and affordable price. Further, the sustainable development of housing has assumed a greater significance in recent years in view of the fact that there has been a shrinkage of the supply of developed land and related services like potable water and transportation. A cost-effective strategy is one of the key elements of today's housing growth. The decongestion measure as suggested by the policy would diversify not only the economic and settlement activities but also reduce the pressure on major urban areas, and the same should be taken up with all concern and priority. It is needless to mention that such a measure would ensure a balanced growth and bring about a change in the availability of housing-related services in small and medium urban centres. Similarly, with regard to the question of employment, a lot needs to be done in professionalizing the employment activities. This would call for training and re-training of the construction labourers on a massive scale, which would no doubt hike the cost of labour.

Finally, if industrialists are persuaded with fiscal incentives, housing deprivations of industrial labourers could be minimized by including the cost of housing in their industrial project costs. In this regard, state governments need to play a critical role in modifying their policies.

SHELTER FOR ALL, 2000

The Global Strategy for Shelter of the year 2000 has been a guiding document prepared by Habitat of the UNCHS for the benefit of public policymaking by the member countries. This policy was adopted by the UN General Assembly almost a quarter century back (UNGA 1988). The purpose of the resolution has been that shelter problem is a global problem that needs global efforts to reach solutions and that each country can meet its shelter problem by applying a set of common principles with its individual efforts of social, political, cultural and economic contexts. The other major purpose has been to urge governments to develop appropriate national and subnational strategies for shelter in the light of the guidelines provided. Among many other resolutions, one of the critical roles identified by the assembly was that women as income earners, homemakers and heads of households should participate in the elaboration of housing policies, programmes and projects of governments. The main objective of the strategy is to facilitate adequate shelter for all by the year 2000, especially by improving the conditions of the disadvantaged and poor.

Before its influence on public housing policymaking is discussed, it is indeed necessary to ponder over its suggestion with regard to the development of an information system on various aspects of land, housing and other issues of relevance to the policymaking. It should be admitted that most of the countries did not give attention to this critical requirement of development of an information system and pursued the development activities on the basis of unreliable, irrelevant and unrealistic data. It goes without saying that the policies evolved over these databases have been ineffective in terms of meeting the multidimensional housing needs. Therefore, it emphasized that a reliable database on key variables is an important component of national shelter strategies. By using such data, the performance of the shelter delivery system, policy adjustments, malfunctions/setbacks and economic interventions can be affected from time to time (UN Habitat 2000). These data need to be collected at regular intervals with appropriate statistical techniques and methodology in coordination with the land registration/information system. The following key variables are suggested to collect the data:

1. demand for housing due to population growth, migration and economic development;
2. housing prices, land prices and rents in different districts;
3. housing investments and rents;
4. the availability and distribution of credit;
5. the amount of land in residential use;
6. the number of units in the different price ranges of the housing stock;
7. location of housing and employment centre;
8. transport expenditures;
9. vacancies and the rate of demolition of the existing stock;
10. income and affordability; and
11. public revenues available for infrastructure construction, maintenance and subsidies.

This strategy has four important components upon which the national shelter strategies are expected to be evolved: (a) creditable housing finance, (b) rental housing stock, (c) public infrastructure networks and (d) subsidized housing for the poor. Mobilization of finance for housing is the obligation of the government to promote and mobilize savings, reduce costs, improve the efficiency of financial intermediation and assist the free movement of the capital. It shall be the component of a shelter strategy, and the cost of housing finance should be at the lowest possible consistent with sound financial and economic principles. While deciding the cost of housing finance, the cost of deposit rate, servicing costs and cost of risk (default, fluctuating interest rates, liquidity and prepayment) should be the basis. The creditable housing finance strategy should be built around traditional sources with twin concepts of self-help and personal savings and has to be mobilized to its full potential. However, poor income-generating opportunities should be supplemented to ensure personal savings for housing finance. The institutional finance should have short-term borrowing and long-term lending, which can be achieved through multiplicity of financial instruments (mortgage bonds, life insurance endowment contracts, pension and PFs). The HFS in many countries has been made to compete for funds with the general financial sector, which has not considered housing as a priority and made housing finance rates unattractive. It is appropriate to review such policies and to take measures to mobilize savings and ensure financial viability. As far as possible, HFIs should not be the channels of housing subsidies of the government, as the same threatens the financial integrity of the lending institutions. Finally, HFIs (government agencies, community-based cooperatives and others) suffer from defaults; enforcement becomes very difficult and cumbersome for various reasons, and evictions become obvious, although not easy tasks, due to humanitarian, community and political considerations. The policy suggests that communities, especially the people close to the borrowers, should be involved for loan recovery purposes.

Considering that rental housing has been an integral segment of the overall housing stock in urban areas, rental housing is built by state enterprises and is rented on extremely low rates and uncared for maintenance. In other forms of production of rental housing (private sectors and market economies), the management is said to be more efficient, and people in need regardless of their income level have foregone buying own houses. This would certainly call for other governments to promote rental housing in their national strategies to encourage formal and informal sectors to pave the way for augmented financing as well as to cater to the cheap rental options. Such a strategy would facilitate LIGs in developing countries to find decent and affordable housing accommodation close to their workplaces. The social legislations of the governments intended to protect the interest of weak groups should not hamper the production of new rental housing units, and review of such policies (including rent control legislations) is indeed necessary keeping the efficiency, compassion, equity, subsidy, etc., in view.

Public infrastructure networks are used by all and cannot be bought and sold like other commodities, and they will have to be provided by public agencies, public enterprises and other public authorities. These include road, electricity, communications, water supply, drainage, sewerage waste disposal and others. It must be borne in mind that housing production and development of the infrastructure are entirely dependent upon the availability of serviced land, and artificial shortages of the same need to be overcome through a planned programme. Financing for infrastructure needs to be collected from two people: (a) from the users and (b) from adjoining land and structure owners due to increasing value resulting from infrastructure improvement. Direct and indirect taxation of the beneficiaries should be employed by the developers, if the collection of user charges is impossible, as part of the development strategy. Local authorities in developing countries need to strengthen their mechanisms of collection of user charges and property taxes as means of financing infrastructure development.

The national shelter strategies must focus on addressing the housing needs of the poor and disadvantaged, as part of an overall strategy, on the principle of compassion, equity and social welfare. The shelter subsidy system for housing poor and disadvantaged sections should be seen like any other expenditure for income support programmes, education and health, as it gives the greatest opportunity to those who need it. The subsidy system should be transparent, measurable and efficient so that it reaches the intended beneficiaries at the lowest administrative cost and free from other social and economic costs. Moreover, such a subsidy system should not endanger the financing system or the subsidy-granting organizations that may face a financial collapse. There shall be a special welfare fund to assist the poor possibly with financial guarantees to meet defaults in the payment of user charges for housing and infrastructure and to increase security of the loans. The policy also cautioned, based on the contrary practices against the poor, to review the housing subsidy system not only in terms of their scale and impact but also to avoid reaching such subsidies to high-income members and deprive the poor and disadvantaged ones.

The Indian response to the Global Shelter Strategy guidelines has been a mixed one in the sense that it has achieved four major successes, and at the same time, it has made a beginning with regard to the other four. Having made a beginning, the NHP of 1994 attempted to promote housing activities in rural and urban areas by focussing on the homeless poor households. The housing norms for rural areas in terms of the plot size were pointed out. Slum rehabilitation, conservation of existing housing stock, rental housing, development of affordable building materials, infrastructure development, supply of serviced land for housing and many other critical concerns have been dealt with half-heartedly. Similarly, housing finance has lacked the direction for vertical and horizontal growth. Especially, the system had to compete with the general financial sector for the resource, as there were no HFIs or a strong resource mobilization strategy. The housing finance available from SCBs was selective and unaffordable apart from the investment rigidities. The roles of the governments at various levels had not been defined, as if the responsibility of housing was confined to a single level. Although priority to households below poverty line, landless families, displaced families, SCs and STs, women-headed households, physically handicapped and other disadvantaged people was given in public housing benefits, the public action itself was handicapped due to the then economic crisis. With the revival of the economic situation and realization of the unattended issues of the housing sector, the NHHP (1998) has shed light on most of the outstanding issues. It is important to note that given the fast urbanization and rural labour shift to urban areas, the urban housing segment has witnessed an exclusive and dedicated NUHHP, 2007 (GoI 2007b). It has promoted largely affordable housing apart from capturing most of the guidelines of the Global Shelter Strategy. Apart from clearly defining the roles of the government (centre and the states), it has clearly spelt out the responsibilities of the urban local bodies (ULBs) and other agencies and, importantly, suggested specific actions with regard to infrastructure and critical inputs for housing development. The organization of the HFS with NHB as its apex body is an important development. It has four important players, namely HFIs, SCBs, RRBs and cooperatives, to meet the financial needs of the homeless. The role of the NHB is quite big in terms of support to all the major players through its refinancing programmes, and it has been playing a major role in the application of funds under rural–urban housing funds of the Central government. The credit of developing the Indian information system on housing must go to the Census of India and the NSSO. The Census of India has started presenting a comprehensive information/data since 1991 for each decade. Housing need on account of population growth, new family formation and demolition due to dilapidatedness; housing infrastructure such as drinking water, electricity and sanitation; and housing shortage in general and for the disadvantaged groups in particular have been some of the selected critical variables for the entire country (national and sub-national levels). Similarly, the NSSO has been conducting sample surveys by and large on the same variables of housing, while different statistical techniques are being used to collect, process and present the findings frequently. The data inputs have helped public policymaking in the housing sector of the country. Finally, the influence of the Global Shelter Strategy is even more visible with regard to social housing for the urban poor, targeting the EWSs and the LIGs. Four different strategies have been evolved: (a) in situ slum upgrading; (b) affordable housing through credit-linked subsidy; (c) subsidy for beneficiary-led individual house construction; and (d) National Urban Livelihoods Mission (NULM). These initiatives have aimed at ensuring new housing units, incremental housing, equitable supply of land and housing services to all the homeless poor.

India is yet to go a long way with regard to total compliance of the Global Shelter Strategy. Undoubtedly, non-development of rental housing, ill-development of housing infrastructure, lack of cost-sharing habits and misuse of the poor designated benefits, continued dominance of men in decision-making and cultural inhibitions have been certain urban housing realities. Unfortunately, an affordable rental housing segment in urban India is still a far-reaching goal, as this sector has been left to itself or to the whims of a few wealthier individuals. Government participation is limited highly to the essential public servants. The NUHHP is lacking a clear road map for the development of healthy rental housing. It is disappointing as far as the development of housing-related infrastructure in urban peripheries is concerned, as even the basic needs of the human settlement, such as drinking water, proper sanitation and solid waste collection, have not been provided over decades by the urban development administration. What is lacking is not the preparedness of the communities to share the cost of the development of infrastructure but the indolence on the part of the service providers. The situation of women's participation in housing-related decision-making is not entirely different. It is rather a disappointing reality, as the economic empowerment is still deprived for the majority of women. It may not be inappropriate to mention that only a small portion of women have started employing themselves in the urban informal employment sector and sharing the family burden (supplementing the income and sharing payment of rents, education and health expenditures). They have yet to attain the level of earning to their full potential and savings for their housing. When such is the situation, women's participation in decision-making is an unfulfilled agenda. Even in this case, the NUHHP, except for replicating the global strategy statement, failed to give a road map for the same, which only indicates non-participation of the women Parliamentarians in articulating the critical need. Last but not least, misuse of the benefits, especially financial subsidies meant for the poor by the non-poor, is dangerous in the housing sector. This has not only resulted in depriving the benefits for the deserving poor but also limited the success of mainstreaming the poor, besides affecting the financial efficiency of the exchequer. Overlapping of the benefits meant for the poor is also a serious concern due to political interference in the distribution and lack of transparency.

NATIONAL URBAN HOUSING AND HABITAT POLICY, 2007

Ever since policymaking for housing began in India, due prominence has been accorded for urban housing development in general and in meeting the housing needs of the urban poor in particular. The HFS—a critical input for housing development—largely confining its operations and coverage of the customers (salaried sections) in urban areas is itself conspicuously evident. The GOI contemplated two policies for the housing sector—NHP of 1994, approved by the Parliament and NHHP (1998). Although these two policies did not draw strict compartmentalization of housing development between the urban and rural areas, there have been attempts to put in place various mechanisms for the promotion of development in urban areas. In other words, these housing policies were designed in such a way that highlighted the development features of urban areas (moderately good design, high cost, mostly standard, modern building material-oriented and connected with all housing services). But while doing so, they have bypassed the typical characteristics of housing in rural areas (low cost-oriented, largely substandard, locally available material-based, unconnected housing services, etc.). Invariably because of the inroads they are into, urban areas have largely benefitted by the policy elements and special attention given to them, such as supply and access to the developed land by the government and public authorities, expansion of private sector investment, special thrust on slum dwellers and housing the urban poor, conservation of the housing stock, development of housing finance, clear demarcation of roles of local governments, fiscal concessions and innovative/cost-effective building materials. To be precise, these initiatives have augmented the supply of the developed land on a large scale across all the sections of the needy by the government, public sector authorities, private sector, cooperative actions, etc. Similarly, housing finance, as has emerged with the presence of the public sector, private sector and corporate institutions, has targeted the regular income class and salaried sections, as these sections were found in large numbers in urban areas. Fiscal concessions of the government have further facilitated the urban homeless families than the rural ones. There have been financial assistances for redevelopment of the existing housing stock and rental stock, as there is a huge demand in urban areas.

One of the paradigm shifts in the approach of the NHHP, 1998, was the added dimension of the habitat-related issues like living environment and healthy environment, besides emphasizing on mere housing development. The other feature of the policy has been that it declared housing for all as a priority area for all the housing needs, including the poor and deprived sections, and considered that housing activity would be an engine for a substantial generation of employment in the country. This policy was specifically intended to create surplus in housing stock to cater to various shelter options; provision of housing services as priority; access to basic sanitation; partnership among the private, public and cooperative sectors; and development of road connectivity and transportation, among many other elements. It is needless to say that these elements of the policy have been the urban realities when compared with rural areas. The private sector did create sufficient housing stock, particularly in high-rise buildings/flats, although some of them are not affordable to the MIGs and LIGs. But this is not the case of either the government/public sector or cooperative sector or the case of rural areas, wherein the housing activity is by and large confined to social housing schemes or to individual efforts. The cooperative housing sector has the least exposure in rural areas despite being a century-old movement. Development of housing services, such as drinking water, sanitation, and electricity connection, has been the housing culture of the urban areas, including social housing schemes meant for the urban poor and slum dwellers., whereas, in the rural areas, these services are being developed at different points of time and on a compartmentalized basis. While the commitment is one and half decades old, rural areas have yet to catch up with the urban culture of housing development, largely on account of the indifferent attitudes of the government and people. One of the characteristic features of the Indian housing sector is the multiplicity of institutions (state and local governments, housing boards, corporations, development authorities, cooperative societies and the private sector) in the case of urban areas.

The above-mentioned measures have been furthered by an exclusive policy—NUHHP, 2007—here, the policymakers have taken cognizance of three major factors for consideration, namely (a) growing urbanization; (b) urban poverty and housing poverty; and (c) balanced development of urban and rural areas. It can also be said that the policy-driven action strategy is in response to the emerging urban scenario of the country in the years to come (GoI 2007b). The NUHHP is aimed at (a) urban planning and upgrading the master, regional and zonal plans, respectively, by the state governments, ULBs and development authorities in order to adequately provide housing and amenities to the urban poor; (b) creating affordable housing stock in the ownership and rental housing segments with capital and interest subsidies to increase the affordability of the vulnerable and EWSs; (c) increasing the flow of funds from the government and private sources with suitable fiscal incentives to the target groups for fulfilling housing and infrastructure needs; (d) development of microfinance for housing and SHGs among social housing beneficiaries as a strategy of demand-driven approach, which emphasizes on cost-and-subsidy recovery of financial policy; (e) increasing supply of serviced land for the EWSs and LIGs and, more so, for the SCs/SCs, other backward communities/minorities/disabled/women-headed households by suitably restructuring the institutions; and (f) ensuring employment generation, PPPs, healthy environment by promoting renewable energy resources and effective solid waste management with the help of modern technologies. The policy emphasized the need to forge a partnership between the Central government and state governments, ULBs and other agencies to implement the goals and aims of the NUHHP through action-oriented initiatives. For this purpose, the policy prescribed a clearly demarcated role for the Central government, state governments, local bodies, banks and HFIs, cooperatives and private sectors.

The Central government:

- acts as a facilitator and enabler with actionable steps taken by the other stakeholders such as state governments, ULBs, cooperatives and NGOs;
- advises state governments to implement the NUHHP in a time-bound manner;
- promotes balanced regional development by decentralizing functions related to the housing sector and promotes action plan for water, drainage, sanitation, sewerage, power supply and transportation;
- promotes systematic planning at the city, metropolitan, district and regional levels;
- develops housing finance policies to enable accelerated flow of resources and financial instruments and designs suitable fiscal

concessions for housing purposes to EWSs and LIGs, including promotion of FDI in the sector; and
- develops a national land policy to ensure availability of the serviced land for development.

The state government would create a supportive environment that includes:

- preparation of the State Urban Housing and Habitat Policy (SUHHP) and act as a facilitator and enabler with ULBs, the private sector, the cooperative sector and NGOs for slum development projects and for integrated townships projects;
- ensuring suitable flow of financial resources for EWS/LIG beneficiaries;
- preparation of medium- and long-term strategies for tackling basic amenities such as adequate water supply, drainage, sewerage, sanitation, solid waste management, power supply and transport connectivity;
- promotion of incentive-based production and availability of local building materials;
- preparation and upgrading master plans, metropolitan plans, district plans and zonal plans for adequate availability of land for the urban poor;
- simplification and rationalization of the legal and regulatory frameworks to boost housing and infrastructure facilities; and
- promotion of PPPs for housing and infrastructure projects, in situ upgrading of slums, optimum utilization of land, integrated townships, urban extensions, special economic zones, skill training, skill upgrading of construction workers and encouraging cooperative group housing activities, NGOs and CBOs, ULBs, employees organizations, etc.

The ULBs/development authorities/housing boards would:

- take up master, district and regional plans, prepare inner-city development scheme, extensions, in situ upgrading of slums, check unauthorized colonies and new slums;

- identify housing shortage and prepare the action plan with appropriate provision for EWSs/LIGs and vulnerable sections for better affordability by the poor;
- promote industrial estates with labour housing colonies having necessary services and develop capacity-building programmes; and
- promote residents' welfare associations, CBOs for fixing of urban boundaries, maintenance of services, monitoring encroachments, cleaning of streets/lanes, solid waste disposal, etc.

Banks and HFIs shall:

- develop financial inclusion policies for EWSs and LIGs to encourage housing finance and adopt more flexible credit appraisal norms;
- develop financial products to encourage slum improvement programmes and housing finance from EWSs/LIGs with insurance coverage;
- evolve special programmes for vulnerable sections like loans for house sites and provide subsidy support of the Central and state governments; and
- promote MFIs, SHGs and cooperative societies for mobilization of savings and for financing housing activities among the EWSs and LIGs and, finally, suggest policies.

Cooperative societies and private sectors will:

- undertake land assembly and related development of basic services to meet the residential needs of all and poorer sections in particular;
- design PPPs for slum reconstruction with suitable subsidies; and
- augment housing stock in the ownership and rental segment to overcome shortage of EWSs/LIGs.

SPECIFIC ACTION AREAS

Keeping the urban growth, the need for housing the homeless in general, and EWSs and LIGs in view, the NUHHP has identified eight specific areas that need special attention in urban areas. They include

(a) land; (b) finance; (c) legal and regulatory framework; (d) technology support, (e) infrastructure; (f) employment in housing sector; (g) slum improvement and upgrading; and (h) sustainability. A reasonable size of land assembly, development and disposal shall be done by public and private sectors as per the norms of the metropolitan district and regional plans. Every such project with appropriate legal stipulations and incentives shall earmark 25 per cent of the floor area ratio (FAR) to EWSs/LIGs for housing. A special action plan shall be prepared for urban slum dwellers, SCs/STs/EWSs/PHs and minorities. Cooperative group housing societies and employees' welfare associations shall be encouraged for beneficiary-led housing projects, as these organizations are citizen-based and non-profit-oriented. Second, plan allocations and other assistance of the state for housing and infrastructure shall be matched up according to the action plan of the project. Incentives shall be provided for financial institutions, HFIs and banks for lending the rental housing projects. A Model Rent Act should be prepared by the GOI that emphasizes on a mutual agreement between the landlord and tenants. Companies and employers are encouraged to invest in rental housing. MFIs shall be promoted to increase flow of finance for the urban poor transparently without charging usurious interest. HUDCO is directed to increase investment under EWS/LIG housing. The National Shelter Fund should be under the NHB to provide subsidy support to EWS/LIG housing. RBI and the Ministry of Finance should encourage FDI from NRIs and persons of Indian origin. Special financial and spatial incentives should be developed for inner-city slum development schemes. Third, the states should repeal such acts that are obstructing the release of surplus land for housing; bring reforms for stamp duty and property tax; enact the Model Cooperative Housing Act, Town and Country Planning Act and Apartment Ownership Act; computerize land and property records with geographical information system (GIS); and create awareness about the Securitization and Reconstruction of Financial Assets and Enforcement of Security Interest Act (SERFAESIA), 2002 and the Debt Tribunal Act (DRT), 1992. ULBs should follow a single-window approach for approval of building plans. Fourth, the development of GIS-based city maps of all urban areas, use of low energy-consuming appliances, rainwater harvesting technologies and use of prefabricated building materials and cost-effective building materials in all construction and housing are some of the directions of the policy under technology support. Fifth, under infrastructure development, states should encourage all cities with over 100,000 population to prepare 'Habitat Infrastructure Action Plan' and to develop mass rapid transit system (MRTS) at the sub-regional levels around metropolitan cities. Sixth, protection of water bodies; norms for growth of city beyond reasonable limits; reduction of migration into mega and metro cities; and development of green belts and recreation areas such as lakes, gardens and zoos for public visits have been a few points, among many, for sustainable cities. Seventh, provision of quality training to construction workers, including women, to improve and upgrade their skills on a decentralized pattern, provision for occupational health and safety of all workers and crèches and temporary accommodation with all facilities are the main employment-related directions. Finally, along with the critical role of the JNNURM in improving the slums, in situ development of slums, security of tenure, affordable housing and basic services to the urban poor, special slum improvement projects and inner-city slum development should be taken up under the in situ rehabilitation approach. Formation of group CHSs, SHGs, CBOs and NGOs should be organized for land pooling and provision of thrift and credit for housing and services in slums.

The NUHHP is an exclusive policy design prepared by the government, keeping four un-avowed objectives in mind: orderly urban living in the country, inclusive urbanization with a view to mainstreaming urban EWSs/LIGs and slums, definition of mandatory roles across all the stakeholders and identification of specific action areas. Having taken the mandatory responsibilities, the respective stakeholders should execute them without losing any more time in order to achieve the overall goals of the policy. Being almost a decade old, it is indeed necessary to mention that most of the sub-national governments have not enacted their respective SUHHP by identifying their priorities and action plans. Similarly, the HFS and its partnering institutions have not developed any thrift-based savings for housing and amenities, particularly from EWSs/LIGs/other urban poor. Instead, their lending operations for housing have been mainly on the basis of high-cost market borrowings. Although the activities of the private sector have been on the rise, voluntary institutions like housing cooperatives have been handicapped due to augmented competition and indolent attitudes. If this is the overall situation with regard to compliance of the policy, less said the better in the case of ULBs, which have been struggling for their existence.

AFFORDABLE HOUSING DEVELOPMENT STRATEGIES, 2017

It is indeed necessary to answer two pertinent questions in the housing sector of the country—'should there be a special thrust or focussed road map policy for the development of affordable housing?' and 'whose responsibility should it be to provide housing for the poor/ unaffordable homeless households?' A straightforward answer is yes in the case of the first question in all the societies or countries that have the presence of the poor or unaffordable sections. In the case of the second question, it shall be the duty of the state represented by the government under the welfare functions. Because housing market with large number of private producers always lose sight of the poor and unaffordable sections, as the supply housing units cater only to the income class and the affordable sections. In other words, the housing market hardly cares and shows concern for the homelessness or housing needs of the marginalized sections, as their primary aim is to earn profit from the construction business. At the same time, owing to the poor socio-economic status, poor and unaffordable sections rarely mobilize and organize themselves to form community organizations. People's organizations—popularly 'cooperative societies' as the third option—are hardly being organized to meet their housing needs, more pertinently in rural areas and backward regions. With these two very important limitations, the onus shall be to develop affordable housing in the high-income and market-led economies (Hulchanski et al. 2004), which has been incidentally built up from the late 20th century. Although the housing market generally functions with the second sector (market players) and the third sector (cooperatives or community organizations) from time immemorial, the first sector (government) shall have the responsibility to provide housing for the poor and unaffordable sections. This shift has prompted and pressured to produce affordable housing benefits, instead of creating unaffordable housing units, which generally lead to the market glut and low occupancy or housing vacancy. The disappointing reality has been that most of the developing economies have been at different stages of organizing their own housing markets and would not have thought of an exclusive stream for supplying housing at an affordable price to the poor and vulnerable sections. India's position also was no different from any other low-income economies, as it did not have a housing market at all to supply critical housing inputs like land and finance at an affordable price. From pre-independence time, India has engaged itself in delivering housing benefits largely from the cooperative/third sector, which was organized with the help of a Parliament legislation in 1912. This has paved the way for expansion of CHSs across the length and breadth of the country. Then, from the post-independence time, the government as the first sector became the second largest provider of housing with a series of social housing interventions for the various targeted groups. This regime was continued with ad hoc approaches till the commencement of the watersheds in the housing sector from the late 1980s.

Significantly, there has been a paradigm shift in India's approach in the delivery of housing benefit to the needy with a number of new initiatives. Establishment of the NHB in 1987 (Indian Parliament 1987) and thereafter the first-ever NHP (Indian Parliament 1994) were the milestones. The chief business of the NHB is to promote, establish and support HFIs and provide loans and advances to HFIs and SCBs. Similarly, the goal of the NHP was to reduce homelessness and to provide a larger supply of the developed land and finance to different income groups. In fact, the housing market as the second sector has started taking shape and is functional as an outcome of these legislations. However, the disappointing reality is that none of these sectors have proved effective in terms of providing housing benefits to the people to whom they are expected to serve. The first sector has never matched its actions to the total housing needs of the poor and unaffordable homeless households at any point of time. The second sector (housing market with its sub-markets for land, labour and finance) has been undoubtedly playing a critical role in the production of housing benefits. It has even created housing surplus, especially in the sky-rise/vertical structure. But the biggest stumbling block for the market is the housing glut and housing vacancies due to unaffordable costs of the housing units. The third sector, which is suffering from the organizational and managerial issues after the independence, has now been crippled for want of state patronage. The cooperative housing movement, with the creation of over 2 million housing assets from its time, is beset with sustainable contribution and loss of focus. With this emergent scenario, it can be said that the country has produced housing surplus, on the one hand, and is facing housing shortage simultaneously, on the other hand. This divergent environment needs an effective public corrective intervention in terms of financial packages for housing development with subsidy. That apart, the need of the hour is also to arrest the ineffectiveness in the functioning style of the three major sectors meant to deliver housing benefits. Especially, such action is imminent to alleviate the housing poverty, which is mostly experienced by the poor and unaffordable sections, especially in urban areas.

With the backdrop of almost no action/programme for the development of affordable housing, the national government has initiated a series of measures from the first term of its office, which is believed to be mitigating housing problem of the poor. In this regard, 'Housing for All' (2015) is one of the missions declared and implemented, which is intended to provide central assistance to the implementing agencies. It is aimed at building 20 million houses by the year 2022, with a provision of credit-linked subsidy to the beneficiaries of all income range, except for HIGs. Evolving a PPP model for affordable housing (2017) and the development of affordable housing for the homeless, including the LIGs, through a number of refinance schemes of the NHB effective from 2018 have been very important milestones. These three strategies are the major shifts or paradigms as compared to the interventions hitherto for housing development. The earlier strategies, being largely ad hoc in nature, have hardly focussed on the development of affordable housing with a clear road map. Very pragmatically, these interventions emphasize and facilitate to undertake repairs, renovation and upgrading of the existing dwelling units that are in dilapidated condition. This is in all measure a paradigm of making the intention very clear for the benefit of the poor, as they have been facing housing threats. Additionally, new impetus for the construction/purchase of new housing units for the poor living in crowded housing with housing adjustments is yet another paradigm. In other words, the strategies are in tandem or compatible with the housing needs of the poor.

Pradhan Mantri Awas Yojana-Housing for All: PMAY-HA aims at ensuring housing for all by 2022 by constructing 20 million houses in rural and urban areas (GoI 2016). The subsidy-linked credit is being offered to the EWSs, LIGs and MIGs and with the family income ceiling of up to ₹300,000, ₹600,000 and ₹1.8 million, respectively. These beneficiaries are entitled for the interest subsidy of ₹600,000 and ₹1.2 million, respectively, to construct 3 square, 6 square and 16–20 square carpet area. Subsidy is also made available for the extension of the room, kitchen and toilet in the existing house. PMAY was introduced to boost increased supply of affordable houses and also as a counter-strategy for the real estate sector. Central and state governments share funding responsibility of 60:40 ratio. The then IAY has been merged with PMAY in 2016, with retaining all its features. It mainly provides financial assistance to the homeless and households living in dilapidated houses to construct standard houses in the entire rural India, except in Delhi and Chandigarh. Beneficiaries include SCs and STs, freed bonded labourers, Non-SCs/STs and minorities under below poverty line, kin and widows of paramilitary forces, ex-servicemen and individuals killed in action. The beneficiaries are selected by the gram sabhas of village panchayats. Unlike rural areas, the urban PMAY has a broader canvass on a mission mode basis, considering the poor situation of urban housing. It is being implemented in four components (a) in situ slum redevelopment—with a grant of ₹100,000 per house after taking land as a resource and by private participation; (b) subsidy of beneficiary-led individual house construction—for individuals of EWS categories with the state to prepare separate projects; (c) affordable housing through credit-linked subsidy—for EWSs' and

LIGs' new house or incremental housing; and (d) affordable housing through credit-linked subsidy for MIGs—with PPP. The beneficiaries include EWSs with an annual income cap of up to ₹300,000, LIGs (₹300,000–600,000) and MIGs (>₹600,000 to 1.8 million).

Public–Private Partnership Model for Affordable Housing: Affordable housing is an ideal situation, where housing units are available at an affordable cost for the consumers/needy, and its promotion is an important but effective mechanism to solve the problem of housing that the country is facing. As the literal meaning goes, housing units are necessarily developed in the PPP mode by sharing all the input costs such as land, capital and risks between them. In a way, it is a win-win situation for the public and private sectors in the sense that the burden of housing production is jointly shared between the producers (public and private) and the consumers after aligning the land availability and pooling of the financial investment. The consumers at the end meet their lifetime housing dream at an affordable price (Sengupta 2004). One of the recent changes in housing governance is the realization of the benefits of PPP models in order to increase the availability of affordable housing and to put in place the public intention to achieve a housing equilibrium (demand and supply) if not housing surplus (more supply than the demand). The strategy (GoI 2017) enshrines three very important dimensions of challenges and the strategic choices: (a) enhancing access to low-cost land; (b) cost reduction through construction and operations; (c) access to finance and capital markets; and (d) housing risks' mitigation strategies. With regard to the first, the policy suggests five different options such as:

- portion of land for affordable housing against permission or approval of the government for intensive utilization of land or land incentives;
- cross-subsidy transfers from high-end housing buyers to the low-end consumers against the permission to build high-end housing;
- unlocking unutilized/underutilized government-owned lands to the private sector to build houses;

- redevelopment of underutilized urban areas and makeshift temporary structures, ramshackle single-storey tenements and corrugated iron (CI) sheet roofs mostly in urban slums; and
- change of land use of agricultural lands on a self-propelled basis for affordable housing with a low or no dependence for subsidies or cross-subsidies. Such initiatives shall provide trunk infrastructure consisting of roads, water, sewage and electricity to be structured through PPP and public sector projects.

Regarding cost reduction, the policy suggests strongly to use technology and better management and construction practices in order to achieve cost-efficiency in the PPP housing projects. On-time delivery and lower cost would add to the increasing supply of affordable housing. It expects to achieve economies of scale by undertaking large projects and involving a large number of private partners. Third, the private sector is expected to bring in private investment for a fair return from it for affordable housing, necessarily to meet the land and construction cost, in addition to the government subsidies and incentives. Upon successful delivery of the houses to the allottees, the investment is recoverable. Rental and leased units being part of affordable housing could be a good source of recovering the maintenance cost. In doing so, the private sector can act as a financial intermediary and facilitate bringing the affordable housing customers into the debt market, besides being the microfinance lenders. Finally, given the risks in the affordable housing projects at the pre-construction, construction, allocation and operation–maintenance phases, the policy suggests for a flexible environment of the regulatory requirements, especially in matters of FAR, land-use conversion and approvals from regulatory authorities.

Refinancing schemes for affordable housing: One of the conspicuous developments of the NHB, which was created by an Act of Parliament in 1987, has introduced a good number of refinancing schemes in recent times for the development of affordable housing in the country (see Table 4A.1). This initiative in all measures is the first of its kind in the history of housing development. There have been two forms of housing development interventions: state-driven approach from almost the independence period for the poor and vulnerable homeless families and market-driven approach for affluent sections mostly, especially from the mid-1980s. Unfortunately, these approaches have kept people away from their reach in terms of effectiveness in coverage and absence of low priced/economical units. Precisely, while producing housing units for dwelling, the price of the same was not kept lower or at the level that most people can buy for self-occupation. A serious problem of the state-driven strategy has been the limited coverage of the housing needy, owing to inadequate public action as well as financing, resulting in a huge backlog and growing housing poverty. The market-driven strategy—alternative to public action—has created surplus in housing stock, especially in the sky-rise structures; however, most of them are unaffordable due to high cost, resulting in a housing glut. It is indeed necessary to note that the country has been experiencing housing shortage, on the one hand, and housing surplus, on the other hand, simultaneously. Under this juncture, the only way to meet the challenge was to promote demand for housing, especially by the homeless households and to encourage the middle- and low-income families for owning housing units for dwelling. As a fillip measure, the NHB has rolled out refinancing schemes with the un-avowed objective of increasing demand for housing in the market, especially for the ready-to-occupy ones.

An overview of the refinancing schemes (NHB 2018) clearly indicates that the NHB has developed these products by roping the HFCs, SCBs, small finance banks (SFBs), RRBs, urban cooperative banks (UCBs), and SCBs, including the apex cooperative housing societies (ACHS). The bank has rolled out four different but effective interventions, namely regular refinance scheme (RRS), affordable housing fund (AHF), refinancing the households affected by natural calamity (RHANC - Kerala) and special refinance for low-income groups in urban areas (SFLIG-U). What is of interest is that these schemes have many compatible features vis-à-vis the housing problems *per se* of the country. First, all the four refinancing schemes have been designed to finance new construction, including purchase of new dwelling units and to refinance repair/renovation and upgrade. Undoubtedly, the refinance intervention for repairs, renovation and up-gradations are altogether a new additional dimension, which is in response to replace the dilapidated units, which have been accounting to more than 50 per cent of the housing need or the poverty. Pertinently, an exclusive scheme for the LIG families for both the purposes, especially in the urban areas, is an added feature of the intervention. Further, given the reconstruction challenges in Kerala, designing a specific interventional programme is a welcome measure. Second, one of the laudable features in the application/scope of the schemes is the inclusion of rural areas for well-known reasons such as severity of the housing problem of the poor, inhibition of the institutional interventions and non-availability and/or limited financial services for rural housing. It is surprising that of the four schemes, three have been designed to lend refinancing services in rural areas and the other one for the urban areas exclusively. Because rural areas deserves effective and feasible interventions, as they had only ad hoc interventions for housing all along, which have left the incidence of housing sufferings untouched altogether. Despite the three schemes designed for refinancing for rural areas, the effectiveness would be marginal due to inhibitions and institutional rigidities, and urban areas would continue to garner the benefits under the schemes. Third, going by the family income limits contemplated to be the beneficiary, the schemes have been aimed at extending the financial services to the poor, LIGs and MIGs in both urban and rural areas. A total of ₹600,000 for urban and ₹300,000 for rural areas as the family income limit would certainly pave the way for the maximum utilization of the benefits by the targeted groups to keep others away from misusing the benefits. Interestingly, fixing the family income at ₹300,000 by earning livelihood from the informal sector for refinancing purpose in urban areas deserves appreciation in all measures. This would certainly give the targeted families who generally live in temporary huts in the pavements, public parks and other similar places a ray of hope to live in improved housing.

Fourth, designing four different loan ceiling slabs for the heterogeneous group of beneficiaries is another feature. The RRS availed through HFCs, SCBs and SFBs has contemplated refinancing facility of up to ₹20 million and ₹5 million and 3 million for the UCBs,

RRBs and SCBs. The unstated intention of this is to cover varieties of housing needy in urban and rural areas. Typically, in the case of the SFLIG-U, the scheme that has been offering loan facilities of up to 80 per cent of the loan-to-value ratio is indeed a big financial support for the low-income households in urban areas. Fifth, the most concerning feature is the concession on interest to the vulnerable and weaker sections of the country. Under RRS, interest concession is provided for up to a loan of ₹1 million Similarly, loans are provided in rural areas for women-headed households/single women, disabled, third gender, SCs and STs and for those raising loans for green housing. With this package, the long-time dream of owning a roof over the heads of these marginalized people becomes a reality. The other concern that is being shown is lending a helping hand towards the reconstruction of houses destroyed in recent natural calamities. The affected families are due to get the refinancing loans at concessional rates of interest at 4.93 per cent, which is by and large base-level price of the fund. The financial burden is being met from the 'AHF' created with the NHB from 2018 to 2019, which only mirrors the concern of the entire country. Yet other positive concession made available to the urban low-income households is refinancing through MFIs and SHGs, which have been the special status institutions as business promoters enjoying a concessional rate of interest against the borrowings. The loans are sanctioned with mortgage of the title deeds, and the interest rates are determined by the NHB itself from time to time. Sixth, it is interesting to observe that there is no hard and fast rule with regard to the interest for the loans under refinancing schemes. If the RRS carried both floating and fixed interest on the loans, the AHF and RHANC-K carry concessional rates at 4.93 per cent. It goes without saying that fixing such lowest levels of interest to the loans is to encourage the target households to come out of the housing poverty and to ensure safe dwelling. Finally, the refinancing loans can be availed from a short-term to a long-term period of up to 15 years. Since RRS covers the entire gamut of the poor, loans can be availed up to 15 years. But in the case of the AHF and RHANC-K, the term of the loans is fixed for 7 years, whereas, under SFLIG-U, the maximum term would be given of up to 15 years with 5 years of moratorium initially.

APPENDIX A

Table 4A.1 *An Overview of the Refinance Schemes of the National Housing Bank (NHB) for Primary Lending Institutions (PLIs)*

Name of the PLI	*Housing Finance Companies (HFCs), Scheduled Commercial Banks (SCBs), Small Finance Banks (SFBs), Regional Rural Banks (RRBs), Urban Cooperative Banks (UCBs) and State Cooperative Banks (SCBs)*			
Name of the scheme	Regular refinance scheme (RRS)	Affordable housing fund (AHF)	Refinance households affected by natural calamity in Kerala (RHANC-K)	Special refinance for low-income households (Urban; SRLIH)
Purpose of the scheme	Construction and purchase of dwelling units Repairs, renovation and upgradation of dwelling units	Refinancing individual housing loans	Construction, repairs and reconstruction of the houses of affected households	Construction and purchase of dwelling units repairs, renovation and upgrading of dwelling units
Eligibility of refinance	No limit on loan size of HFCs, SCBs and SFBs of up to ₹2 million, ₹5 million and ₹3 million in the cases of RRBs, UCBs and SCBs, respectively. Applicable to urban and rural areas Ultimate borrower could be anybody	Applicable to Urban & Rural Areas Family income up to ₹600,000 in Urban and ₹300,000 in rural	Family income up to ₹600,000 in Urban and ₹300,000 in rural	Family income up to ₹300,000 from Informal sector. Loan up to ₹500,000 or 80% of loan-to-value ratio

(Table 4A.1 Continued)

(Table 4A.1 Continued)

Name of the PLI	*Housing Finance Companies (HFCs), Scheduled Commercial Banks (SCBs), Small Finance Banks (SFBs), Regional Rural Banks (RRBs), Urban Cooperative Banks (UCBs) and State Cooperative Banks (SCBs)*			
Tenure	1–15 years	7 years	7 years	5–15 years
Type of interest	Floating and fixed	Fixed Rate at 4.93%	Concessional rate at 4.93%	As notified by the NHB from time to time.
Concessions	Loan of up to ₹1 million Loans in rural areas Loans for women Loans to third gender Loans to disabled Loans to Scheduled Caste/ Scheduled Tribe beneficiary owners Loans for green housing	Implemented through all the PLIs like HFCs, SCBs, SUCBs, RRBs, SCBs, SFBs, ACHFSs and ARDBs	The loan amount is being refinanced from the Affordable Housing Fund created at the NHB from 2018–2019 by the Government of India	Implemented through Microfinance institutions (MFIs) or self-help groups (SHGs) Prepayment is provided to the extent of loan amount prepaid by the beneficiary to the HFC Mortgage of title deeds of the property as security to the loan

Source: Compiled from the Booklet on Refinance Schemes of National Housing Bank: 2018.

5

Major Development Issues of Contemporary Urbanizing India

India's human settlement issues have come to limelight only after four decades of its independence and especially after the development of a nationwide database by the Census of India from the 1980s. An understanding of the various dimensions of human settlements per se in general and urban areas in particular also began from the 1980s. Till then, neither was the importance of a full-fledged database realized by the public policymakers nor was the public intervention during the period in accordance with the actual situation of the ground realities. Human settlements, among many things, are concerned with housing the people and providing access to basic amenities such as drinking water, lighting, sanitation, clean environment and solid waste management. Unfortunately, the Indian urban administration had never attempted to understand this concept by itself nor was encouraged by the development of the database. This has prompted ad hoc development interventions on various urban issues, including human settlements. At this juncture, the first-ever sensitization by the Vancouver Human Settlement Deliberations in the 1970s has influenced the need for the development of a comprehensive database on various issues of human settlements in India. This has paved the way for making of a first-ever housing policy in the mid-1980s. More so from the 1990s, separate collection, compilation and presentation of data on all the aspects of human settlements, including housing development, access to amenities and slums, at the subnational and national levels, have further led to a comprehensive understanding. That apart, it has facilitated in capturing growth of housing stock by types, housing need/demand and development of housing amenities in both rural and urban contexts, thanks to the Census of India and to the external influences to put up to a public attempt for the policy-led housing development in India. Since then, India's human settlement sector not only has been witnessing a number of changes due to the corresponding public policies, supported with data reflection introduced from time to time, but also has attempted to contemplate separate public interventions for urban and rural India by capturing the essential features, characteristics and needs.

With the increase in the pace of urbanization, its impact on human settlements and public policy responses to effectively manage the emerging situation has been the major realization of the first decade of the 21st century in India. India's urban population (as estimated by the Habitat report) would be in the order of 45.24 per cent by 2025, with an annual growth rate of 3.08 per cent (UNCHS 1996), owing to a large-scale migration or shift of rural labour workforce and also due to an expanding urban informal sector, which has paved the way for employment expansion and income increase. In fact, the estimated urban population growth is threefold higher than the national annual growth of 1.05 per cent by 2025. Also, homelessness (as a principal consideration of human settlements) has always been coexistent in the history of Indian housing administration in particular. Urban India has been facing a bane of poverty to the tune of around 27 per cent of the population, and around 6 per cent of the families are currently facing a housing shortage.

It is obvious that the poverty-stricken people cannot afford to overcome their housing problem independently, as they cannot afford primary housing inputs like developed land. Added to this, the financial distress of the poor due to the housing finance system has been another problem, which has kept away the homeless people from availing the financial services of formal financing institutions such as the SCBs, financing companies, cooperatives and others. In the absence of financial support, most of the homeless and the poor in particular either postpone the construction of good houses for their dwelling or completely drop the dream of owning houses. Finally, given India's emerging urban trend (growing urbanization, poverty and increasing housing shortage), a new development environment has been created not only to respond to the emerging scenario but also to develop a balanced as well as an alternative urban settlement strategy. A review of the recent history of housing administration clearly indicates that the urban housing sector has been affected by a series of reforms in two tranches. The first tranche (1987–2000) has witnessed three milestones, namely the adoption of a public policy on housing (NHP); organization of the housing finance system, with HFCs and SCBs as the main suppliers of financial services for housing purposes; and, the decision to offer a number of economic sops like tax rebate and interest rebate on housing loans to the house owners. These initiatives have laid a strong foundation in promoting housing activities, especially on the owner segment. Also, it is needless to mention that these initiatives have benefitted urban homeless households in general and salaried/income class in particular as compared to others. Similarly, from 2001 onwards, conscious efforts were made to develop the urban housing sector and to enhance the urban living standard of people by keeping poorer sections in focus. Notable development during this period was that bold initiatives were contemplated to ensure housing for all the deprived households in urban areas. These initiatives have undoubtedly brought conspicuous changes in increasing the quality of the housing stock. Despite these notable changes, housing poverty (quantitatively and qualitatively) persisted in the urban areas, as discussed in the following pages.

The understanding of slums—a serious concern of urban areas—and the development of the database at both international and national levels in the past decade have prompted several insights into the world of slums. This understanding in the Indian context has facilitated two very important and consequent changes: (a) evolving public policy commitments of governments for the overall improvement in living and environment conditions of slums and (b) the development of schematic interventions for mainstreaming of the slum population into the urban process and thereby to achieve inclusive urbanization. The Global Report on Human Settlements (UN Habitat 2003) in this regard has significantly enhanced the understanding of slums in different countries in terms of their incidence in the development context, searching adequate policy responses and proposing agenda for the improvement of slums, based on international experience. These initiatives have successfully sensitized the incidence and magnitude of slums in the 21st century besides laying road maps for the eradication of slums in those countries. In the case of India, the efforts for the development of slums and their improvement have almost coincided with the commencement of development planning in the early 1950s and with the advent of industrialization in urban areas. Moreover, a schematic approach for the development of slums was clearly laid down in the Second Five-Year Plan (1956–1960) itself (Planning Commission 1956), although public understanding of the growth and incidence of slums began in the mid-1970s. The first-ever attempt to understand the socio-economic conditions of slums was made by the NSSO in its 31st Round (NSSO 1977), subsequently in the 58th Round (NSSO 2003) and then in the latest one—65th Round (NSSO 2009). There has been a significant improvement in the approach of the survey during every round of the survey. In the first round (31st Round), only Class I towns were covered, having 1971 census population of 100,000 or more and two Class II towns, namely Shillong and Pondicherry. The second survey (1993—NSS 49th Round) was conducted after a lapse of 16 years and also included rural areas into its coverage, and based on the declarations of the municipalities, corporations, local bodies or development authorities, the slums were classified as 'declared' and 'undeclared'. Again, after almost 10 years, the third round of survey (NSS 58th Round) was conducted in 2002, limiting its scope to only urban areas in terms of availability of facilities rather than their adequacy. The last survey (65th Round) portrayed the geography of the slum area, approach roads, electricity, drinking water, sewerage, drainage, garbage disposal and their assessment of improvement over the years in the notified and non-notified slums in terms of the whole of the Indian union. The efforts of the surveys conducted over the past three and a half decades have laid the foundation for evolving a national consensus through a Draft National Slum Policy (DNSP; Government of India [GoI] 2003), enshrining the essential strategic interventions by both the Central and state governments across the country. In fact, the DNSP has been a guiding force for a number of states to evolve their own policies and action plans for the eradication of slums in their respective states. This apart, the Ministry of Housing and Urban Poverty Alleviation has been implementing a major scheme, namely RAY, which envisages secured housing facility with access to amenities for the slum dwellers and improvement of living and environmental conditions in slums. What is significant is that these strategies are aimed at the long-cherished dream of India, which is of being free of slums in the coming years (GoI 2007a).

Further, there has also been a concentration of slums and squalor along with degraded environment in and around major urban areas, especially in the metropolitan and megacities of the country. To put it frankly, slums are not only located in core business districts but also in the urban peripheries. Migrants who have travelled to urban areas for better prospects have found slums to be safer for their settlements as well as for affordable (rental) housing facilities and related services. The increasing employment opportunities, expansion of the urban informal sector, guaranteed income and better services in the post-independent period have been largely responsible for the growth of urban slums. It goes without saying that political patronages have also equally played their part in the growth of the filthy environment in urban areas. The Habitat initiatives for sensitizing about the growing urbanization together with the sustainable policies in the urbanizing countries and the Global Shelter Strategy (UNCHS 1998; UNGA 1988) have clearly emphasized on the development of the housing sector as a significant component of economic welfare of people and to address the housing and necessary amenities for the poorer sections, more so in slums. However, in the Indian context, although growth of slums has been synonymous with urbanization, this subject had not attracted academic attention of social scientists for comprehensive understanding across the geographical spread of slums and their socio-economic conditions. Therefore, by and large, the academic literature on slums was confined to stray writings for want of reliable, analysable and official database. Attempts of research studies on slums by a few scholars, notwithstanding, have had their own limitations, particularly with regard to coverage of slums and methodologies. The share of the population in slums and its distribution by different sizes of urban areas and housing conditions of the slum dwellers have been captured in the mid-1980s (Cherunilam and Heggade 1987). Slums in million-plus cities of the country according to households; housing characteristics, including access to amenities; and the government policies for slums have been captured in metropolitan cities such as Calcutta, Delhi and Madras (Chennai), as they were the main cities in terms of urban slums (Gupta 1985). In addition to these three metropolitan cities, the study also covered Greater Bombay, Hyderabad, Ahmedabad, Bangalore, Kanpur and Poona. What is significant is that there have been an increasing number of million-plus cities (27) spread over 13 states with a notable population size. Also important is that a good number of states have registered more number of a million-plus cities reportedly having housing slums. For example, the state of Maharashtra has slums in 7 cities with a population of 1 million, including Greater Bombay, followed by Uttar Pradesh (5 cities with a population of 1 million), Gujarat (3 cities with a population of 1 million), and Madhya Pradesh and West Bengal (2 cities each with a population of 1 million). The 2001 census figures indicate eight more cities with a population of 1 million having housing slums. The National Institute of Urban Affairs (NIUA 1988) has furthered the comprehensive understanding of slums in India and their relationship with the growth of India's urbanization between 1971 and 1981. All these studies have not only brought to the fore the growing incidence of slums in the country but also have contributed towards a clear understanding of the multifaceted dimensions of the slums. Further, the continuous efforts on the part of the NSSO, the Census of India (Census of India 2001a) and the Ministry of Housing and Urban Poverty Alleviation have contributed conspicuously to evolve slum improvement strategies within a broad policy framework. Except for the analysis of the availability of the social infrastructure, housing and demographic outcomes (Chandrasekhar 2005), there are hardly any attempts to capture the changes that have taken place in slums in the two different points of survey periods. These initiatives at the national level and the development interventions by the states that have been historically facing the slum problem have contributed towards a significant and positive impact on people from all walks of life in slums. The understanding and interventions have resulted in a dwindling number of slums in the country, coupled with the overall living and environmental improvement in slums. In fact, these developments have been the testimonies of the change. Capturing these changes in the housing and living environment fronts in the slums across two different periods and to identify the main drivers is of paramount significance, which is attempted in the following paragraphs.

A good urban living necessarily encompasses connectivity of all the major housing services to all the households in conducive as well as human-friendly conditions. Also, for an equally decent urban living, meeting these services uninterruptedly and proportionately for an increasing population is especially a necessary condition. Otherwise, if these two critical needs are not met, the service gaps would result in deprivation in the short run and their poverty in the long run, apart from making urban living non-liveable. In other words, total coverage of the urban population/families, with all the basic housing services, is the necessary criterion to ensure smart urban living. The development of the urban housing services to meet the total needs of the urban population/families is as important as urbanization itself. If it does not progress with the increasing population/families, such urban growth amounts to mal-development, lopsided development and development failure. A related literature survey also supports this argument that the housing amenities/services showed a positive relationship among safe drinking water–sanitation–other services and health–overall welfare improvement and adverse impact if these services are not safely and adequately provided. It further recognizes that drinking water and sanitation are central to good housing, living condition and health, besides being central to prosperous economies (Dieterich and Henderson 1963). Also, access to water supply and sanitation is a fundamental need and a human right, apart from being vital for dignity and health of all the people, and poor water supply and sanitation would lead to health hazards such as diarrhoea, intestinal infections, blindness and schistosomiasis (WHO and UNICEF 2000).

For common understanding, urban services mainly encompass safe water for drinking; electricity mainly for lighting; sanitation (toilets) for decent defecation; households' bathroom connectivity for decent showering purposes, particularly for women; and drainage connectivity to avoid water logging and filthy environment around living places. Ensuring these facilities not only enables a hygienic environment but also promotes good health of the people. Drinking water, as a basic necessity, acts as a lifeline and is a natural gift, which is being supplied to the people through various methods for their survival. Electricity is an economic good, which is produced by various players (mainly the government) and has been an indicator of a modern way of life; it is a production agent of goods and services. It has been a prominent input of household economic activities as well. Sanitation within the housing unit mainly caters to dwellers' needs, particularly the needs of women, children and others round the clock, and is a critical but inseparable utility in the urban living environment. Irrespective of the agency that undertakes the development of the urban housing environment, ensuring a decent level of urban services is inevitable. If this critical requirement is not accomplished, not only is there any meaning to urban living, but it also accounts for deficient or ill-housing, which would have a negative price impact on the project. Unlike the rural practices, which paved the way for the development of housing amenities on a compartmentalized basis (at different points of time and according to one's own convenience) due to the cost factor, generally, in urban areas, development of housing services takes place simultaneously and jointly along with the construction of houses, irrespective of the cost consideration, administrative formalities or inconvenience.

Despite the important aforementioned considerations, urbanization in India, ever since it commenced, has not paid adequate attention to the development of urban housing services, which are on par with the urban population expansion and attained the equilibrium level. There has always been a deficit in the provision of urban housing services vis-à-vis the urban population/families. If this is the overall situation, perspective planning and development (creating urban housing services according to future growth) have been altogether missing in the development administration, not because of a lack of interest but for want of huge financial implications. It is observed that the progress achieved notwithstanding, especially after 'The International Drinking Water and Sanitation Decade 1981–1991', short coverage of the urban people is a reality in India, as the water supply and sanitation sectors are financially unviable, insufficient and of low quality (World Bank 1999). Further, inadequate water services, low-quality services and constraints have been the most common attributes of the public water system in major and other urban areas. Urban water supply to all, including the poorer segment, is continuing to face difficulties such as inadequate funding on the part of the public authorities, high-cost supply, pilferages, jurisdictional conflicts, improper mechanism to recover water user charges and others. Similarly, households' sanitation is continuing to be a distant dream of the squatter settlements on account of ill-financing and poor collection efficiency of solid waste (Planning Commission 2008). Furthermore, less said the better about urban solid waste, in which urban development administration has consciously contributed to the colossal growth of the problem. Although there has been a realization in managing solid waste, the efforts have ended up with ineffective administration due to the half-hearted approach of the stakeholders such as public, local administration and household/community participation.

Despite these macro-development concerns in the human settlement issues of the country, mainstream scholars have not evinced interest in undertaking research in this important sector (urban housing poverty, urban slums, amenity deficiencies, solid waste management) of the Indian economy. Moreover, studies highlighting the supply- and demand-side problems of the housing sector, dwindling number of slums, provision of amenities and solid waste management from the overall ground perspectives and failures in the development initiatives are by and large missing. Further, the policy introduced in the urban housing sector since 2001, impact assessment on housing poverty, dwindling slums, improvement in housing amenities, gaps in the development administration and the current challenges have not been studied in the urban set-up. This research assesses the development progress of the urban housing sector during 2001–2011 in terms of the housing stock created and access to principal housing amenities to the families. It also identifies the development gaps mainly with regard to housing shortage and deprivation of the amenities at the national and subnational levels. Similarly, the underlying importance is to understand the actual position of mainstreaming of slums and solid waste management in terms of the development challenges and to ponder over what is due to be achieved to wholly eliminate poverty and deprivation and to achieve slum garbage-free urban environment. This would not only help in achieving the goal of total coverage of the population but would also lead to achieve a smart way of living, as forecasted in the SCM of the national government. The official data source, as presented by the Census of India (2011) and the NSSO (NSSO 2009; 65th Round), has been used for this purpose. The data on access to urban services and gaps in the development from the first source and, similarly, the second source on the issues related to urban slums and environment, are collated, owing to its compatibility. With this backdrop, this chapter has identified four very important but selected human settlement issues of the urban areas, namely (a) incidence of urban housing poverty; (b) deficiencies in housing amenities; (c) mounting solid waste and failure in its management; and (d) inherent but waning slums. The following pages discuss these issues in greater detail.

PART I
HOUSING POVERTY AND AMENITIES DEPRIVATION

The changes in the urban housing front in terms of overall increase in the housing stock, quality (standard) stock (Mahadeva 2002b, 2006) and, as a result, a proportionate increase in access to housing amenities in the last decade have left behind two important challenges (a) the housing poverty and (b) deprivation of housing amenities, especially among the unaffordable sections. It is not that these challenges are unmanageable/unmet, but the volume of developmental interventions has not been proportionate to the needs of the urban homeless households. In order to infuse effectiveness of the urban housing administration, this research has analysed the urban housing poverty in general and by its classification—relative and absolute poverty. Before the nature and incidence of poverty across the country is discussed, it is indeed necessary to note two realistic observations. First, it should be noted that not all the urban areas of 29 independent states and 6 UTs of the country have been facing the same incidence of housing poverty, although the problem is widespread. Instead, only 13 independent states have become the centres of housing poverty, in the sense that they accounted for the major portion (85.65%) of the total housing poverty of the country (the detailed discussion will follow subsequently). This finding obviously leaves the rest of the other 16 states and 5 UTs, which have accounted, respectively, for 13.9 per cent and 0.45 per cent of the urban families facing the housing poverty (Table 5.1). Second, the overall housing poverty can be classified into (a) absolute poverty: families living with relatives and friends by sharing the housing accommodation, which is also called

Table 5.1 *Housing Poverty by Source in Selected States of Urban India, 2011*

Sl. No.	State and Union Territory	Overcrowded Families	Families Dwelling in Dilapidated Houses	Total Housing Poverty	% of the Families Facing the Poverty
1	Uttar Pradesh	0.459 (61.36)	0.289 (38.64)	0.748 (15.65)	10.04
2	West Bengal	0.194 (31.65)	0.419 (68.35)	0.613 (12.84)	9.65
3	Maharashtra	0.239 (54.07)	0.203 (45.93)	0.442 (9.26)	4.09
4	Madhya Pradesh	0.191 (64.75)	0.104 (35.25)	0.295 (6.18)	7.67
5	Tamil Nadu	0.114 (39.04)	0.178 (60.96)	0.292 (6.12)	3.27
6	Andhra Pradesh	0.151 (60.16)	0.100 (39.84)	0.251 (5.26)	3.70
7	Bihar	0.093 (40.09)	0.139 (59.91)	0.232 (4.86)	11.52
8	Delhi	0.133 (59.64)	0.090 (40.36)	0.223 (4.67)	6.84
9	Karnataka	0.090 (46.63)	0.103 (53.37)	0.193 (4.04)	3.63
10	Punjab	0.076 (40.86)	0.110 (59.14)	0.186 (3.90)	8.88
11	Kerala	0.019 (11.73)	0.143 (88.27)	0.162 (3.39)	4.47
12	Rajasthan	0.101 (64.33)	0.056 (35.67)	0.157 (3.29)	5.08
13	Haryana	0.081 (57.86)	0.059 (42.14)	0.140 (02.93)	8.00
Total and % in the Incidence		1.941 (86.46)	1.993 (84.88)	3.934 (85.65)	6.68

(Table 5.1 Continued)

(Table 5.1 Continued)

Sl. No.	State and Union Territory	Overcrowded Families	Families Dwelling in Dilapidated Houses	Total Housing Poverty	% of the Families Facing the Poverty
	*Total of all other states	0.294 (13.10)	0.345 (14.70)	0.639 (13.90)	5.60
	Total of all union territories	0.010 (00.44)	0.010 (00.42)	0.020 (00.45)	3.07
	Total urban India	2.245 (48.88)	2.348 (51.12)	4.593 (100.00)	5.82

Source: Census of India (2011). Tables on Houses, Household Amenities and Assets, Series 1, Registrar General and Census Commissioner, Government of India, New Delhi.
Note: *Other states include Arunachal Pradesh, Assam, Chhattisgarh, Goa, Gujarat, Himachal Pradesh, Jharkhand, Jammu and Kashmir, Manipur, Meghalaya, Mizoram, Nagaland, Odisha, Sikkim, Tripura and Uttarakhand. Similarly, union territories include Andaman and Nicobar Islands, Chandigarh, Daman and Diu, Dadra and Nagar Haveli, and Puducherry. However, Lakshadweep is not included in the table, as the housing shortage is less than few hundreds; figures in million.

housing adjustment and (b) relative poverty: families living in dilapidated/unsecured housing structures and facing all forms of threats and not able to renovate the structure and upgrade frequently owing to their poor status. It goes without saying that absolute housing poverty would have arisen on account of a shortfall in the new construction vis-à-vis the need for new housing units, particularly among newly formed families. Indeed, it is highly important to note that the incidence of housing poverty is almost equally existent and attributed for absolute as well as relative, in the country, although a few states have had an upper hand in one or the other forms or both.

The total urban housing poverty or the number of families facing housing shortage is in the order of 4.593 million in the country—2.248 million due to absolute terms (housing adjustment) and 2.348 million due to relative terms (dilapidated dwelling). Roughly, about 6 per cent of the urban families have been facing a shortage in housing, as is evident from Table 5.1. The disaggregated scenario depicts clearly that the housing poverty is confined largely to 13 major and independent states with a total incidence of 3.934 million units (85.65%), 16 other states have accounted for 639,000 units (13.90%) and the UTs accounted for 20,000 units (0.45%). Further, in terms of the urban families facing housing poverty, it is quite high in the case of 13 states (6.68%), it is below the national average in the case of 16 other states (5.60%) and it is far below in the case of the UTs (3.07%). This only means that housing development efforts of the public, private, voluntary and cooperative actions have not been commensurate with the housing needs of the urban homeless families; the actions are very conspicuously disproportionate among the 13 major states, moderate in other states and very negligible among the UTs. Therefore, it is highly discriminatory to assess the housing poverty of the country in its totality, without analysing from the regional perspective. Further, between the two types of poverty, the relative segment has an edge over absolute poverty, for example 2.348 million families (about 51%) are dwelling in dilapidated units facing threats in 2011, with minimum basket of housing, as their dwelling units do not ensure safe housing throughout the year and around the changing climatic conditions. Especially during the rainy season, the dwellers of the dilapidated units always face one or the other kind of life threats such as falling roof, falling walls, and houses getting washed off. Having been largely poor, the majority of these families are unable to upgrade their dilapidated units. Furthermore, the incidence of the absolute homelessness is equally bothersome, since as many as 2.245 million families (49%) are facing this problem. This means that those many families have resorted to housing adjustment with their relatives and friends, knowing fully well about their direct contribution to crowded dwelling and pressure they exert on the existing housing services. In fact, a good number of families consciously prefer crowded dwelling in many urban parts, as joint living provides many benefits such as sharing cost of the maintenance, social life, caring children care for tender population and aged people.

An understanding of the urban housing shortage of 13 major states is extremely necessary for the regional planning and development, which clearly points out that the incidence is widespread and voluminous. These 13 states can be categorized as highly vulnerable with limited housing production from the market. This group of the states is led by Uttar Pradesh, which has recorded the highest number of housing shortage in the entire country. These states have together accounted for a total housing shortage of 3.934 million units, which is 85.65 per cent of the national incidence and shares the total shortage between crowded and dilapidated units at 1.941 million units (86.46%) and 1.993 million units (84.88%), respectively. Further, 7 of the 13 states have recorded the highest percentage of the urban families facing shortage above the group average. For example, Bihar had the highest percentage (11.52%), followed by Uttar Pradesh (10.04%), West Bengal (9.65%), Punjab (8.88%), Haryana (8.00%), Madhya Pradesh (7.67%) and Delhi (6.84%).

DEPRIVATION OF HOUSING AMENITIES

The importance of housing amenities need not be explained again. Clearly, the number of families deprived of housing amenities (drinking water, sanitation and lighting together) in urban India has officially declined from 8.58 million in 2001 to 5.62 million in 2011, which is one of the positive changes. This means that as many as 2.96 million families have been provided with these facilities, which have helped them to overcome the deprivation (Table 5.2). In relative terms, urban families deprived of housing amenities, which was in the order of 16.14 per cent in 2001 has declined to 7.15 per cent in 2011—a net reduction of almost 9 per cent. The uncovered families are in the order of 5.620 million and are largely migrants, subsistence earners and located mostly in inaccessible places, and would have resorted to unsafe sources/means, as the public interventions have not reached them. Depending on un-piped drinking water sources (wells, springs, rivers, canals, tanks, ponds, etc.), open space defecation and use of carbon dioxide-emitting materials such as kerosene, burning oils, cow dung and firewood for lighting have been the common practices. Thus, it is necessary to note adverse implications like deterioration of people's health conditions and environmental degradation in urban areas. Further, the incidence of urban families depending on unsafe sources for fulfilling the housing amenities is even more conspicuous at the subnational level, despite many regions having successfully

Table 5.2 *Deprivation of Selected Housing Amenities in Urban India—2001–2011 (Drinking Water, Toilet and Lighting)*

Sl. No.	State and Union Territory	Deprivation of All the Three Amenities—2001		Deprivation of All the Three Amenities—2011		Change (+ or –)	
		Urban Families	% in Total Families	Urban Families	% in Total Families	Urban Families	% in Total Families
1	Andhra Pradesh	0.440 (5.13)	10.52	0.390 (6.94)	5.78	–0.050	–4.74
2	Arunachal Pradesh	0.010 (0.12)	10.42	—	4.55	–0.010	–5.87
3	Assam	0.150 (1.75)	20.14	0.040 (0.71)	3.73	–0.110	–16.41
4	Bihar	0.350 (4.08)	26.46	0.220 (3.91)	11.07	–0.270	–15.39
5	Chhattisgarh	0.200 (2.33)	25.10	0.170 (3.02)	13.64	–0.300	–11.46
6	Goa	0.030 (0.35)	18.12	0.010 (0.18)	5.56	–0.020	–12.56
7	Gujarat	0.380 (4.43)	10.14	0.270 (4.80)	5.00	–0.110	–5.14
8	Haryana	0.100 (1.17)	9.67	0.080 (1.42)	4.39	–0.020	–5.28
9	Himachal Pradesh	0.010 (0.12)	9.79	0.010 (0.18)	4.22	—	–5.57

(Table 5.2 Continued)

(Table 5.2 Continued)

Sl. No.	State and Union Territory	Deprivation of All the Three Amenities—2001		Deprivation of All the Three Amenities—2011		Change (+ or –)	
		Urban Families	% in Total Families	Urban Families	% in Total Families	Urban Families	% in Total Families
10	Jharkhand	0.320 (3.73)	29.91	0.180 (3.20)	11.76	–0.140	–18.15
11	Jammu and Kashmir	0.030 (0.35)	6.41	0.030 (0.53)	5.02	—	–1.39
12	Karnataka	0.500 (5.83)	13.94	0.330 (5.87)	6.11	–0.170	–7.83
13	Kerala	0.440 (5.13)	26.80	0.050 (0.89)	1.44	–0.390	–25.36
14	Madhya Pradesh	0.490 (5.71)	17.10	0.360 (6.41)	9.47	–0.130	–7.63
15	Maharashtra	1.400 (16.32)	17.39	1.110 (19.75)	10.26	–0.290	–7.13
16	Manipur	0.020 (0.23)	20.79	0.020 (0.36)	12.87	—	–7.92
17	Meghalaya	0.010 (0.12)	15.38	0.010 (0.18)	5.17	—	–10.21
18	Mizoram	0.020 (0.23)	20.73	0.010 (0.18)	7.76	–0.010	–12.97
19	Nagaland	0.020 (0.23)	23.88	0.010 (0.18)	8.70	–0.010	–15.18

20	Odisha	0.400 (4.66)	31.19	0.190 (3.38)	12.79	–0.210	–18.40
21	Punjab	0.090 (1.05)	5.97	0.050 (0.89)	2.58	–0.040	–3.39
22	Rajasthan	0.300 (3.50)	13.54	0.230 (4.09)	7.54	–0.070	–6.00
23	Tamil Nadu	1.210 (14.10)	20.48	0.830 (14.77)	9.28	–0.380	–11.20
24	Uttar Pradesh	0.740 (8.62)	14.23	0.460 (8.19)	6.20	–0.280	–8.03
25	Uttarakhand	0.030 (0.35)	8.21	0.020 (0.36)	2.53	–0.010	–5.68
26	West Bengal	0.650 (7.58)	14.32	0.360 (6.41)	5.73	–0.290	–8.59
27	Chandigarh	—	—	0.010 (0.18)	4.39	0.010	4.39
28	Delhi	0.240 (2.80)	9.94	0.160 (2.85)	4.97	–0.080	–4.97
29	Puducherry	—	—	0.010 (0.18)	5.83	0.010	4.36
	Total	**8.580**	**16.14**	**5.620**	**7.15**	**–2.960**	**–8.99**

Source: Census of India (2011). Tables on Houses, Household Amenities and Assets, Series 1, Registrar General and Census Commissioner, Government of India, New Delhi.
Note: Figures in million.

brought down the deprivations. A few regions could be mentioned that have outperformed achievement over the national average of 9 per cent. Kerala has arrested the deprivation of housing amenities by more than 25 per cent, followed by Odisha (18.40%), Jharkhand (18.15%), Assam (16.41%), Bihar (15.39%), Nagaland (15.18%), Mizoram (12.97%), Goa (12.56%), Chhattisgarh (11.46%) and Tamil Nadu (11.20%). But at the same time, many of these regions have continued to exhibit deprivation exceedingly more. Chhattisgarh continues to face the brunt in a huge order at 14 per cent, followed by Manipur (12. 87%), Odisha (12.79%), Jharkhand (11.76%), Bihar (11.07%), Maharashtra (10.26%), Madhya Pradesh (9.47%) and Tamil Nadu (9.28%). It should also be noted that the other regions have underperformed in mitigating the deprivations in their respective urban areas.

MOUNTING SOLID WASTE AND FAILURES IN THE MANAGEMENT

Uncontrolled and unchecked growth of urban solid waste is a disappointing reality in urban India, irrespective of the size. There have been failures on the part of both the urban development administration and the community in this regard, in the sense that these stakeholders have consciously contributed not only to the colossal growth of the problem but also to a contemporary challenge. If, on the one side, urban households/urban population have not been adequately engaged in controlling the generation of solid waste, urban development administration has largely neglected the collection and segregation of the waste, on the other hand. At the same time, less said the better about the management of solid waste as the public administration is yet to address this issue fully. The biggest problem has been that urban development administration is yet to gear up with the financial resources as well as adoption of wrong locations (amidst residential localities) for the management of solid waste, on account of not taking the community into confidence at the planning and execution levels. These errors in management have obviously invited the wrath of the communities. Although these issues have been recently realized by the urban administration to manage solid waste, the success was very limited and the measures taken were ineffective due to the half-hearted approach of the stakeholders such as public, local administration and household/community participation.

The second very important concern of the emerging urban India is the volume of solid waste *per se*. The related literature provides two dimensions in this regard—(a) its incidence and (b) its collection practices. It is estimated that over 10,844 metric tons per day of waste quantity is being generated in the state capitals and in cities with more than 1 million population in the country, at the rate of 0.35 kg per capita per day. The capital cities of Bangalore and Ahmedabad have been, respectively, in the top positions among the state capitals, with waste generated at 1,669 metric tons and 1,302 metric tons per day and 0.39 kg and 0.37 kg per capita per day, respectively (Asnani 2006, 160). Similarly, 23 major states of the Indian union with 299 cities generated a total municipal solid waste (MSW) in the order of 48,134 ton/day, at 38 kg per capita per day (Sharholy et al. 2008, 460). The state of Maharashtra has topped the list with the highest MSW at 8,589 ton/day or 17.84 per cent in total, followed by Uttar Pradesh (5,515 ton/day or 11.46%), Tamil Nadu (5,021 ton/day or 10.43%), West Bengal (4,475 ton/day or 9.30%), Delhi (4,000 ton/day or 8.31%), Andhra Pradesh (3,943 ton/day or 8.19%), Gujarat (3,805 ton/day or 7.91%), Karnataka (3,118 ton/day or 6.48%), Madhya Pradesh (2,286 ton/day or 4.75%), Rajasthan (1,768 ton/day or 3.67%), Bihar (1,479 ton/day or 3.07%), Kerala (1,220 ton/day or 2.53%) and Punjab (1,001 ton/day or 2.08%). If these 13 states together accounted for a total MSW of 46,220 ton/day or 96.02 per cent of the total in the country, the other 10 states have accounted only for 1,914 ton/day or 3.98 per cent of the total incidence.

Equally important is that municipalities have been shouldering the responsibility of collection, processing and management of solid waste in urban areas. In this regard, municipalities have faced two disappointing realities. Solid waste generated by all the urban households irrespective of their type and location has not been collected. The solid waste collection arrangement data clearly show that only 63 per cent of the urban households have been covered for the collection, and municipalities covered only 48 per cent, followed by residents (13%) and others (2%), whereas the other households

Table 5.3 *Solid Waste Collection Arrangements by Types of Houses in Urban India*

Houses by Type	Number of Households (Million)	Waste Collection Arrangements by Source (%)			
		Municipalities/ Corporations	Residents	Others	No Arrangements
Pucca	60.9	63.9	12.9	3.7	19.5
Semi-pucca	4.1	43.5	15.6	2.5	38.3
Kutcha	1.4	35.5	11.5	0.6	52.4
Total	**66.4**	**47.64**	**13.34**	**2.28**	**36.74**

Source: NSSO (2010). Report No. 535 (65th Round), Housing Conditions and Amenities in India 2008–2009, Government of India.

(roughly 37%) have been deprived of the arrangement (Table 5.3). Further, it is evident that the incidence of uncovered households is very large among the unserviceable kutcha houses, which are largely found in urban slums and filthy living environment. The municipal inefficiency in the collection of solid waste has been countered by a number of alternative methods such as (a) door-to-door collection (waste pickers, PPP in small towns and full privatization); (b) recycling, processing and scientific disposal (waste pickers and municipalities); and (c) awareness generation and campaigns (schoolchildren and households; NIUA 2015).

DEVELOPMENT OF SMALL AND MEDIUM TOWNS

The emergent urban patterns and the disparities that have crept in the process of urbanization have been well sensitized by the government, and the response has been positive in terms of the schematic interventions in the late 1970s. Integrated Development of Small and Medium Towns (IDSMT) was introduced as a national commitment and a centrally sponsored scheme (GoI 2009) with all measures to redress the disparities of urban development. The un-avowed objectives were to decongest the major urban centres and to make the other urban segments settlement friendly. The IDSMT intends to promote orderly urban development, irrespective of the size and the development scale (see Table 5A.1). What is particularly true is the intention of the scheme to provide financial assistance to such small towns that are as small as 20,000 people to up to a population of 500,000 and an elected body in office to supervise the urban development. Being the funding partner, state governments have been given the responsibility to select and recommend the towns for the development assistance under the scheme. Equally significant is the number of components identified for the purpose of financing under the scheme, which covers the entire gamut of the facilities a town or city needs to ensure a decent outlook and for orderly living of the people. Interestingly, the project funding is defined keeping absorption capacity at ₹10 million to towns having a population of up to 20,000, ₹20 million to towns having a population between 20,000 and 50,000, ₹35 million to towns having a population between 50,000 and 100,000, ₹55 million to towns having a population between 100,000 and 300,000 and, finally, ₹75 million to towns between 300,000 to 500,000. Further, the funding pattern is such that both Central and state governments provide higher grants as assistance (80%) to the smallest towns (<20,000 population) and 60 per cent assistance in the case of towns with a population of up to 500,000. In all the cases, the elected body of the local bodies are expected to raise loans from HUDCO or from financial institutions that could be ranging between 20 per cent and 40 per cent of the defined project costs. Second, the Urban Infrastructure Development Scheme for Small and Medium Towns (UIDSSMT) of 2012 is yet another initiative of the government, which was subsumed in 2015 with a sub-mission of JNNURM. With the launching of the UIDSSMT from 2005 to 2006 and subsuming of the same with JNNURM, no new towns were covered under IDSMT. Especially from 2007–2008 onwards, Central grants have been stopped completely to IDSMT. But what has disturbed the corrective actions of the government is that the process of development of the small and medium towns has been completely halted without attributing any reasons nor has it been made known as to what is happening to the ongoing process of the development. There is also no clear indication of targets and components defined under UIDSSMT.

Thirty years of implementation of the IDSMT (1979–1980 to 2006–2007) has impacted the selected small and medium towns in its own way, if not the country as a whole. The scheme has benefitted

68 towns on an average in 28 states, although a majority of the states have responded very poorly. In many cases, the development response for the schemes was far below the national average. Equally, UTs have also responded positively and effectively to the scheme (Table 5.4). With this intervention, as many as 1,907 small and medium towns (1,382 in 10 major states, 512 in the remaining 18 states and 13 in the UTs) have reportedly completed the selected developmental works within their purview. The country has incurred a total expenditure of ₹18.13 billion at an average of ₹600 million every year during the period of its implementation. It must be noted that the IDSMT, being a centrally sponsored scheme, assistance from the Central government constituted the substantial expenditure at around 60 per cent, and the remaining was borne by the state governments, as their share. In other words, higher the participation of the state and the Centre with their share of resources, the larger is the development of the towns at the sub-regional level and vice versa. But what disturbs the implementation is that not all the states have received the scheme with the intention of development of the small and medium towns in their respective states, which is to a larger extent evident. This group of states have implemented the scheme equally with their own resources and have accounted to over 72 per cent of the towns in total achievement and have incurred more than 81 per cent of the total expenditure. It can also be said that these states have contributed about 47 per cent (on an average) of the total expenditure in the implementation of the scheme, which is certainly above the national average. This only speaks of the development interest and promotion of people's welfare at the cost of the financial challenges. Equally important to note is that Uttar Pradesh and Maharashtra have together led the development success of the IDSMT, in terms of the number of towns covered and the total expenditure, apart from receiving maximum central assistance. Similarly, among the UTs, Pondicherry has garnered the major benefits when compared to other UTs. It has accounted for a very large number of towns with a total expenditure of ₹74.4 million with most of it (59%) met by itself under the scheme. Perhaps no other UT has received the impetus the way Pondicherry received. In this regard, what matters is the political will showcased among the 10 major states and UTs with the participation of own resource contribution, in addition to the central assistance received for the scheme.

Table 5.4 *Performance of IDSMT in India—2018 (₹ Million)*

No.	State	No. of Towns Covered	Total Expenditure	Central Assistance	State Assistance
01	Uttar Pradesh	206	1,769.2	1,065.2	722.9
02	Maharashtra	178	3,438.5	1,263.7	848.3
03	Tamil Nadu	172	1,648.6	916.4	634.4
04	Karnataka	169	1,105.6	876.5	578.8
05	Madhya Pradesh	146	1,033.0	642.2	459.9
06	West Bengal	121	1,568.2	951.2	690.2
07	Gujarat	115	1,244.2	758.8	489.4
08	Andhra Pradesh	90	1,222.7	652.7	440.8
09	Rajasthan	78	1,307.5	485.3	280.4
10	Odisha	67	430.6	294.2	189.6
	Total	1,382	14,768.1	7,906.2	6,861.9
	Total of all other states	512	3,255.3	2,792.8	462.5
	All union territories	13	106.3	55.6	50.7
	Grand total	1,907	18,129.7	10,754.6	7,375.1

Source: Integrated Development of Small and Medium Towns (IDSMT) Scheme: Performance Details, Ministry of Housing and Urban Affairs, Government of India. Website: mohua.gov.in/integrateddevelopment.idsmt.pdf

Against the active participation and the success achieved, 18 states, which have been lagging behind in the implementation of the scheme, have undertaken the development of only 512 towns at an average of 28 towns, which is more than twofold less than the group of 10 states. This unsatisfactory or disappointing outcome could be explained by two specific reasons: (a) unwillingness to participate owing to their mandatory share of the total expenditure towards the development and/or (b) not interested in the development of small and medium towns at all in their regions and to bring in improvement in the walks of life of the people. If the latter is the case, it only means that the majority of the states have failed to exhibit the political will for the sub-regional development. The exhibition of half-hearted interest and concerns to the scheme could perhaps be one of the reasons for the lack of widespread impact of the scheme in these states.

PART II
SLUMS AND THE DEGRADED ENVIRONMENT

Urban degradation refers to such portion(s) of areas, where people live substandard life disgracefully and shamefully, which is contemptible. Discrediting themselves, the localities where the people live are dirty in all measures, with congested street and housing and mostly without access to even basic human needs. Generally, slums have been considered as degraded environments, as they imbibe most of the features of degradation. Slums have been defined differently according to their contextual understanding. But three definitions are very important to understand, including the official one, which is comprehensive and imbibes all the characteristics. Slums are such parts of the city that may be unfit for human habitation either because the structures therein are old, dilapidated, grossly congested and out of repair or because it is impossible to preserve sanitation for want of sanitary facilities, including ventilation, drainage and water supply, or because the sites by themselves are unhealthy (Singh 1978). The official definition has been that a slum is a compact settlement with a collection of poorly built tenements, mostly of temporary nature, crowded together usually with inadequate sanitary and drinking water facilities in unhygienic conditions (NSSO 2003, 58th Round). The DNSP 2003 defines a slum as a compact area with a population of 300 or about 60–70 households, poorly built congested tenements, unhygienic environment and inadequate infrastructure lacking proper sanitary and drinking water facilities (GoI 2003). Notwithstanding their economic conditions, the urban poorest of the poor who generally live in slums have greatly contributed to the urban economy in terms of labour force, consumption, governance, public voice, etc. (Seetharam and Reddy 2014).

An understanding of the world of slums from the viewpoint of the geography, demography and human settlements at both international and national levels in the past few decades (i.e., 1980s and 1990s) brings out two very important and consequential findings. First is evolving workable/feasible public policies by governments for the overall improvement in housing and living conditions of the slums. Second, is evolving schematic interventions for mainstreaming of urban slums in order to include them into the rest of the urban areas, which is also termed as inclusive urbanization. In designing these goals and interventions, the UN has played its own significant part in sensitizing such governments that have been facing the prevalence of slums, more so in the developing countries, since the 1970s. In this regard, the Vancouver Declaration (UN Habitat 1976) is a landmark to direct and ensure socio-economic and living environment improvement in all human settlements, irrespective of their location in urban or rural areas with public investments, including subsidies, incentives and grants. Further, the Global Report on Human Settlements (UN Habitat 2003) has placed a huge significance in understanding the slums in different countries in terms of their incidence in the development context and proposing agenda for the improvement of slums based on the experience of the number of countries, including India. These initiatives have successfully sensitized about the growing incidence and magnitude of the slums in the 21st century, besides laying road maps for the eradication of slums in those countries and to achieve inclusive urbanization.

In the case of India, the efforts for the development of the urban poor who are generally referred to as slum dwellers or informal settlements (Sen 2014) and their improvement have almost coincided with that of the development planning process in the early 1950s with the advent of industrialization in urban areas. There were seven important strategies promulgated for the improvement/development of slums as laid down in the Second Five-Year Plan itself (GoI 1956; Shivalingappa 1975): first, acquisition and clearing of slum areas; second, acquisition of private lands and allotment of independent sites; third, acquisition of private open lands to rehabilitate the slum dwellers; fourth, construction of small independent houses on house sites for allotment of slum families; fifth, construction of small twin houses for two slum families; sixth, construction of multi-storeyed buildings to rehabilitate the slum dwellers; and, seventh, environmental improvements in the slums that are located in the government, municipality, corporation and city improvement trust board lands. But the disappointing aspect was that these strategies have had very limited impact over their objectives on account of (a) displacement of slum dwellers from their workplaces as well as their social network, (b) litigations by private landowners and (c) inadequate public funding. With regard to the last issue, the national government being the principal supplier of finance for the cause of the slums, it had channelized public investment through SHBs, city improvement trusts, town planning authorities and slum clearance boards, which was entirely inadequate to meet the total challenge. Subsequently, the responsibility was entrusted to the HUDCO to administer the public investment for the development of slums in the country. It must be noted that these strategic interventions of the government were by and large ad hoc in nature and were not necessarily based on the various dynamics of the urban slums from their ground perspectives. A hard reality has been that the public understanding of the slums and their incidence across urban India had never been attempted by any authority until the mid-1970s.

The NSSO has attempted to understand the socio-economic conditions of slums for the first time in 1976–1977 in its 31st Round and subsequently in 1993 (49th Round), in 2002 (58th Round) and the latest in 2009 (65th Round). Many changes were introduced in the methodology and coverage between the first two and the last two rounds of the surveys. In fact, the pathetic world of slums was exposed only after the various NSSO surveys undertaken with a significant improvement in the approach in every round. In the first round, only Class I towns having 1971 census population of 100,000 or more and Class II towns, namely Shillong and Pondicherry, were covered. The second round surprisingly included rural areas into its coverage. Further, the slums were classified as 'declared' and 'undeclared' based on the declarations of the local authorities. Again, in the third round held in 2002, slums were surveyed, limiting only to urban areas, in terms of availability of the facilities in slums for the past three and a half decades rather than their adequacy. In fact, the findings of this survey have not only sensitized the public policymaking but also have evolved a national consensus over the slums, besides prompting to prepare the DNSP 2003' by the national government, enshrining the essential strategic interventions by both the Central and state governments across the country. In fact, the DNSP has been a guiding force for the subnational levels (or states) to evolve their own policies and action plans for the eradication of slums in their respective regions. This apart, the Ministry of Housing and Urban Poverty Alleviation has initiated and has been implementing a major scheme called RAY', which envisages a secured housing facility with access to amenities for the slum dwellers and improvement of the overall living conditions in urban slums. Interestingly, it is this very scheme that has forecasted a 'slum-free urban India' in the coming years (GoI 2007). Finally, the latest survey (65th Round) portrayed the slum areas geographically and assessed the availability of approach roads, electricity, drinking water, sewerage, drainage, garbage disposal and their improvements over the years in the notified and non-notified slums in India.

INCIDENCE OF SLUMS

Without denying the contribution of the NSSO in understanding of the geography and demography of the slums, the Census of India being the second authority has equally contributed significantly by way of collecting and presenting the data on the traits and characteristics of urban slums for public consumption. Accordingly, urban India has registered 2,822 slum-reported towns out of the total number of 8,027 towns (Census of India 2011b). This means that over one-third (35.16%) of India's urban geography is inhabited by slums. These slums have been housing over 35 million households out of the total number of urban households of 167.82 million, which works out to roughly 36 per cent (Table 5.5). Based on the official data, the Indian states and UTs can be classified into three categories over the issue of slums: (a) higher incidence; (b) lower incidence; and (c) no slums. If the first category is housing around 25 per cent of the total slum households, the second category accommodates around 11 per cent. Together, the incidence of the slum households is reportedly in the order of over 35 per cent. There are seven states in the first category, which have 912 slum-reported towns (34%) with 30 million households dwelling in these towns. This apart, these states reveal a few other traits. Sikkim, as one of the states in the category, has the smallest number of towns (9), and over three-fourths (77.78%) of them are reportedly having slums; however, the average number of households living in the slums is marginally less than the group average of about 25 per cent. Madhya Pradesh, being the second largest state, has more than 63 per cent of its towns (302) registered with

Table 5.5 *Number of Slum Towns and the Households (High Incidence) in India*

Categorization of States and Union Territories	No. of States and Union Territories	Total No. of Towns	Slum-Reported Towns	Total Urban Households (Million)	Households in Slums (Million)	% of Slum Households to Total
Higher incidence	7	2,686	912 (33.95)	120.05	29.83	24.85
Andhra Pradesh	–	353	124 (35.13)	6.78	2.42	35.7
Chhattisgarh	–	182	94 (51.65)	1.24	0.40	31.9
Madhya Pradesh	–	476	302 (63.45)	3.85	1.09	28.3
Sikkim	–	9	7 (77.78)	–	–	24.1
Odisha	–	223	76 (34.08)	1.52	0.04	23.1
Maharashtra	–	534	187 (35.02)	100.81	24.49	22.7
West Bengal	–	909	122 (13.42)	6.35	1.39	21.9
Lower incidence*	24	5,270	1910 (36.24)	47.77	5.23	10.95
No slums**	4	71	Nil	Nil	Nil	Nil
Total	35	8,027	2,822 (35.16)	167.82	35.06	20.89

Source: Census of India (2011). Housing Stock, Amenities and Assets in Slums, India Series 1. Registrar and Census Commissioner, India.
Notes: * Details presented separately; ** includes Manipur, Daman and Diu, Dadra and Nagar Haveli, and Lakshadweep.

slums; the share of the households living in the slums is much more than the group average (28.3%). This is also the case of the state of Chhattisgarh with around 52 per cent of the towns having slums with 32 per cent of the households. Andhra Pradesh tops the group with the highest number of households (35.7%) living in the slums, which is almost one and a half times more than the group average. Finally, all the other states (Odisha, Maharashtra and West Bengal) have registered a lower incidence of slum households, which is below the group average. However, it is indeed necessary to remark about the state of Maharashtra that has not only recorded the highest number of urban households, but it also has households in slums within the group. Maharashtra accounted for 84 per cent of the urban households in the group and also accounted for 82 per cent of the slum households.

There are 24 other states and UTs recording lower incidence of urban slums. Slums have been reported in 1,910 towns (36.24%) out of the total number of 5,270 urban towns in the group. There are 5.23 million households living in the slums that work out to roughly 11 per cent of the households (Table 5.6). With this, it can be said that 36 per cent of the urban households (national average) live is the slums, as evidently discussed. The incidence of slums is evidently higher in five regions with Pondicherry topping the list by recording 60 per cent of its towns inflicted by slums, followed by Karnataka (59.37%), Haryana (48.70%), Tamil Nadu (45.94%) and Himachal Pradesh (37.29%). Similarly, the incidence of slum households is largely registered in three major states, namely Tamil Nadu with 1.45 million or 28 per cent, followed by Uttar Pradesh (0.99 million or 19%) and Karnataka (0.73 million or 14%). These three states alone constitute to around 61 per cent of the slum households in the group. Contrarily, a good number of states have recorded lower incidence of slum towns as well as the lowest incidence of slum households, from the perspective of group average. In seven independent states and two UTs, the incidence of slum households is less than 10 per cent, as can be seen in Table 5.6. Finally, the third category of the states (1) and UTs (3) is absolutely free from the incidence of slums. Interestingly, though the geography is very small as compared to the country, this part of the country has not recorded even a single slum, despite having 71 urban towns with a very negligible number of households living

Table 5.6 *Number of Slum Towns and the Households (Low Incidence) in India*

S. No.	Name of State	Total No. of Towns	Slum-Reported Towns	Urban Households (Million)	Households in Slums (Million)	Slum Households (%)
1	Jammu and Kashmir	122	40 (32.79)	0.52	0.01	18.8
2	Haryana	154	75 (48.70)	1.75	0.33	18.6
3	Puducherry	10	6 (60.00)	0.02	0.01	17.0
4	Tamil Nadu	1,097	504 (45.94)	8.93	1.45	16.3
5	Uttarakhand	115	31 (26.96)	0.59	0.01	15.1
6	Tripura	42	15 (35.71)	0.24	0.01	14.4
7	Punjab	217	71 (32.72)	2.09	0.30	14.2
8	Mizoram	23	1 (04.35)	0.12	Negligible	14.0
9	Karnataka	347	206 (59.37)	5.32	0.73	13.7
10	Nagaland	26	7 (26.92)	0.12	Negligible	13.3
11	Uttar Pradesh	915	260 (28.42)	7.45	0.99	13.3
12	Rajasthan	297	107 (36.03)	3.09	0.38	12.4
13	Delhi	113	22 (19.47)	3.26	0.38	11.8
14	Chandigarh	6	1 (16.67)	0.23	Negligible	9.7
15	Bihar	299	71 (23.75)	2.01	0.20	9.6

16	Meghalaya	22	6 (27.27)	0.12	Negligible	9.4
17	Andaman and Nicobar Islands	5	1 (20.00)	Negligible	Negligible	8.9
18	Himachal Pradesh	59	22 (37.29)	0.17	Negligible	8.6
19	Gujarat	348	96 (27.59)	5.42	0.36	6.7
20	Arunachal Pradesh	27	5 (18.52)	0.01	Negligible	6.1
21	Jharkhand	222	31 (13.96)	1.50	0.01	5.3
22	Assam	214	31 (14.49)	0.99	0.05	4.8
23	Goa	70	3 (04.29)	0.20	Negligible	2.4
24	Kerala	520	19 (03.65)	3.62	0.01	1.5
Total		5,270	1,910 (36.24)	47.77	4.23	10.95

Source: Census of India (2011). Housing Stock, Amenities and Assets in Slums, India Series 1. Registrar and Census Commissioner, India.

in these towns. With this reality, it is indeed a disappointing feature that only a limited portion of urban India is slum-free.

Cities with one million and above population (COMP) have been the major centres of slums in all measures, according to the official declaration, owing to the reasons explained already. Interestingly, over the years, not only has there been an increasing number of COMPs, but there is also an increase in the slum population from 1,078 million in 1971 to 1,770 million in 2001 due to excessive concentration of manufacturing and service sector investments. However, one striking feature is that the percentage of slum dwellers in COMPs in the total population receded to 24.10 per cent from 28.69 per cent—a net decline of 4.59 per cent is an encouraging trend (Gupta 1985, 92). There are 27 COMPs, and these centres have been housing 17.70 million slum population—over half of the total incidence of the country (Table 5.7). This apart, the most disheartening reality is that out of the total COMPs, Greater Mumbai alone accounted for a lion share of 6.48 million (36.61%) population living in the slums. The other two COMPs that have registered the highest population in their municipal corporations are Delhi (1.85 million or 10.45%) and Kolkata (1.49 million or 8.42%). In other words, these three major COMPs accounted for over 55 per cent of their population in municipal corporations living in slums. It goes without saying that the remaining 24 COMPs house the rest of the slum dwellers. Another flip side is the slum population in the total population of the municipal corporations of the COMPs. It is a fact that over 54 per cent of the population of Greater Mumbai Municipal Corporation live in the slums, which is almost double the incidence of all COMPs. Other COMPs that have given shelter for slum dwellers over and above the average is Faridabad (46.50%), Meerut (44.10%), Nagpur (35.90%), Kolkata (32.50%) and Thane (27.80%).

Slums have been historically known for occupying municipal and public lands as the first choice for their settlement for security reasons than private and other vacant lands due to the risks involved. But in recent years, the settlement dimension of the slums has changed a bit according to the NSSO. The municipal and public lands (railway lines) have been the obvious choice for slum settlements (69%), as

Table 5.7 *Slum Households in Cities with One Million and Above Population*

State and Union Territory	Name of Million Plus Municipal Corporation	Slum Population in the Municipal Corporation (Million)	% in the Total Population of the Municipal Corporation
Maharashtra (7)	Greater Mumbai	6.48	54.10
	Pune	49	19.40
	Nagpur	74	35.90
	Thane	35	27.80
	Kalyan–Dombivli	03	2.90
	Nashik	14	12.90
	Pimpri–Chinchwad	12	12.20
Uttar Pradesh (5)	Kanpur	37	14.40
	Lucknow	18	8.20
	Agra	12	9.50
	Varanasi	14	12.60
	Meerut	47	44.10
Gujarat (3)	Ahmedabad	47	13.50
	Surat	51	20.90
	Vadodara	19	14.20
Madhya Pradesh (2)	Indore	26	17.70
	Bhopal	13	8.70
West Bengal (2)	Kolkata	1.49	32.50
	Howrah	12	11.70
Delhi (1)	Delhi	1.85	18.70
Tamil Nadu (1)	Chennai	82	18.90
Karnataka (1)	Bangalore	43	10.00
Andhra Pradesh (1)	Hyderabad	63	17.20
Rajasthan (1)	Jaipur	37	15.90
Punjab (1)	Ludhiana	31	22.50
Bihar (1)	Patna	01	0.30
Haryana (1)	Faridabad	49	46.50
(13)	**Total (27)**	**17.70**	**24.10**

Source: Census of India (2011). Housing Stock, Amenities and Assets in Slums, India Series 1. Registrar and Census Commissioner, India.

these lands have continued to be soft destinations. But it must also be noted that there is growing public assertion over these lands by the public authorities themselves. It is also evident that urban slums have been found increasingly as well in private vacant lands (17%) and other lands (14%; projects and construction sites). Based on the geographical spread, urban slums can be classified into three categories: (a) slums that are spread between <0.5 hectare and 2 hectares; (b) slums spread between 2 hectares and up to 8 hectares; and (c) slums spread over more than 8 hectares. It is important to note that 82 per cent of the slums are located in the first category, 16 per cent in the second category and only 2 per cent in the third category. Political bargaining and development consideration of the slums have been often said to be the reasons for the emerging realignment strategy. With regard to the location of the slums, it is further evident that industrial and commercial places have come to be the preferred destinations in recent years for obvious reason of employment. In fact, the number of slums located next to industrial and commercial places has increased to 36 per cent during the aforementioned period. As a result of the emerging trend, the pressure on the in and around residential areas has been eased to some extent, although they continue to house the slums in large numbers (64%) for want of connectivity of the utilities for the slum dwellers.

SLUM DEVELOPMENT POLICIES AND SLUM-FREE CITIES

The development strategies of the urban slums can be categorized into two regimes based on their characteristics of interventions: (a) ad hoc approach (1956–1996) and (b) pragmatic approach. The main differences between these two are the policy shift and the volume of interventions (schemes and public investment) from the first to the second. Under the first, the thrust was to clear the slums, which was hampered largely due to dislocation of the slum dwellers, whereas under the second, the thrust has been to in situ approach or to improve the slums wherever they are located. This approach is also known for multi-schemes coupled with an adequate flow of public funds. Further, the improvement strategies in the first regime were pursued almost without a national commitment and a clear road map for the slum development. The next regime was a windfall for the world of urban slums in India, during which a national consensus in the form of DNSP was evolved for the eradication of slums. Also, a dedicated scheme (RAY) has been designed exclusively to improve the housing and living conditions of slum dwellers. These three development strategies of the urban slums are portrayed in the following paragraphs.

The government has exhibited its commitment for the slums through two different schemes, namely slum clearance scheme (1956) and slum improvement scheme (1972). The first scheme mandated the government to compulsorily acquire slums and redevelop them by demolishing unfit housing stock and replace them with new dwellings. Further, rehabilitation, which was a second component of the scheme, essentially emphasized to rehouse the slum dwellers in such a way that they should not be away from their place of employment. Subsequently, the shift in policy and approach in the second scheme emphasized on improvement in environment through the provision of tap water, sewer and storm water drains, community baths and latrines, paved roads, street lights, etc. (Gupta 1985, 100). The consensus for the improvement of slums than demolition and clearance of slums was built keeping three very important reasons in view: (a) high cost involved in land acquisition for rehabilitation of slums, demolition and redevelopment; (b) avoid dislocation of slum dwellers, upkeep their socio-economic fabric and resentments; and (c) huge subsidy involved in the construction of new houses (GoI 1956, 561). The in situ strategies of upgrading and improving slums have been pursued, as they caused least disturbance both to the dwellers and to their livelihood (GoI 2003).

The National Slum Development Programme (NSDP) was introduced in 1996 to provide ACA to the states and UTs for providing physical amenities such as water supply, storm water drains, community latrine and bath, widening and paving existing lanes, sewers and street light. The scheme also had a component of shelter upgrading or constructing new houses. The Planning Commission used to allocate the funds under the NSDP, based on the slum population of the states/ UTs and between 1996–1997 and 2004–2005, ₹24,960 million was spent. Similarly, Valmik–Ambedkar Awas Yojana (VAMBAY) 2001 aimed to provide shelter or upgrade the existing shelter for people living below poverty line in urban slums, with a view to achieving 'Shelter for All' as well as the Habitat goal of 'Slumless Cities'. SC families being the main target at 50 per cent, the scheme was to cover 30 per cent of the families from the backward classes, 15 per cent of the families from other weaker sections and 5 per cent from physically handicapped persons. A net total subsidy of ₹9,336 million was released for the purpose of implementation of the scheme. The NSDP and VAMBAY were subsequently subsumed with a new scheme called the Integrated Housing and Slum Development Programme (IHSDP) 2005. The related literature indicates that the scheme has had a holistic slum development approach with a healthy and enabling urban environment by providing adequate shelter and basic infrastructure facilities to the identified urban slum dwellers. The IHSDP had a number of good features such as (a) the scheme was made applicable to such cities and towns that are not covered under JNNURM (2005); (b) the land for the relocation of slums should be provided by the state governments; (c) title of the land should be jointly in the names of husband and wife; (d) the ceiling cost of housing unit is ₹80,000, with 12.5 per cent more in special category/hilly states or difficult far-flung areas; (e) housing unit shall not be less than 25 square metres, with a two-room accommodation along with kitchen and toilet; and (f) beneficiary contribution shall be 12 per cent and 10 per cent in the case of SCs/STs & BCs/PH respectively. Finally, the commitment of the government for land pooling and sharing, slum improvement, in situ slum rehabilitation along with secured tenure, affordable housing and basic services, inner-city slum redevelopment programmes, etc., has been clearly stated (GoI 2007b).

Much before the introduction of IHSDP, one of the significant initiatives of the GOI was to articulate a DNSP (GoI 2003) as a road map for the development of slums in the country. Being the first-ever national consensus after independence, the states and the UTs were given free hand to adapt the DNSP as per the local conditions of their regions. First, the DNSP has been aiming at including slums and slum dwellers into the mainstream of urban life/urban living by developing and improving them through organized public efforts and by stakeholders' participation. The policy has embodied itself with a number of goals to achieve: (a) slum upgrading and improvement, instead of slum clearance; (b) institutional reorientation to provide efficient basic services to slum dwellers through public–community mobilization; (c) re-visioning the urban development process and making towns/cities fully democratic, economically productive, socially just, environmentally sustainable and culturally vibrant to reach cities without slums; (d) ensuring equity and distributive justice by promoting balanced, equitable and sustainable development; (e) continuous supply of serviced land for high-density occupation by LIGs in order to proliferate slums; (f) enhancing effectiveness of slum development/improvement activities by collaborative efforts between urban local bodies and stakeholders, especially in resource allocation, service delivery and urban governance; and (g) greater participation of community/civil society in planning, capacity building and development.

The DNSP suggests the following strategic interventions for overall improvement of slums: (a) listing and registration of slums/informal settlements, registration of slum dwellers with identity cards to get an entitlement for basic services and other assistance; (b) delisting such slums that have reached acceptable norms of the basic service on a sustainable basis and assessment of slums for every two to three years for delisting purposes; (c) embargo on declaring the slum lands as untenable unless such settlements offer undue risks for human habitation and are against public interest. While fixing such embargo, the district magistrate, after consulting the ULBs and the technical experts, shall hear to resident community in public; (d) ensuring full property rights to all slum dwellers in government-owned lands and the private lands housing the slums, jointly in the name of the spouse, subject to formation of recognized residents' associations. Sale or transfer of ownership rights, although allowed with a fee, the policy strongly advocates obviating from the same; (e) unless the present slum settlement is untenable, which only calls for rehabilitation/resettlement, upgrading and improvement are the primary concerns. In the event of rehabilitation as enshrined in the policy due care must be taken, (f) modification of planning instruments (master plans, land-use plans, urban development plans, urban poverty alleviation plans, departmental plans and the schemes) to ensure all the slums are integrated into urban areas and formulation of integrated municipal development plan (IMDP) in order to ensure adequate and sustainable level of infrastructure and services to all in an equitable manner. For these purposes, bottom-up planning is suggested, with priorities of needs and indication of contribution towards the costs of the different stakeholders; (g) improving the quality of life by improved environment and by physical infrastructure development as one of the tools of convergence of the slum dwellers into the urban mainstream. Community-based approach, targeting women and children, household-based service delivery, contracting the environment upgradation activities and piped and hand pump supply of water, individual sanitation and cluster latrines, separate pedestrian and vehicular ways, storm water drains, household electricity and solid waste collection are the physical infrastructure development to be attained towards their standard norms; (h) improving access to preventive, promotive and curative health services and health insurance in partnership with community and private to ensure greater outreach. Similarly, incentive-based preschools and non-formal education, day crèche facilities, discouraging child labour and upholding their rights and exclusive public distribution system need to be provided with; (i) bringing municipal services under the Consumer Protection Act to ensure their quality and reliability in slum settlements. It is mandatory to have a special consumer panel at the municipality level, which comprises members of different settlements to redress; (j) strengthening livelihood needs of the urban poor through vocational, self-employment facilities, providing improved access to raw materials and marketing support, legal rights and redressal system and organizing savings and credit groups on the lines of SHGs to increase access to formal sources of credit by the ULBs; (k) financing sustainable slum improvement through public funding by both the state—slum development fund (SDF)—and municipalities—municipal convergence fund (MCF), besides private sector funding. Institutional financing, extending tax base, user charges, sharing cost by community and selling land title are the other suggested sources; and (l) improving creditworthiness, strengthening municipal governance, shelter upgrading and monitoring and evaluation of the strategic interventions are the other considerations apart from obtaining illustrative feedback by the slum dwellers on water, sanitation, access to credit and on their housing.

Slum-Free Cities

Creation of a conducive environment in urban areas that is free from slum is one of the ambitions of the national government. This need not be misunderstood that slums would be eradicated completely, but they would be redeveloped in all measures on par with the rest of the urban areas, in terms of the living environment, human settlements, access to amenities, hygienic environment, etc. To realize this dream, RAY was introduced as a central assistance scheme (CAS) to undertake in situ development of the slums, wherever they exist. Construction of affordable housing for the slum dwellers and upscaling their dwelling condition are its main focus. RAY has a three-pronged critical objectives to achieve: (a) tackling the twin problems of shortage of urban land and housing the urban poor; (b) redressing failures of the formal system that have come in the way of slum development and put an end to the creation of new slums; and (c) subsuming slums with rest of the urban system and achieve parity in basic amenities. With the prominent vision for SFCs in urban India, RAY pointed out four critical and priority issues such as urban planning, land, housing and infrastructure financing. One of the paradigms of RAY is that city master plans (CMPs) should give up the exclusionary model that earmarks land for HIG/MIG, commercial, institutional recreation and other uses but excludes EWS/LIG, which has facilitated income classes and excludes the poor from access to land besides throwing them out of the land market. To put an end to this process, RAY points out that the CMP should make provision for EWS/LIG as a distinct category. The approval of city authorities must ensure that 'small lot zoning' (creating plots for EWS/LIGs) is ensured in layout for housing. Regarding land, the JNNURM should reserve 25 per cent of the developed land in all new housing colonies for EWS/LIG housing as compensation to non-allocation of land for these sections. Similarly, as is the global practice, the occupied land or a part thereof should be allocated for the slum dwellers to have access to housing and basic amenities. Given the massive needs for affordable housing, it is necessary to involve the private sector to create affordable housing stock on ownership, rental or rental and ownership basis, in addition to public actions for housing the slum dwellers. The government should also earmark resources for affordable housing for the urban poor. Finally, banks and HFIs should give up their reluctance to finance EWS/LIG segments, and governments should work out suitable fiscal, legal and institutional mechanisms to ensure flow of capital for the priority scheme.

In order to realize the SFC dream, the RAY mandates two action plans—one for the state and the other for city that has slums. The SSFPA should be annexed with a legislation of the state assembly covering all legislative issues necessary for redevelopment or rehabilitation of slums, including spatial norms, city(ies) identified to be covered in five years, phases, approaches (integrated or holistic) and notified or non-notified for upgrading of slums for each identified city. The objective of such a plan should be to ensure decent housing with all basic civil infrastructure and services with total sanitation (individual toilets). The plan should be flexible and beneficial—a built housing model that is prepared separately for upgrading the existing slums and action for preventing new slums. It should also be appended by legislative and administrative changes to enable urban land expansion and town planning regulations to reserve EWS/LIG housing. The other mandates are to prepare SSFPA for the entire state by the respective governments and UTs, assign legal title to slum dwellers over their dwelling space through legislation for property rights and bring about necessary reform to make urban development inclusive. The SSFPA thus prepared and after approval by state assemblies should be submitted to the Central government for funding under RAY. The other action plan is that SFCPA shall be prepared by the municipal commissioner/executive officer of the ULBs, based on the guidelines of the state government. SFCPA is prepared for each city based on (a) the survey of all slums; (b) the mapping of slums; (c) integration of geospatial and socio-economic data; and (d) identification of the development model for each slum, as per the guidelines of the state government and the nodal agency of RAY. SFCPA would be prepared depending upon the availability of lands, construction of affordable houses, infrastructure, etc., and after identifying the gaps in these parameters between the city and slum levels. Based on the decision about upgrading/in situ development or relocation of the existing slums, slum-free plan would be implemented with timeline and phasing, which would be monitored. The GOI, besides financing the SSFPA and SFCPA of state governments and municipalities, respectively, also supports for conducting slum surveys, slum database, slum mapping, expert consultancies, NGOs/CBOs, biometric identification of slum dwellers and providing hardware and training programmes, etc. Further, the national steering committee, besides monitoring the entire process of SSFPAs in a time-bound manner, considers all the proposals, including sanctioning of funds and reviewing the physical and financial progress under the RAY.

Slum Improvement and Their Waning

Urban slums and their unfavourable environment conditions have been synonyms in the Indian context ever since they existed. In fact, slums have always been enjoying the dubious distinction of being the centres of degraded environmental conditions, though various public initiatives have led to a number of changes in all walks of life of the urban slums and their dwellers. This is especially true for housing, access to housing amenities and the living environment of the slums. Further, the waning number of slums (both notified and non-notified), after having achieved development parameters vis-à-vis the rest of the urban areas, is another noticeable change. With these changes, the public intervention for inclusive urbanization has begun to yield initial positive results over the years, which in itself is a testimony officially. Based on the materials used for the construction of houses, the National Buildings Organization (NBO) has classified that there are three housing structures, namely standard, substandard and dilapidated (NBO 1988). Standard units are those that are constructed by using burnt bricks, solid blocks, sand–cement mix, etc., for walls and roof made of CI—cement concrete, tiles, slate, etc. People with regular income and institutional financial assistance prefer constructing standard housing units. Second, substandard units are constructed by using standard materials to construct either walls or roof, but not both. These structures are used to be constructed by those having irregular income of their own and are not qualified to avail financial services. Finally, dilapidated structures are constructed by using locally available materials that are not standard construction materials for walls as well as for roof. Such structures become dilapidated over the years on account of lack of proper maintenance and frequent upgrading. These units are generally 'some sort of housing constructed out of distress', which need to be rebuilt at short intervals, as they are unsafe for dwelling and may not provide safe shelter round the year. Dwelling in such structures is subject to the changing climatic conditions. These units are usually built by the poor who are not able to afford construction of other structures. Interestingly, there has been a significant shift towards construction of standard housing units, which could be partly due to upgrading of the existing substandard units. As a result of this shift, there has been a corresponding decrease in the substandard and dilapidated stock in the slums (Table 5.8). The net increment in the standard housing units was 9.50 per cent on account of the overall increase to 57 per cent from 47.50 per cent. Owing to this important change, the total substandard and the dilapidated housing stock have declined by 6 per cent and 3.50 per cent, respectively. Substandard housing units, which were constituting 35 per cent in 2002, have reduced to 29 per cent in 2009, and dilapidated units have reduced from 17.5 per cent to 14 per cent. What is striking is that the shift towards incremental standard housing units has mostly emanated from the un-notified slums than the notified ones. The standard housing stock in the un-notified slums has increased from 30 per cent to 50 per cent, as against a marginal fall in the case of the notified slums. Proportionately, the share of the substandard and the dilapidated stock in the un-notified slums has been wiped out by 11 per cent and 9 per cent, respectively, which is far above the national average. While in the case of the notified slums, the share of the substandard housing stock has marginally declined, but the dilapidated stock has rather increased to 7 per cent, which is twofold more than the national trend.

The situation with regard to access to housing amenities (drinking water, electricity, latrine/sanitation and sewerage) by the urban slum

Table 5.8 *Change in Housing Conditions of the Urban Slums: 2002–2009 (%)*

Housing Types in Urban Slums	*NSS 58th Round (2002)*			*NSS 65th Round (2009)*			*Change*		
	Notified	*Un-notified*	*Total*	*Notified*	*Un-notified*	*Total*	*Notified*	*Un-notified*	*Total*
Standard	65.00	30.00	47.50	64.00	50.00	57.00	–1.00	20.00	9.50
Substandard	30.00	40.00	35.00	29.00	29.00	29.00	–1.00	–11.00	–6.00
Dilapidated	5.00	30.00	17.50	7.00	21.00	14.00	2.00	–9.00	–3.50

Source: NSSO, Government of India, Conditions of Urban Slums—2002, NSS 58th Round and NSSO Government of India, Some Characteristics of Urban Slums, 2008–2009: NSS 65th Round.

dwellers is not very encouraging. There is only a marginal increment during the period, and the deprivations are conspicuously persisting (Table 5.9). Though there is considerable coverage of slum dwellers with drinking water supply through tap and tube wells, (95%), the rest have no alternatives but to use drinking water from open wells and other sources, whose quality cannot be assured. Irrespective of the quality and adequacy of the piped water supply, tap connections to houses in un-notified slums have increased by 6 per cent additionally. Similarly, in the notified slums, another 7 per cent of the slum houses have been supplied water from tube wells. But one of the positive aspects is that the number of slum dwellers depending on unsafe drinking water sources (wells and others) declined to 5 per cent in 2009 from 7 per cent in 2002. Next to drinking water, the other important concern is sanitation in the slums. Based on the availability of latrine facility, slum dwellers can be classified into two: one with access, irrespective of source of availability and the others without access. Obviously, it is the second category that resorts to open defecation as the only option. What is evident officially is that slum dwellers with access to latrine facility have increased to 80 per cent from 66 per cent, and as a result, the incidence of open defecation due to non-availability of latrine facility has reduced from 34 per cent to 15 per cent. Moreover, in un-notified slums, the incidence of open defecation came down to around 20 per cent from 51 per cent, which is worth noting. While enhancing access to latrine facility to slum dwellers, community-based latrines have played a significant part in both the notified and un-notified slums. The community source covered more than half of the slum dwellers, as against 37 per cent in 2002. Yet, 'other' source (possibly pay-and-use initiative) covered additionally about 12 per cent of the slum dwellers with latrine facility. In fact, the total coverage by other sources has increased from a mere 4 per cent to over 16 per cent, especially in the un-notified slums. Finally, household sharing latrines have eroded together from 25 per cent to 19 per cent in the total coverage. Being the economic good and given its contribution to economic and domestic activities, the necessity of electricity for households hardly needs any emphasis. Although the number of households without electricity has dropped over the years, electricity connections to slum

Table 5.9 *Change in Housing Amenities of the Urban Slum Dwellers: 2002–2009 (%)*

Housing Types in Urban Slums	*NSS 58th Round (2002)*			*NSS 65th Round (2009)*			*Change*		
	Notified	*Un-Notified*	*Total*	*Notified*	*Un-Notified*	*Total*	*Notified*	*Un-Notified*	*Total*
Drinking water									
Tap	84.00	71.00	78.00	79.00	77.00	78.00	–5.00	6.00	0.00
Tube well	10.00	22.00	16.00	17.00	17.00	17.00	7.00	5.00	1.00
Well	2.00	2.00	3.00	1.00	2.00	2.00	–1.00	0.00	–1.00
Others	4.00	5.00	4.00	3.00	3.00	3.00	–1.00	–2.00	–1.00
Latrine facility									
Owned	21.60	3.80	12.70	13.10	7.20	10.20	–8.50	3.40	2.50
Sharing	13.70	11.30	12.50	10.40	7.10	8.70	–3.30	–4.2	–3.80
Community	41.90	31.50	36.70	53.80	46.40	50.20	11.90	14.90	13.50
Others	5.80	2.80	4.30	12.70	19.70	16.10	6.90	16.90	11.80
No latrine	17.00	50.60	33.80	10.00	19.50	14.70	–7.00	–31.10	–19.10
Electricity									
Within households	11.00	25.00	18.00	16.00	26.00	21.00	5.00	1.00	3.00
Sharing street lights	84.00	53.00	68.50	76.00	53.00	65.00	8.00	0.00	–3.50
Only street light	4.00	6.00	5.00	7.00	15.00	11.00	3.00	9.00	6.00
No electricity	1.00	16.00	8.50	1.00	7.00	4.00	0.00	9.00	–4.50

Source: NSSO, Government of India, Conditions of Urban Slums—2002, NSS 58th Round and NSSO Government of India, Some Characteristics of Urban Slums, 2008–2009: NSS 65th Round.

houses have increased only to 21 per cent from 18 per cent. This also means that over three-fourths of the slum dwellers have been deprived of electricity. However, in the absence of household electricity, households depending upon street lights, as a source of lighting, have continued to be at alarming levels. One of the possible reasons for higher deprivation of electricity could be that most of the slum dwellers are unable to afford cost of the installation as well as the consumption charges. Finally, household connectivity to sewerage is of paramount importance in order to keep housing environment tidy and hygienic, more so in urban slums. In this regard, it can be said that higher the household connectivity to sewerage, better is the hygiene as well as better living environment, and vice versa. Households' connectivity to sewerage facility in slums has increased to 26 per cent in 2009 from 22.5 per cent in 2002, with a net increase of 3.50 per cent. A notable feature is that the success in additional connectivity of households to sewerage has taken place almost at the same scale for both notified and un-notified slums. With the unsatisfactory coverage, still a large segment of the households (74%) have remained unconnected to sewerage facility, and the consequence of this huge exclusion could be largely attributed to an unfavourable living environment in the urban slums.

The public initiatives to improve the conditions have also brought some more respite in the walks of life of the slums, although they need to go a very long way. Development of all-weather roads, development of approach roads to slums and garbage collection are three of the several other environmental issues in which public initiatives have made some headway. Slums with all-weather roads have increased to a little more than two-thirds as compared to 54 per cent in 2002, and the net increase is in the order of 13.5 per cent (Table 5.10). Un-notified slums have attracted a good deal of public effort in the development of all-weather roads than the notified slums. The un-notified slums have achieved an overall increment of 20 per cent, which is more than the national average in the development of all-weather roads than a mere 7 per cent increase in the notified slums. Similarly, the development of motorable roads has correspondingly increased by a net 22.50 per cent to 65.50 per cent from 43 per cent. If the un-notified slums have put up a 3 per cent increase in the development

Table 5.10 *Change in Living Conditions of the Urban Slums: 2002–2009 (%)*

Housing Types in Urban Slums	NSS 58th Round (2002)			NSS 65th Round (2009)			Change		
	Notified	Un-Notified	Total	Notified	Un-Notified	Total	Notified	Un-Notified	Total
All-weather roads									
Motorable	73.00	55.00	43.00	73.00	58.00	65.50	0.00	3.00	22.50
Non-motorable	55.00	12.00	35.50	19.00	18.00	18.50	–36.00	06.00	–17.00
Garbage disposal									
Municipality	79.00	42.00	60.50	75.00	55.00	65.00	–4.00	13.00	5.50
Others	5.00	12.00	8.50	15.00	22.00	18.50	10.00	10.00	10.00
No collection	16.00	46.00	31.50	10.00	23.00	16.50	–6.00	–23.00	–15.00
Source of services									
Government	92.90	83.04	90.23	91.55	86.36	88.96	–1.35	3.32	–1.27
NGOs	2.54	4.29	3.11	4.10	5.91	5.00	1.56	1.62	1.89
Residents	4.20	11.14	6.00	2.00	3.27	2.64	–2.20	–7.87	–3.36
Others	0.36	1.53	0.66	2.35	4.46	3.40	1.99	2.93	2.74

Source: NSSO, Government of India, Conditions of Urban Slums—2002, NSS 58th Round and NSSO Government of India, Some Characteristics of Urban Slums, 2008–2009: NSS 65th Round.

of approach roads from 55 per cent to 58 per cent, the notified ones have remained at where they were at 73 per cent. Over 83 per cent of the slums have had the benefit of garbage collection, which is 14.5 per cent over 69 per cent in 2002. But the most important fact is that though municipalities have stepped up their efforts over the years, the real success has come from the other initiative, especially the outsourcing method, through which the volume of garbage collection increased to 22 per cent as against 8.5 per cent in both the notified and un-notified slums.

Despite the positive changes that have taken place, a few of the environmental problems have been continuously daunting the urban slums of the country. Water logging in urban slums is one such problem, the incidence of which has rather increased. It goes without saying that the public initiative for arresting the water-logging problem has hardly brought any improvement from the prevailing conditions. Much to the dismal position, the incidence of water logging, as faced by urban slums, increased to 47.5 per cent from 45 per cent, and the incidence has mostly heralded in the case of notified slums, while in the un-notified slums, the problem remained mainly unattended. One of the reasons for the continued degraded environmental conditions could be that urban slums have been excessively depending upon the state action or public intervention for their improvements. This is evident from the fact that the government is the principal and critical source/provider of various services in the slums, although there was a marginal decline in the same from 90 per cent to 89 per cent. In other words, the role of market forces and NGOs though have made inroads in a very small way in the improvement of urban slums, the volume of services provided by them has increased from 3.77 per cent to 8.40 per cent during the assessment period. However, what is deplorable is that the residents' participation level in the provision of various services in the slums has eroded from 6 per cent to less than 3 per cent, which may be on account of increasing scale of the other players. Further, even in the case of peoples' participation in slums, the situation is not different, as the residents' association activities in the slums is completely standstill at 24 per cent. Moreover, in the case of notified slums, the residents' associations have minimized their existence from 35 per cent to 28 per cent, whereas the situation in un-notified slums is much better, as the associations' activities have been on a revival path.

Interestingly, there have been a number of mixed outcomes in minimizing the development gaps between the non-slum urban areas and the slums. In a number of cases, the non-slum urban areas have been far ahead in their achievement as against the slums. Slums, at the same time, have also been ahead of their achievement against the rest of the urban areas. If the first success is largely due to market intervention and household initiatives, the second success is largely due to public commitment and facilitation. These differences in the achievement are presented in Table 5.11. Marked differences between them and across different parameters were evident. The non-slum urban areas are ahead in terms of electricity, separate kitchen at home, flush latrine, separate washroom and connectivity to closed drainage. These provisions are ensured at the time of the planning and execution while constructing the houses, by and large, on a priority basis. Seldom the people neglect these comforts and consider these facilities are part of comfortable living and settlement. The best part is that they never look for anybody's support and intervention. But it is not the case with the slums. As the slum dwellers are largely poorer sections, these facilities are generally expected to be provided by the government, and the possibility of their contribution is very bleak. Despite these limitations, slums have achieved some degree of success in the number of cases like standard housing stock and provision of treated water, and in a few cases, the development gap is very marginal. What is significant to note is the presence of the dilapidated housing stock in a large number of slums as compared to that in non-slum urban areas. With almost three-fold increase, the dilapidated stocks are in the order of 14 per cent of the total as against 5 per cent, which is 9 per cent higher than the non-slum areas. Similarly, the incidence of drinking untreated water and using kerosene for lighting is very high in slums. Lack of household kitchen, washrooms and toilets in several houses of the slums is the other reality. These deficiencies along with the lack of access to drainage have led to the practice of open defecation and filthy environment mainly around the houses

Table 5.11 *Development Gaps in Housing Amenities in Urban Areas and Slums, 2011 (%)*

S. No.	Housing Amenities	Non-slum Urban Area	Slums	Difference (+ or –)
	Type of housing stock			
1.	Standard	53.4	57.0	3.6
2.	Substandard	41.2	29.0	–12.2
3.	Dilapidated	5.4	14.0	8.6
	Access to drinking water			
1.	Treated tap water	61.3	65.3	4.0
2.	Untreated water	8.3	8.7	0.4
3.	Covered well	1.8	0.8	–1.0
4.	Uncovered well	5.0	2.3	–2.7
5.	Hand pump	11.7	12.7	1.0
6.	Bore well	9.2	7.6	–2.4
7.	Others	2.4	2.7	0.3
	Access to energy			
1.	Electricity	93.1	90.5	–3.4
2.	Kerosene	6.1	8.2	2.1
3.	Solar energy	0.2	0.3	0.1
4.	Other oil	0.1	0.2	–0.1
5.	Any other	0.2	0.2	0.0
6.	No lighting	0.3	0.5	0.2
	Access to kitchen and fuel			
1.	Has kitchen	82.0	67.3	–14.7
2.	Does not have kitchen	17.5	32.1	14.6
3.	No cooking	00.5	00.5	0.0
4.	LPG	67.9	51.3	–16.6
5.	Kerosene	06.2	14.0	7.8
6.	Others	24.7	33.3	8.6

S. No.	Housing Amenities	Non-slum Urban Area	Slums	Difference (+ or –)
		Access to sanitation		
1.	Flush latrine	75.7	57.7	-18.0
2.	Pit latrine	7.3	6.2	-1.1
3.	Night soil to open drain	1.1	1.6	0.5
4.	Service latrine	0.5	0.6	0.1
5.	Public latrine	4.1	15.1	11.0
6.	Open defecation	11.3	18.9	7.6
		Access to freshness		
1.	Bathroom	79.8	66.6	-13.2
2.	Bathroom without roof	8.4	14.5	6.1
3.	No bathroom	11.8	19.0	-8.8
		Drainage connectivity		
1.	Closed drainage	46.1	36.9	-9.2
2.	Open drainage	35.8	44.3	8.5
3.	No drainage	18.8	18.8	0.0

Source: Census of India (2011). Housing Stock, Amenities and Assets in Slums, India Series 1. Registrar and Census Commissioner, India.

in slums. With this marked difference in the levels of development, urban areas cannot afford to have two different and distinct worlds within its boundary. These distinct differences would always be a set back to the process of inclusive urbanization as well to achieve development parity.

However, despite the marked differences in the scale of development within the urban world, the process of achieving SFCs or inclusive urbanization has been set into motion, as is evident. This means that the potential slums have achieved a marked improvement in their environment and qualified to be included with the urban

Table 5.12 *Dwindling Urban Slums in India, 2002–2009*

Urban Slums	*Number of Slums Due To Be Subsumed*		
	Notified	*Un-notified*	*Total*
Total numbers	26,166 (50.62)	25,522 (49.38)	51.688
Subsumed with rest of urban areas	1,385 (5.29)	1,306 (05.12)	2,694 (5.21)
Balance to be subsumed	24,781 (94.71)	24,213 (94.88)	48,994 (94.79)

Source: Some Characteristics of Urban Slums, 2008–2009: NSS 65th Round, NSSO, Government of India.

areas. The process of diminishing number of slums has been a reality to some extent, as per the NSS estimates. Significantly, an interesting aspect is the diminishing number of both the notified and un-notified slums almost on the same scale. Although the process set in has to go a very long way in changing the characteristics of the slums, a huge majority of the slums have to give up their hard stand to seize their present identity and to improve themselves to be part of the urban world. The latest NSSO data have confirmed the process of urban inclusion by a dwindling number of slums over the survey (Table 5.12). Accordingly, the number of urban slums that has dwindled are in the order of 2,694, as a result of the reduction of slums to 48,994 in 2009 from 51,688 in 2002. Of which, 1,385 (51.41%) and 1,309 (48.59%) were, respectively, of the notified and un-notified slums that have ceased of their identity. This only indicates that the slum improvement/development interventions are taking place across the notified as well as the un-notified slums almost equally, without making any distinction. The notified slums, which were in the order of 26,166, have dropped to 24,781 and, similarly, un-notified slums from 25,522 to 24,213 during the period of reference. With this change, what is largely needed on the part of the public action is the 'mission-mode approach' to the process of inclusive urbanization and slum-free environment with reinvigorated thrust to augment the pace and process.

APPENDIX A

Table 5A.1 *An Overview of Public Actions for the Reduction of Disparities and Development of Small and Medium Towns*

Name of the Scheme	*Objectives of the Scheme*	*Selection Method of Towns*	*Components for Funding*
Integrated Development of Small and Medium Towns (IDSMT)—1979 (A centrally sponsored scheme and amended up to 2004–2005)	• Improving infrastructure facilities in small &medium towns • Decentralizing economic growth and employment opportunities • Increasing availability of serviced sites for housing, commercial and industrial uses • Integrating spatial and socio-economic planning and Promoting resource generating schemes to improve the local bodies financial position	• Applies only to towns/cities with up to 500,000 population • Towns are to be identified by the state government/UTs according to their urban strategy • Applies to only such towns where elections to the local bodies have been held and elected bodies are in position	• Strengthening roads like ring, arterial, bypass/link roads and small bridges with street lighting • Sites and services • Development of bus/truck terminals • Construction of/upgradation of storm water channels • Solid waste management • Development of market complexes/shopping centres • Provision of tourist facilities • Development of parks, slaughterhouses, gardens, playground marriage halls, pay and use toilets, etc. • Cycle/rickshaw stands • Traffic improvement schemes • Construction of retaining walls in hill station towns • Social amenities for the poorer sections

(Table 5A.1 Continued)

(Table 5A.1 Continued)

Name of the Scheme	*Objectives of the Scheme*	*Selection Method of Towns*	*Components for Funding*
Urban Infrastructure Development Scheme for Small and Medium Towns (UIDSSMT) – 2012 and subsumed in 2015 with a sub-mission of JNNURM	• Improve infrastructure facilities in towns and cities • Urban sector reforms • Enhance public–private partnership in infrastructure development • Promote planned integrated development of towns/cities	NA	NA

Source: Collated from the Scheme Design of the Ministry of Housing and Urban Affairs, Government of India website.

6

Towards a Pragmatic Urban Housing Sector

Among all the other dimensions of poverty in India, housing poverty occupies a very significant place in the development discourse. This is because of the fact that owning a house, besides giving overall security for the family members and to their belongings, gives sociopolitical identity in a particular place(s), apart from economic benefits. Despite these associated benefits, India has been lagging behind in ensuring decent and safe housing to its population, especially to its citizens facing homelessness for various reasons. Lack of effective and need-based public interventions for housing development for the poor and disadvantaged sections is very conspicuous ever since the independence. Simultaneously, the housing market that has taken shape from the mid-1980s is yet to have a widespread impact on its operations to cover the entire homeless families of the country. Especially, the HFS, which is a critical input supplier (Mahadeva 2008, 2009), has failed to meet the financial needs with innovative approaches. These two prominent restrictions and setbacks have kept the housing poverty alive in the country, both quantitatively and qualitatively. The homeless families and people at the same time have resorted to housing adjustments as well as unsafe dwelling in the absence of adequate and safe housing interventions over the years. It is reported that roughly about 20 per cent of the households are facing housing poverty from both the dimensions. Experiencing these two kinds of housing poverty has both pleasure and pain for the homeless people, especially for the disadvantaged poor sections, owing to their flexible attitudes and unaffordable costs. Because of the advantages and disadvantages associated with both forms of dwelling practices, housing poverty is being experienced even to date. Invariably, housing adjustment has number of benefits such as scale of economy, social life, common care of the elderly and children, and sharing responsibilities. However, the disadvantages of housing adjustment like inadequate space and crowded housing, which exert pressure on the housing amenities such as water, toilet (sanitation), electricity and other common utilities, should not be relegated or neglected. Further, privacy for married couple, more so to the newly married ones, is a distant dream in housing adjustment. Similarly, unsafe housing, being largely low cost in nature, can be considered as some sort of housing associated with the poor economic status. Drinking water, sanitation, electricity, etc., are generally connected with free or subsidized housing services. The biggest disadvantage of an unsafe dwelling is the housing risks involved, like weak structure and collapse, as the dwelling is subject to unfavourable climatic conditions. Despite the safety aspect, human comforts and dignity would not have been considered at all.

In this regard, the NUHHP has failed in wiping out the housing adjustment practice completely, which occurs always with the formation of new families. Otherwise, contemplating an exclusive policy for distinct situations is laudable to address the hitherto neglected issues of a sustainable habitat in urban areas. The specific objectives of the policy; target group approach for public assistance; special areas of action; clear demarcation of roles and responsibilities of the ULBs and Central and state governments; additional thrust for strengthening the cooperatives, etc., are welcoming initiatives. It is also very clear from the discussion that there are hard realities related to housing in terms of the incidence of housing shortage in urban areas experienced by all homeless in general and the poor and LIGs in particular. Inappropriate and ineffective policy interventions followed ever since the independence can be directly attributed to this situation. Needless to mention, narrow definition, misconception in participation and non-development of a broad-based HFS have been noted as the three major inconsistencies. In light of these inconsistencies, various components in the national shelter policies as suggested by the Global Shelter Strategy and other related initiatives were discussed. The debate emphasized on the need to set clear objectives to ensure adequate housing for all households; reorganization of the shelter sector, including meeting the housing needs of special groups, mobilization and distribution of financial resources; redevelopment of existing (dilapidated) housing stock; and, finally, the involvement of ULBs in the management of housing stock. Further, it is argued that owing to incompatible actions, the country is continuing to face the housing problem and challenges in spite of the positive changes that have taken place, especially in the financial and housing production fronts between 1991 and 2001. However, it was brought to the fore as to how the development initiatives of the 1990s have had hardly any impact on arresting the housing problem in the case of a large number of major states due to a lack of even spread of development benefits. Unfortunately, the incidence of the housing problem has aggravated further in the already most affected states. Finally, regional variations in terms of housing shortage are distressing in major states in the sense that the situation is highly alarming. The incidence of housing shortage in 12 major states is in the order of over three-fourths (83%) of the total. In this section of the book, issues that need careful consideration in public policymaking for effective addressing of the housing problem in the immediate years to come are discussed. The critical issues include the need for compartmentalized housing strategies, need-based development of housing input, reorganization of the housing market and special concerted efforts for minimizing the incidence of shortage in major states that are worst hit. It becomes effective and meaningful if these issues form the basis of public policymaking in housing in the years to come. Also, keeping the sustainable urbanization and comfort as well as dignity in the urban human settlement in view, the following specific policy implications are offered to facilitate the change in housing development.

Undoubtedly, the policies for the promotion of affordable housing targeting the LIGs, MIGs, EWSs and the poor homeless households are a paradigm shift in the history of housing development of the country. Unlike the ad hoc approaches followed hitherto, which were intended to supply new housing units and have known for the short supply, targeting the families living in the crowded housing and living in the deficient/dilapidated units is a significant change in the approach. It goes without saying that it is these two forms, which are generally attributed as quantitative and qualitative dimensions of housing poverty, are being targeted for eradication. Given the nature and magnitude of the incidence, appropriate interventions would take a sufficiently long time to exhibit the impact over the targeted households. But it is important to note that the country has made a beginning to develop affordable housing for the unaffordable sections, including the homeless poor, if not solving this problem in the short run. Similarly, targeting the poor families that cannot afford a decent shelter by themselves is a welcoming feature. These initiatives, apart from offering the financial support to the targeted sections, ensure households participation in the process of building their homes by mobilizing the financial resources. Also, they would be sensitized to facilitate themselves to associate with the financial institutions, especially with the SHGs or MFIs. These small financing institutions qualify the homeless to get refinanced, obviously inculcating the habit of saving for various purposes, including housing. Interestingly, the prospects for realizing the overall goals of the interventions look very positive by excluding the affordable sections or high-income households from the ambit of these approaches. These infused changes in the approach for the development of affordable housing should impact the poor rather conspicuously and should minimize housing insecurity as well as ensure housing comfort with adequate space and access to housing amenities. But what is needed is the strict targeting of the poor families by the implementing authorities and vigilant implementation of the schemes to ensure that the benefits reach only the genuine households and at the right time. Such vigilance is imminent, especially for the homeless families earning a livelihood from informal activities, as they move from place to place frequently. The second paradigm is the benefits targeting the vulnerable poor who would have depended on earning a livelihood from the informal sector in urban areas. This would certainly have a positive impact on the informal settlements or urban slums and the pavement dwellers over their housing. The national initiative to share the housing distress owing to the natural calamity in Kerala has come at a right time to express solidarity of the rest of the Indians out of the AHF created from the financial year 2018–2019. Third, other than the families earning a livelihood from informal activities and affected by the natural calamity, the policy's focus on helping out the other households in the general segments facing homelessness is a significant milestone. The policy has targeted and identified women, third gender, SC and ST households, rural households and other vulnerable groups under this segment. They can very well avail the financial services, ranging between ₹2 million and ₹5 million, at a concessional rate of interest or at the floor fund cost for a loan term of up to 15 years. Undoubtedly, this would facilitate housing graduation and housing expansion.

PRIORITY TO DEVELOP SECOND AND OTHER TIER CITIES AND TOWNS

As evidently shown, the emerging urbanization of the country although looks positive in terms of the investment and employment opportunities from all the three sectors (public, private and cooperative), the hard reality of the same is that the development is highly skewed or tilted. Undoubtedly, Class I cities have become the centres of urbanization and have been attracting migration. The geographical expansion of Class I cities is increasing at an alarming level, coupled with the demographic increase in the population. The hard fact is that no other size class of cities and towns has expanded the way Class I cities have in the decades of review of the study. This trend in urbanization is worrisome to the public administration as well as to the urban management. In the first place, the present trend has introduced unmanageable pressure in terms of the density of population, which is at present more than threefold and twofold of averages of the all class sizes and Class II cities, respectively. The reasons for the same have already been explained in the respective section. But the fact that cannot be suppressed is the urban administration, particularly the city corporations and other statutory bodies face several managerial problems, as has been the case for many issues. It could be rightly said with one or two examples that about one-third of the households have not been supplied with drinking water from a piped source for want of adequate capacity in water resources and lack of infrastructure. The deprived households in these urban centres have been made to depend on the groundwater source mostly and on other water supply methods, which are not cost-effective. This apart, households connected with a piped water source have been facing other problems such as drinking water being supplied on a rationing basis, on an hourly basis or a weekly basis, which is very common in most of the major cities. Similarly, non-collection of the total households' solid waste by the municipalities for various reasons is a cause of serious concern from the governance point of view. Lack of adequate workforce, non-satisfactory working environment, lack of segregation and treatment infrastructure for the solid waste and other issues have limited the public action. Yet non-development of the storm water drainage system and non-connectivity of households to drainage in major urban areas, let alone the other urban areas, have been a serious environmental hazard. Water logging has been very common, especially around the households in such areas, which have been facing the problem of lack of development of a drainage system. These unpleasant scenes are quite common but natural in the informal settlements in the major cities. Second, as a result of the major centre-centric urbanization, owing to investment and employment opportunities in the manufacturing and tertiary sectors, second- and other-tier cities have been suffering from economic as well as infrastructure development. Lack of development and the lacunae have not only left these urban areas in the lurch without prospects for growth but also have given rise to urban mobility of the people, especially with the next-tier cities. Based on the public information, these urban centres are naturally capable enough to observe the population influx as well as the investment. But what is due in the development discourse and needed is the political will to develop these urban centres as an alternative to urbanization. Finally, one of the development outcomes in the urbanization of the country has been the discrimination and disparity between the major cities and the other urban areas, which have cropped up from almost the beginning of the process. It is very conspicuous that the development divide and disparities between the major cities and rest of the urban areas are such that the former group is far ahead of the latter group in terms of revenue and investment. The latter ones have the same organizational set-up and institutional mechanisms with varied capacities and functioning styles. But, at the same time, these centres have untested capabilities to absorb the investment.

While examining the public interventions as a redressal measure, this chapter has brought to the fore the main characteristics of the IDSMT and UIDSSMT in terms of their objectives, components and other features. Besides, an attempt is also made to capture the success and limitations of the development. The purpose of pondering over all these issues is to recapitulate and re-sensitize the development process, including the public commitments in terms of the policies and the expenditure to ensure both orderly and decent urbanization process. This is because urbanization is an unstoppable and inescapable course of development for any country, irrespective of its standing. Equally, the public action must ensure and create a necessary condition on a sustainable basis for human settlements across all sizes of the towns. From these perspectives, the present trend in the urbanization process needs to be modified or reversed. Class III cities to Class VI towns with the population range, respectively, between 50,000 and 5,000 cannot afford to be neglected any longer, as has been the case all along the commencement of the process. Unfortunately, owing to the continuous inattention, these centres have acquired the images of neither urban nor rural area, which needs to be changed with a strong public commitment and institutional mechanisms. The social and economic infrastructure development in small and medium towns with public–private investments has many benefits. This would not only minimize migration to the major cities but would also facilitate reverse migration, which has already started owing to various pressures. Most importantly, this process would decongest the state capitals and other major cities. The development of infrastructure coupled with investment can create employment opportunities, which would have multiplier effects such as increasing income, purchasing power and living standards. Above all, such initiatives would pave the development of magnetic centres in city peripheries for the purpose of human settlements. Failing to do so would only result in increasing congestion, manifold increase in all forms of poverty, deprivation of amenities and degradation urban establishments as urban India is experiencing currently. Yet another limitation of small and medium towns is the excessive dependence on the government for the investment and allowing private investments. Public authorities need to explore the possibility of financial incentives and sops to the private and corporate world in promoting the investment in small and medium towns. Second, the decision of shunning the exclusive IDSMT scheme has damaged the development process in its own way. Although the IDSMT was inefficient, its repeal has shattered the only hope for the development of neglected segments of urban life since 2005–2006. Subsequently, no new towns were selected and funded for development, and these towns continue to face the pain of distress and deprivation in all measures. That apart, it must be noted that of the total number of 4,224 towns (small and medium; Census of India 2001b), IDSMT has developed only 1,854 towns or 42 per cent of the total and left behind the remaining 2,370 towns, which still need to be developed. At the same time, it is neither clear regarding whether the UIDSSMT is given the responsibilities of the IDSMT nor are there any alternative means of development of small and medium towns. The complete eschewing of a scheme, which was yet to make significant inroads into other unattended towns and impact the walks of life of the hitherto neglected towns, has led to further marginalization. Undoubtedly, IDSMT with laudable objectives has lived up to its mission, even with all the funding limitations, but the complete erasing of the scheme without an alternative in place is preposterous. Keeping the need and necessity in view, the following specific policy imperatives are offered for public action.

First, apart from the development of magnetic centres for want of decongestion and development of the neglected cities, meeting the emerging challenges and to create a human-friendly urban living environment in the other centres is the need of the hour to ensure sustainable urbanization, which will happen very fast. The Report on the Urbanizing World of the UNCHS (1998) has clearly indicated that India's urban population by 2025 would be in the order of over 45 per cent. Given the saturation that most of the state capitals and major cities have reached in terms of the resources and the development interventions, undoubtedly, adoption of urban development decentralization is the need of the hour in the country. This is warranted not only to face the challenges of future urban growth but also to ensure orderly urban life in terms of basic infrastructure. What India should do is that it need not have to create new towns but develop the existing ones in large numbers. The IDSMT, which was designed with multi-pronged objectives, needs to be reintroduced. Medium and small towns would serve as immediate service centres (especially for education and health) at the sub-regional levels besides the immediate centres of absorption for the rural migrants. Second, mere development of the medium and small towns alone does not suffice decent and orderly urban life, but equally essential is the upgrading of the existing services provided by authoritarian bodies such as housing boards, water supply and sewerage and municipalities. These statutory authorities should ensure that all the urban settlements developed by public authorities, private builders, cooperative societies or individuals are connected and integrated. The housing development approach should accord equal importance for the replacement of dilapidated and unserviceable units as well as increasing the supply of good houses corresponding to the need (Mahadeva 2006). Regarding sustainable and efficient water supply, it is all the more necessary to share the financial burden between the public authority and the users (World Bank 1999). Also, rectification of the pilferage and unauthorized and un-priced consumption in the current supply mechanism should be attended to. Alternatively, urban families that depend on the unsafe water sources for drinking should be financially supported (one-time grant or subsidy or both) to adopt the necessary technology to get water treatment/purification at the household level to make it fit for consumption. Additionally, the state should ensure that families living in urban areas should harvest the rainwater compulsorily to facilitate recharging of the groundwater level by providing financial assistance. It is indeed necessary to popularize the use of solar energy for lighting for the deprived families, as the progress achieved in this regard is far from satisfaction. The government needs to work on meeting the initial capital expenditure for solar energy for those who cannot afford this facility by themselves. Above all, there shall be a mission-mode action plan for the eradication of open defecation by providing sanitation to deprived families in urban areas, as it is an indecent practice and against orderly living. A special drive with financial grants and subsidies by the governments for the urban poor families to put up household toilets is the need of the hour to achieve total coverage. Also, the local authorities must establish community latrines for the floating population under their supervision and management with the support under the corporate social responsibility (CSR) scheme.

Finally, it is very essential that the people should follow the basic tenets of smart living and act smartly in all walks of their living in private, public and society by sharing the financial burden and by promoting clean environment in their surroundings.

REJUVENATION OF THE COOPERATIVE HOUSING MOVEMENT

The movement led by primary societies in India have failed to develop themselves as vibrant institutions after taking a lead in arresting the housing problem of their members in urban India. Even though the cooperative housing movement is as old as the credit cooperative movement, an indifferent attitude from within and outside has greatly impeded the movement's reach. Much of the failures have been attributed to the lack of public action to nurture and promote cooperative societies as alternative agencies to pure public and private actions, a weak internal financial base, below-capacity operation, etc. However, as was done in the past, housing societies cannot be left to themselves. Owing to their special economic advantages, benefits and their necessity to deliver housing benefits at fairly cheaper costs to the poorer sections under changing economic circumstances, the revival of housing cooperatives is a must for a variety of reasons. First, like any other cooperative system (especially credit, consumers, dairy, etc.), the cooperative housing system has a very wide network of organizations (primaries to the tune of over 100,000), in major and medium urban areas, covering a variety of people from all walks of life as their members. If meaningful and action-oriented roles are not assigned to CHSs, their potential and capacity to deliver housing benefits would be wasted. Second, given the well-thought-out and better working environment, CHSs can go hand in hand with other housing development agencies. CHSs need to be given preferential treatment in the allotment of residential plots by the land acquisition and development agencies and finances by the HFIs. The underlying benefits with this arrangement are that CHSs can further spread the benefits to a large number of individuals. Yet another benefit is that housing development agencies can minimize the opportunity costs if their services are delivered to CHSs in bulk. Third, CHSs are cost-effective organizations as they acquire critical inputs like residential plots and finances on a wholesale basis and deliver the same to their members on a cost-equivalent price. Although the element of dividend/profit cannot be totally ruled out, by and large, the price of CHSs on inputs is comparatively less than the market prices. Since most members of CHSs are average middle class or even poor, meeting their housing needs is extremely important through cost-effective mechanisms because the market-promoted institutions do not respond and cater to the needs of these sections as they cannot afford costs and services. At the same time, reducing the role of the government under the new economic regime and inordinate delay in meeting the housing needs of the common man have further prompted the rejuvenation of CHSs. Fourth, the emerging scenario in the housing finance sphere, which is characterized as highly competitive, accommodating and flexible, has increased the access to financial services. Of late, a large number of financial institutions (public–private sponsored subsidiaries), including commercial banks, have entered the domain of housing finance as a fabulous avenue for investment. Having entered the market, the interest war (lending at less price) led by many prominent players has begun as a strategy of survival. In fact, this has even led to a drastic reduction in the lending rates for housing in recent days. Lending rigidities are gradually phasing out. Interestingly, lending terms are being tuned in accordance with consumers' convenience. For example, there are institutions that lend with minimum or without down payment; similarly, there are institutions that allow longer years of repayment of housing loans. All these positive changes have increased avenues and opportunities for CHSs. There are HFIs prepared to lend to CHSs even at less than the market-determined rate of interest and for longer periods if the repayment is guaranteed and regular. Thus, if CHSs are re-motivated and re-tuned to the emerging mechanisms, the existing credit gap for housing for the members can be arrested to a greater extent. Fifth, the response to the NHHP's (1998) call for increased private action in land development for residential purposes was average and sporadic throughout the country. Similarly, the response was very poor as far as legal reforms at the state level are taken as an impetus to housing development. In this context, it is worth mentioning the initiative of Karnataka, which has paved the way for releasing land for residential activities. If the landlords are so convinced that their holdings are uneconomic and give unviable yield, then they are free to convert the holding for non-agricultural purposes. This has helped both the landlords in the urban peripheries as well as the buyers (including groups of individual) to acquire land in bulk for housing activities. Housing societies aimed at acquiring land and developing it for residential activities for their members can re-engineer themselves into a new situation through negotiations. At this juncture, administrative reforms are important in registering of land, which is released for non-agricultural activities, especially for residential purposes of individuals, group of individuals, etc. Further, reduction in stamp duties and administrative costs in the registration of land would be an impetus for housing activities of cooperatives and individuals. At present, stamp duties and the administrative costs continue to be at high levels, and their incidence is largely felt by individuals and PIIs like cooperatives.

Apart from the aforementioned avenues, there are two more avenues for rejuvenation of CHSs in the days to come. They are household-based resource mobilization and increasing direct access to HFIs by the PHSs. These measures give much autonomy and freedom to CHSs, thereby minimizing government intervention and politicization. Besides, independent resource base would facilitate CHSs to supply finance at a cheaper rate. Ever since the beginning of the cooperative housing movement, strengthening the internal financial base of CHSs has been emphasized. It was believed that internal financial soundness would achieve twin objectives of minimizing dependence on external agencies and supply of cheap finances to the members for housing activities. It was also believed to achieve these objectives through mobilization of household savings in the form of deposits, which is one of the tenets of cooperation. Mobilization of household savings not only establishes a cordial relationship between the members and society but also serves as a seed money or down payment for a housing project. But unfortunately, as already mentioned, for reasons not known, most housing societies have not inculcated the habit of saving among their members. Therefore, promoting thrift among their members is belied. The expectation of supplying finances at cheaper cost has continued to be a dream for their members. Untapping of household savings led to an excessive dependence on external financial institutions, which is costlier and burdensome to members. Some of these arguments reiterate the necessities of mobilizing the needed resources within the cooperative fold rather than the capital market. CHSs can mobilize savings by two ways: first, as specific savings exclusively by the members. The proceeds of the savings, after a specific period, could be used as seed money either for land purchase or for house construction, including the renovation of dilapidated houses with refinancing assistance by societies. Second, the general savings should be mobilized like that for any other institution, particularly for commercial banks. The general public as well as the members (if interested) could be the constituency. This type of savings can meet any purposes with refinancing of societies. It goes without saying that the whole gamut of household saving mobilization by members and general public depends on two important preconditions. First is confidence building, and the second is the prudential financial management on the part of the CHSs. CHSs need to be shown as to how they are registered institutions of public interest, their functional performance and locus standi over the years. Confidence building assumes greater significance in light of financial mismanagement in a few state cooperative apex banks. Similarly, the sources and avenues of investment of resources, competitiveness, guarantees, etc., need to be blueprinted.

Time has now come to put forth the idea of establishing direct linkages between the HFIs and PHSs in order to expedite the process of housing loan approvals and to achieve cost-efficiency in the operations. Considering the limited role of the ASs in the cooperative housing structure, the argument for direct linkages gains importance for the three following reasons. First, as already mentioned earlier, there has been increasing number of HFIs and the volume of finance for housing activities, especially with the establishment of the NHB in 1987. Since these institutions are prepared to finance PHSs even at a cheaper rate, and primaries can avail financial services directly on behalf of their members. Second, the presence of the upper tier/ASs has added up the administrative cost to the loans. The current arrangement of financing is that in the absence of their own resources, ASs borrow from different sources to lend the same to PHSs for members' housing activities after charging their administrative and service costs. This has jacked up the cost of credit to the ultimate borrowers. For example, the difference between the borrowing cost and lending cost is around 2 per cent or even more in certain cases. If direct linkages are established between HFIs and PHSs by eliminating the intermediary role of ASs, ultimate borrowers could be facilitated with lower cost on their loans. Third, administrative delays in loan approval and releasing the loans to the primaries can be drastically reduced when a direct relationship is established between the loaner and loanee. The argument for the elimination of an intermediary role of the upper tier in the cooperative housing structure raises a few important questions—what should be the position and role of ASs? Should there be any alternative for ASs? The straightforward answer is ASs should only lead the cooperative housing movement as its spokesperson instead of itself running the business on behalf of the primary societies. It should facilitate borrowings of primaries from different sources. Further, if any worthwhile service towards the cooperative housing movement has to be rendered, there should be three different but properly coordinated wings at the apex level. One wing should be exclusively in charge of looking after the financial facilitation aspects of the entire cooperative housing system—more so of the primaries. This wing can even assess the financial needs of primaries, prepare an action plan for its supply and supervise the investment and recovery of loans. The second wing should recommend to have different land acquisition and development authorities as far as the land requirements of primaries are concerned from time to time. It can even design the guidelines for allotment of residential plots for the members of PHSs. Third and the most important wing should be in charge of coordination between state governments/other agencies and the cooperative housing system. This wing can take up issues that need government consent/approval, such as concession under stamp duty and registration fees for members of PHSs, reservation of developed lands for PHSs and concessional supply of building materials to PHSs.

From the aforementioned discussion, it is evident that CHSs in India have not lived up to their own expectations, let alone responding to societal needs. Over the years, PHSs have failed to convert their organizational strength into capacity. In other words, a huge network of PHSs has contributed only a negligible share in the total housing stock. The cooperative housing system, being in the housing market for over nine decades, is yet to prove its presence and emerge as a key player in the production and distribution of housing benefits to the common man. A number of factors have impeded the cooperative movement, and most of them emanated within the system, although external factors have played their own role. The main factor of these is the weak internal financial base with low share capital and reserves in the working funds. A lower internal financial base has prompted the CHSs to excessively depend on external borrowings from different sources on commercial terms. Disappointingly, even the borrowings have not been exhausted to the capacity of CHSs. Lower capacity utilization on the part of CHSs has further limited the housing activities of members. Although the average number of houses per PHS almost doubled over the years, the percentage coverage of members for housing benefits is continuously declining to a little over one-third of the total membership. This only indicates the disproportionate enrolment of members and their coverage for the benefits. Added to this, the growing incidence of financial indiscipline in the form of overdue payments and bad and doubtful debts has curtailed capital formation. Similarly, the percentage of total business loss of PHSs in the total profit has drastically increased from 78 per cent to over 85 per cent during the period under review. However, in the context of the special characteristics and economic benefits of the cooperative housing system, a total rejuvenation is required to make the CHSs a prominent player in the production and distribution of housing benefits in the market. Also, considering the huge network of institutions and to take full advantage of the emerging housing financial market, CHSs need to be re-motivated. It should be made possible for CHSs to supply the principal housing inputs to their members at cheaper rates. Financial autonomy to PHSs would go a long way in increasing their borrowings with the guarantee of ASs as well as covering more number of members for housing benefit. Elimination of intermediary tiers and establishing direct relationship between HFIs and PHSs would bring about cost reduction. More success can be achieved when the cooperative housing system controls the resources, which could be mobilized through household savings, and the same can be supplied for house construction of the members. At the same time, it is also necessary to initiate measures to recover the overdue payments as the proceeds are going to be the lendable resources. In this regard, apart from all other initiatives for the recovery of overdue payments, educating the defaulting members about how the resources are being mobilized, how repayment matters and what if they do not repay the loans, etc., would go a long way in strengthening the CHSs. Similarly, as far as possible, bad loans and debt loans need to be discouraged.

MOBILIZATION OF THE POOR FOR AFFORDABLE HOUSING

From the viewpoint of sustainable financing for the poor and vulnerable groups to construct affordable housing, four very important but relevant policy implications can be offered. First, mobilizing the homeless poor and unaffordable sections and bringing them under the institutional framework for housing purposes is the need of the hour. Excluding these sections out of the financial institution's reach as it happened all along would only amount to doggedness of the housing problem and housing distress. Above all, not resolving the housing problem of the poor would question the efficacy of the public policy interventions and the presence of the housing-related institutional set-up. Therefore, mainstreaming these sections with the organized institutions can bring about the change. The ACHS—a higher tier in the cooperative housing movement—should initiate action for the formation of PHSs among the poor in all the nook and corners of the country. To empower them, cooperative education should be offered to them, especially on the cooperative principle of thrift/savings promotion. This intervention has two benefits in the sense that it minimizes public dependence, which has supply deficit as well as an unaffordable market, and second, a road map can be drawn to construct their own homes by planning their voluntary savings. The PHSs can also play the role of a catalyst for the implementation of the social housing commitments of the governments meant to target various groups. Moreover, organization of the cooperative movement in the rural and backward regions would be an appropriate and proactive response to the poor development of cooperatives. Second, even more critical intervention is required for the revival of 'savings-linked housing loan' scheme of the NHB and bring it within the affordable housing framework. The housing savings schemes should be reintroduced with the networking institutions of the refinancing schemes. This would not only facilitate every homeless household to save for their affordable housing, but the same can also develop financial relations between the account holders and the service providers. But mere revival does not mean anything; the factor that determines the success is designing the savings products according to the convenience of the various income groups. Such tailor-made products would also bring in the low-cost funds for the operations of the financial institutions besides judging the credibility of the depositors. While doing so, care must be taken to avoid operational aberrations with the implementation partners as experienced already. As far as possible, the NHB should establish financial and functional relations with SHGs and MFIs, as they have been the doorstep organizations in the financially backward regions. Third, apart from creating an environment for sustainable affordable housing, the public actions also must be stepped up in terms of the compatible intervention as well as adequate public finance. Importantly, the government must change its stand to intervene appropriately and must provide housing benefit as a fulfilment of the basic human necessity. It must provide the same beyond the social housing schemes/commitments for the various target groups, which have proved inefficient over several decades. Instead, it must increase the housing supply for the poor and vulnerable sections to the extent of total need with all housing amenities such as drinking water, sanitation, lighting and adequate space Finally, private builders and housing developers should be encouraged with financial assistance and incentives to construct affordable houses for the poor homeless households in the urban areas. Especially, such interventions are imminent in tier one cities or major urban centres with the involvement of the development authorities, municipalities and city corporations in order to meet the total housing needs of the households engaged in informal activities and to infuse the administrative efficiencies. Similarly, in tier 2 and tier 3 urban centres, housing boards and other public authorities must be engaged to implement construction of affordable houses, as the concentration of the poor is very high in these centres.

COMPARTMENTALIZED AND NEED-BASED HOUSING POLICY

As noted earlier, the housing problem in India, as it exists today, has arisen from three different quarters of the households belonging to diverse social income groups. Correspondingly, the public policy and efforts need to be compatible to: (a) supply of new housing units to meet the needs of new families; (b) redevelop the existing dilapidated stock that needs immediate repairs/replacement; and (c) provide temporary housing to urban migrant families. The incidence of crowded living arises mainly due to new family formation, which should be tackled only by augmenting the supply of new housing units in the owner and rental sectors. But, while doing so, it is necessary to ascertain the preferences of the new families (single person, spouse with children, spouse–children and parents, etc.). Also. with regard to costs, whether single or duplex, independent or flat, owned or rental, location, etc., as family preferences may vary across the size of the families. For this purpose, the market should be developed in such a way that it is able to cater to the various housing needs of new families in urban areas. The argument should be like one family one housing unit norm to ensure privacy to the couples, better living environment, better access to amenities and to promote decent and healthy housing. But to cope with this norm, public assistance available to the social housing programmes for poor families must be enhanced sufficiently in order to meet the total demand of the new families. Poor families are likely to take advantage of crowded dwelling (for obvious reasons of cost-saving, social living, etc.), but the 'crowding-out' strategy should be aggressively implemented for reasons stated earlier.

Similarly, pavement dwelling that occurs mainly during an increase in migration needs priority in the housing development strategy, as these persons/families do not have any sort of shelter. As has been done hitherto, the problem can no longer be neglected or ignored, given the implications and ramifications for the urban areas. To arrest the incidence of pavement dwelling, temporary but low-cost housing units with amenities need to be constructed in all the urban centres to house footloose construction workers and other migrant labourers. These units (single/spouse/double occupation) must be developed and managed by local bodies on a use-and-pay basis. Especially, ULBs should be encouraged to earmark resources for exclusive construction of temporary housing units with the initial financial support of upper-tier governments (Central and state), HUDCO, NHB, commercial banks and other financial institutions. In order to make these units self-sustaining, user charges could be collected. Cooperative and private initiatives could also be encouraged on a large scale to produce temporary housing units in urban areas. To effectively administer the housing benefit to migrant labourers, the strengthening of data–labour profile at all potential employment centres is critically required. Critical information may include labour migration by sex, size, source and periodicity of stay; income earnings by source; willingness to pay for temporary housing and amenities; and others. Similarly, on the lines of migrant labourers, the development of a database of slum dwellers is also a need of the hour so as to not only administer housing benefits effectively to slum dwellers but also to eliminate overlapping and to curb other unlawful activities in their habitations. Such a sound database would strengthen the administration to effectively check wrong practices like renting out tenements by the slum allotees.

Besides supplying new housing units for new families and migrants in places of settlements, the public policy also has to focus on redevelopment of the existing dilapidated housing units. Considering their stock and share in the total housing shortage of the country, it is high time to focus on the redevelopment of the dilapidated stock. Unfortunately it is not being undertaken currently by the occupants owing to their challenging economic position and for want of funds. Also, from the viewpoint of cost-effectiveness, the redevelopment of existing stock assumes priority over construction of new units for poor families. Public action should take the lead along with the market in developing a strong focus and mechanism for the redevelopment. At this juncture, it is important to note the cost of upgrading dilapidated units and their recovery. The government and users can jointly meet the cost of upgrading by evolving a saving-linked subsidy/loan scheme with the participation of beneficiaries. This method has many advantages. It promotes thrift and brings about sharing of burden between the state and the beneficiaries besides ensuring quality in construction. Further, the market and financial institutions must be sensitized and made responsive to the housing problems of the country.

DEVELOPMENT OF CRITICAL INPUTS AND AN INCLUSIVE FINANCIAL SYSTEM

Mere compartmentalized housing development strategies do not bring about decent and healthy housing practices unless the same is supplemented with effective supply of critical inputs like land and finance in urban areas. The existing supply mechanisms of both land and finance in urban areas have many deficiencies. Acquisition and development of land for residential purposes by public authorities like SHBs or development authorities have been highly limited or have been completely stopped. The growing indolent attitude of the public authorities in recent years has thrown the poorer sections under the influence of market forces or rendered them homeless for want of an affordable developed land. The growing incidence of indolent attitude has defeated the interest of the poor besides questioning their existence. It is unfortunate that the public development authorities have relegated much before accomplishing their responsibilities and fulfilling the total land needs for housing of the unaffordable sections. Second, there are hardly any incentives available to people's initiatives, developers, and cooperatives for assembling, developing and distributing land/providing housing to the poor. In view of the aforementioned deficiencies, there is a need to introduce specific corrective measures as follows: (a) promotion of joint identification of feasible land by both the state and beneficiaries on a cost-sharing basis; (b) formation of peoples' organizations on the lines of SHGs for land assembling and developing and for distributing of house sites; and (c) making cooperatives as partners/implementers of social housing schemes besides supplying residential lands on a cost-effective basis for the poorer sections, since they have a huge network in urban areas (Mahadeva 2003). Third, PPPMAH, notwithstanding its lofty ambitions, has its own issues in the Indian context. These issues include its acceptability, inclusivity, feasibility and efficacy, given the fact that housing production was hitherto carried out by the government, individual initiatives and cooperatives. The PPPMAH has hardly been experienced and put to test for acceptance by the housing needy, especially the poor and economically weaker sections, since private sector is known to its traits like hidden costs, profits and sustainability issue. Similarly, PPPMAH projects generally cater to the wealthiest needy or the affordable sections, as discussed earlier. Of late, they have also given rise to the gated community culture that mostly keeps away the marginalized and unaffordable housing needy, owing to the risks associated with recovering the maintenance and other costs. Especially, social mixing of all the background needy hardly takes place in PPPMAH projects, and even if it occurs remotely, social distancing by the community is a reality. PPP is a new production mechanism of housing in recent times—the model has sparsely spread only in major urban areas and as such is yet to penetrate into the other tiers in terms of the urban context. Especially in the non-major urban tiers with higher housing poverty and deprivations, the models are yet to be heard of let alone implementation. Lack of transparency with regard to the various costs associated with the land, development of amenities, construction, etc., are some of the other daunting issues of the EWSs and the poor.

Similar to that of land supply, the HFS after its emergence has not been able to broad base its services and is yet to cover all the different income groups, including the LIGs. The existing resource strategies have, by and large, not fulfilled the various housing needs of the people. Therefore, the future housing finance strategies must aim at addressing the needs of the sector and ensure an effective distribution of resources of both the market and public exchequer. Given the scale of various forms of the housing problem, the available resources must be distributed equally for the construction of new housing units to accommodate new families as well as pavement dwellers and for the redevelopment of the dilapidated stock to ensure safe dwelling. Undoubtedly, India has developed the HFS from the late 1980s, but in its strict sense, it has not been highly developed or is a responsive one. As it exists, because of high compartmentalization across different segments, the HFS has not been able to bring about any major breakthroughs in the supply of housing, especially in meeting the financial needs of the poorer sections and in increasing the housing stock in the country. Since the market segment of the system caters to only the white-collared income class, the financial needs of the majority of the vulnerable groups are drawn from either the informal sector or limited government assistance.

There are a number of failures associated with the HFS in India. The first and foremost is the insensitivity of the HFS towards the existing housing problems per se. Lack of a compartmentalized approach in resource application has been a hallmark of the system, since most of the HFIs prefer to extend fresh loans for new construction rather than for renovation/replacement of the dilapidated stock (Smets 1997). It is only one of the conspicuous examples of the missing linkages between the housing problem of India and the HFS. Knowing fully that a higher incidence of dilapidated stock needs total replacement, the HFS has not evolved any strategy for the development of need-based financial products. The other serious concern is the missing focus for meeting common man's financial needs. HFIs operate largely in urban areas, and most part of their resources have been deployed only against guaranteed repayment. Thus, the plight of the common man has been totally left to the social housing schemes as financed by HUDCO in urban areas. It goes without saying that the coverage of families under social housing schemes is far short of the total demand. The other structural deficiency in the housing credit market is the continued predominance of the informal credit market, which is catering to the needs of a large number of people. Given the high-cost services of the informal financing, efforts should have been on reducing the role of the informal credit for housing by increasing the access to credit from formal financial institutions. But this did not happen ever since the organization of housing credit market. In reality, the share of credit from the informal segment has remained unchanged instead of decreasing. For example, of the total housing expenditure during the Ninth Plan period (1997–2002), the share of the informal credit market has been put at more than 80 per cent, whereas the formal sectors' share was only 20 per cent (Planning Commission 1998–2002) as against 84 per cent and 16 per cent during the Eighth Plan period (Planning Commission 1992–1997). All of this is due to the lack of appropriate measures on the part of the formal HFS, on the one hand, and the various advantages associated with the informal credit market, on the other hand. It is also true that the informal financial services are available at the doorsteps of the households and can be availed without any hassles. The fourth important failure of the Indian HFS is the non-development of a savings mechanism. In order to ensure uninterrupted flow of funds for housing activities at cheaper rates, a sound housing-linked savings mechanism is a precondition, and the same is rightly emphasized in the sector policy document (NHHP 1998). But unfortunately, the Indian HFS has failed to evolve a household-based savings mechanism. A well-structured and coordinated housing-related savings would have certainly given an opportunity to the common man to realize his dream of owning a house and would have lessened the burden of public exchequer. In the absence of the same, most of the HFIs, including the housing cooperative societies, have been borrowing the deployable funds from capital market on commercial terms. Although this objective was sought to be achieved by the NHB through its home loan account (HLA), adequate savings could not be generated for various reasons. First, the NHB in the absence of its own institutional network had to depend upon commercial banks for the mobilization of savings, which in turn did not show the needed enthusiasm. This was so because commercial banks were themselves supplying housing finance. Moreover, banks were providing housing finance from their own deposits pool. Second, NHB's savings scheme was not well designed in the sense that targeting was very poor besides the incentive biases. Canvassing for housing savings was, by and large, absent. Although the scheme was open for everyone, saving to some extent was popular only among the taxpayers as they were allowed some exemption from income tax payments. Another discouraging factor was that many people could not opt for savings as housing finance was made available by other institutions, especially from commercial banks even without a savings account. Yet another failure with regard to housing savings is the CHSs. Although promotion of thrift is one of the tenets of cooperation, CHSs have hardly lived up to their own principle (Mahadeva 1992), whereas in the case of all the other HFIs (mainly subsidiaries), although savings have been promoted with higher rate of interest, market borrowing has continued to be a major source of investment.

Fifth, the conspicuous failure of the HFS is the absence of deepening of financial services to all segments of house construction, such as land acquisition, construction and renovation. Having concentrated mostly on new construction, financial services for the other segments of housing activities have yet to claim the needed attention. Especially, a full-fledged financial service for land acquisition is yet to be evolved. So is also the case for the renovation or reconstruction of dilapidated units and for the extension of existing units. Although composite approvals are necessary, which is the need of the hour to further boost housing activities, they have yet to be a common feature in the financial systems. Currently, approvals for land acquisition followed by house construction are considered only in exceptional cases like upper middle and high-income clientele. But these services are restricted not only to short term, but they also carry a higher rate of interest. Sixth, an institution with a conflict of interest in the housing credit market is yet another characteristic in India, although such experiences are uncommon elsewhere. These institutions differ in every aspect of their functioning style starting from resource base to lending practices. HFIs (generally subsidiaries) are guided by the guidelines of the NHB with capital market as the principal source of resources. However, general financial institutions (commercial banks and others) follow operational housing financial services guidelines of the RBI with a strong support of household savings. These institutions are competing with each other to provide credit services, although there has been some overlap on the same. As mentioned elsewhere, the services of the specialized institutions are dearer owing to their lower deposit-linked resource base, but these services are flexible during times of need. They often provide a higher ratio of loans (with low down payment) besides extending the contractual period of loans. In contrast, the general financial institutions discourage these practices at the outset, but under compulsions, they consider higher loan ratio and extension of loan term with a higher rate of interest. Since lending for housing is under close scrutiny of the central bank, general financial institutions are gaining importance owing to their advantage of resources. Finally, a high incidence of housing shortage and a worsening situation are observed in a number of major states. These include Uttar Pradesh, West Bengal, Maharashtra, Madhya Pradesh, Tamil Nadu, Andhra Pradesh, Bihar, Delhi, Karnataka, Punjab, Kerala, Rajasthan and Haryana. Given this situation, there is an urgent need to evolve a special assistance package strategy for these states. Such a strategy should aim at not only mitigating the existing situation of housing shortage but also checking further growth/rise in shortage. This impeding goal should be supplemented with a higher earmarking of financial resources both from the respective states and the Central government. Besides stepping up their efforts, the governments should promote the housing market to play its own role in arresting the housing problem in these states. These states should facilitate the entry of public–private financial institutions with fiscal incentives and evolve a broad-based financing mechanism, including the redevelopment of the dilapidated stock. Moreover, the market should realize and take the benefits to the regions and areas with more business potential.

SUSTAINABLE URBAN DEVELOPMENT FOR THE POOR

This important research has highlighted three very significant facts with regard to the urban slums. First, slums have occupied a significant space of the urban areas of the country, and the incidence is widespread and obviously conspicuous across all the major urban areas, especially in 31 major Indian states and UTs. It is important to note that seven Indian states have accounted for over three-fourths of the total slums in the country, which shows the seriousness of the degraded urban environment, coupled with an extended dimension of poverty. The other 24 Indian states have also equally accounted for the prevalence of slums in their respective urban areas. In other words, except for a small segment, slums have cropped up in every nook and corner of the urban areas. There are 2,822 slum-reported towns from these states, which is more than 35 per cent of the total number of towns, and these towns have been housing roughly 36 per cent of the urban households. The research also astonishingly noted that only a negligible part of the urban areas (one state and three union territories) has been free from the incidence of slums. In other words, not a single slum is registered in these four regions, despite the fact that there are 71 towns in this part of the urban areas, with a negligible number of households (<100,000). Above all, the research has also captured the incidence of slums in COMPs, spread over 27 municipal corporations with roughly one-fourth of the population in the slums.

Second, there has been a paradigm shift in the development approach and strategies for the improvement of urban slums from fringe to wholesome. This paradigm has sought to achieve the twin objectives of subsuming slums and minimizing deprivation level of access to housing and housing amenities. The ground realities notwithstanding, the urban inclusion mission is intended to bring the slum environment on par with the urban areas by establishing connectivity of basic services such as roads, lighting, water supply, sewerage and interface of the people. Though the necessity of the inclusive mission is realized belatedly in the 21st century, the corresponding interventions through specific designs like 'Housing for All' and 'SFCs' have their own impact on people from all walks of life in slums. Especially, the enlightened and pragmatic approaches as followed in the 21st century have brought in a number of changes in urban slums. On the housing front, the development of the standard housing units is itself an indicator of change and is a testimony for housing graduation. Correspondingly, housing graduation has brought down the incidence of other forms of housing stock to a manageable level. Schemes like the NHHP of the GOI have received major impetus for the development of the slums, especially under the IHSDP since 2005. NSP (GoI 2003) is a way forward and a guiding force for achieving SFCs with rejuvenated strategies, empowerment and entitlement for the slum dwellers. The development of household electricity is almost on par with the rest of the urban areas, though the deprivation level is still higher. Similar is the case with drinking water in the slums. Further, RAY, as a major intervention of the national government, has brought greater visibility in the provision of housing and basic amenities to slum dwellers, with an aim to achieve an inclusive urban development. At the same time, efforts to improve the hygienic conditions of the urban slums have had many setbacks, including political will, supported by public finance on the part of the government and non-participation of the people. Based on household connectivity to sanitation and sewerage facilities and the provision of some comforts as discussed already, it is evident that slum development administration is yet to make a significant headway, as the deprivation is continuing at a very high level.

Third, and undoubtedly, the NSSO findings in the measurement of the incidence of slums in different rounds have been the important benchmark for the government in understanding the urban situation. Similarly, transition in the approach of public commitment from ad hocism to pragmatism for the improvement of the world of slums has been another landmark. These paradigms have had a positive effect on the overall walks of life of the slums. Construction of standard housing units to ensure security has been supplemented. Supply of potable drinking water to slum dwellers is almost nearing the stage of total coverage. The incidence of open defecation has been substantially reduced, and the living environment has certainly improved. Above all, the long-term goal of reducing the difference between the urban areas and the slums has evidently occurred besides fulfilling the dream of SFC, even though major changes are yet to occur.

The presence of slums in various sizes is a detrimental factor to achieve orderly urban society because such a society with prevalence of slums cannot be considered inclusive and homogeneous with glaring development disparities, deprivation of basic needs or lack of access to basic amenities. Therefore, there is a need to initiate corrective interventions in order to mainstream India's urban slums. An orderly urban society can be achieved by two methods: (a) controlling of fresh slums and (b) development of all the existing slums in all measures to be on par with the rest of the urban society. The first one demands the urban administration to be very vigilant about the settlements and to ensure planned settlements of the migrants. Moreover, the political will of not promoting unplanned settlements of the people as vote banks is largely needed. The second strategy needs a multi-pronged approach with all the stakeholders' (governments, local bodies, slum dwellers) participation. The government as a principal game changer has to evolve a mission-mode approach, with a time frame to ensure inclusion of all slums into core urban life in order to bring visibility to its commitment for the cause. Otherwise, the inclusive agenda of the government for improving slums would go the same way as it has gone hitherto. The mission mode of inclusion of slums also demands an adequate and uninterrupted public financing on the part of the government, apart from periodic review of the progress of the mission, redressing of the deficiencies/problems and direct financing for the municipalities that are encountering the slums and are involved in the inclusion mission. Local bodies or municipalities cannot be pushed to be in isolation as it happened earlier, but they have a greater role to play as a local government in the inclusion mission of urban slums. These bodies should be given administrative responsibilities for the development of slums with adequate capacities (especially financial) to administer and plan projects, identify new settlements and develop the existing slums under the mission mode.

In fact, evolving the Integrated Development of Municipal Plan is the responsibility of municipalities as per the DNSP, but paucity of information has abstained further analysis. Apart from government and local bodies, community organizations of the slums have a greater role to motivate and sensitize the people about settlement transformation within their place of living besides allowing them to participate in the development, encouraging them to bear all the inconveniences and monitoring voluntary exclusion. Community organizations also need to monitor the inclusionary process of the slum dwellers and settlements to ensure the timely completion of the transformation and also to act as a pressure group on the implementation agencies. This kind of check and balance would ensure accountability on the part of the implementation agencies, including local bodies/municipalities. Evidently, residents' participation in the slums is incredibly low (<5%), which may be on account of increasing operations of the state and other players. Further, this is even more evident in the case of people's participation in the management of slums. The situation is far from satisfactory, as the residents' association activities in the slums have completely stopped. More so, if the residents' associations have minimized their existence in the notified slums, less said the better in the case of un-notified slums. Further, the urban development administration has not recognized adequately the importance of people's participation (slum dwellers) in not only containing the growth of cruel world within the urban areas but also in its all-round development on par with other urban areas. Unfortunately, the absence of the dwellers' participation is evident from the fact that most of the urban slums (two-thirds) do not have their own community organizations, including youth clubs and associations, to play a catalytic role between the service providers (government, municipalities and others) and the stakeholders (beneficiary identification, benefits distribution, connectivity of services, etc.) and to work as pressure groups to meet the development gaps from time to time. With this, the objective of the DNSP to ensure full property rights to slum dwellers along with the participation of the residents' associations is in doldrums. At present, the catalytic role is being played by either outside agencies (like NGOs) on a limited scale or not at all in most cases. Similarly, monitoring of various development activities in the slums is largely in the hands of the government machinery, touts and middlemen, whose participation is always questionable, and many times, the service providers have either their hand in glove or do not want to be monitored or pressured.

Eradication of housing insecurity of the slum dwellers should be given priority in the urban inclusion strategy, both by upscaling housing development efforts and redeveloping the substandard and dilapidated housing stocks in order to develop the needed amenities and to completely eradicate housing insecurity. Also, housing divide (between acceptable and unacceptable housing stock) always breeds the substandard way of living style, which is against the principle of an orderly urban society. Development of housing amenities such as treated drinking water, electricity and sanitation to all the slum dwellers is the need of the hour, if at all the existing disparity between the slum dwellers and other urbanites needs to be erased. As a solution, an integrated housing and amenities development strategy for the slum dwellers would go a long way in ensuring provision of all the basic amenities along with standard housing units. This strategy would only require enhancing the unit cost of construction, besides including the amenity charges. Further, a few of the environmental problems like sewerage connectivity and water logging have been continuously daunting the urban slums of the country. Household connectivity to sewerage is a matter of paramount importance in order to keep the housing environment tidy and hygienic in urban slums. On this front, it can be said that higher the household connectivity to sewerage, better are the hygienic and living environments and vice versa. Unfortunately, still a large segment of the households (74%) have remained unconnected from sewerage facility, and the consequence of this huge exclusion could be largely attributed to an unfavourable living environment in the urban slums. Equally important is that while almost half of the slums are located in low-lying areas, water logging is a common and recurring problem—these incidents have rather increased. It goes without saying that the public initiative for arresting water logging has hardly brought any improvement. One of the reasons for the continued degraded environment could be that urban slums have been excessively depending upon the state action for their improvements, while NGOs and other market forces play an inadequate role; this could be termed as voluntary exclusion of the slum residents in the management of various services.

The government, besides playing a critical role in building slum-free urban India, needs to evolve a strong CSR strategy for the development and mainstreaming of the urban slums. It would not be unreasonable to suggest that if only the corporate world is made a partner of inclusive urbanization with fiscal concessions and financial support, under CSR, several thousands of urban slums can be subsumed with core urban life in the years to come. This would further facilitate the eradication of slums that has already commenced as per the NSSO findings and make urban growth inclusive. Besides, increasing CSR would pave the way for increasing access to the core urban life and interface between the slum dwellers and non-slum urban population.

Finally, setting a very ambitious goal of assisting the construction of 20 million houses for the urban homeless, households of dilapidated houses, slum dwellers and other poorer sections under PMAY-HA is a right move in order to hit the poverty groups because these sections have been facing the housing problem in majority either due to the development exclusions or due to the lack of their own capacity to realize housing dreams. Especially, targeting the households of dilapidated houses for rehousing is the first of its kind in the development history. Similarly, assisting the lower MIGs in the affordable housing stream is another laudable strategy, as these groups have neither been identified with LIGs nor have been identified with upper/HIGs and have not been targeted under any public interventions. However, in situ redevelopment of houses in slums under the PMAY-HA (urban) is overlapping with the existing RAY, which has brought some visible improvement in slums and has mainstreamed a good number of slum dwellers, if not all. Instead, PMAY-HA should focus on providing night shelters and hut dwellings by the ULBs, respectively, for the floating and migrant population in order to eliminate pavement dwelling in urban areas. At the same time, RAY should be revamped in order to target the total coverage of urban slums and the dwellers and to provide urban and housing amenities with additional impetus. Further, the other priority action must be to have the National Housing Finance Inclusion Plan (NHFIP) with a corpus at the hands of the NHB. This corpus shall be developed by the governments with budgetary allocations, CSR funds, transfers of the HFIs and housing-linked savings of the housing cooperatives. This fund shall be used to finance housing poverty eradication programmes of various institutions for the unaffordable poor. The establishment of Housing Development Monitoring Authority (HDMA) to supervise and monitor housing development actions of the urban areas, including the slums, is the need of the hour, given the loaded responsibilities of ULBs. It can audit the performance of all the institutions annually and report their findings to the respective state governments. Such an authority is warranted immediately in the centres of housing poverty, although its presence in other states is equally important.

BIBLIOGRAPHY

Adhikari, Sanchayeeta, and Kushal Deb. 2004. 'State, Civil Society, and Struggle for Shelter of the Urban Poor in Mumbai'. In *Adequate & Affordable Housing for All*, edited by J. David Hulchanski, Robert A. Murdie, and Philippa Campsie. Research Abstracts from the International Housing Research Conference, University of Toronto. Toronto: Centre for Urban and Community Studies.

Asnani, P. 2006. *Solid Waste Management, India Infrastructure Report* (Urban Infrastructure). Oxford: Oxford University Press.

Bai, Thara. 2003. 'Informal Finance for Housing in Rural and Urban Areas of Karnataka'. An Unpublished Doctoral Dissertation. Mysore: University of Mysore.

Cancellieri, A., J. Foscoso, J. Lemoine, M. Mahaut, and R. Paoli. 1990. *Urban Public Housing Management*. New Delhi: Oxford and IBH Publishing.

Census of India. 1991. 'Housing and Amenities'. Paper 2 of 1993, Occasional Paper. New Delhi: Registrar General and Commissioner of Census Operations, Government of India.

———. 2001a. 'Houses, Household Amenities and Assets'. New Delhi: Registrar General and Commissioner of Census Operations, Government of India.

———. 2001b. 'Slum Population'. Volume 1, Series 1. New Delhi: Registrar General and Commissioner, Government of India.

———. 2011a. 'Tables on Houses, Household Amenities and Assets'. Series 1. New Delhi: Registrar General and Census Commissioner, Government of India.

———. 2011b. 'Tables on Houses, Household Amenities and Assets in Slums'. India Series 1. New Delhi: Registrar General and Census Commissioner, Government of India.

Chandrasekhar, S. 2005. 'Growth of Slums, Availability of Infrastructure and Demographic Outcomes in Slums: Evidence from India'. A paper presented during the session on Urbanization in Developing Countries at the Population Association of America's Annual Meeting, Philadelphia, USA.

Cherunilam, Francis, and O. D. Heggade. 1987. *Housing in India*, 1st ed. Bombay: Himalaya Publishing House.

Crook, Nigel, and Tim Dyson. 1982. 'Urbanization of India: Results of the 1981 Census'. *Population and Development Review* 8, no. 1: 145–155.

Dieterich, Bernd H., and John M. Henderson. 1963. *Urban Water Supply Conditions and Needs in Seventy-Five Developing Countries*. Geneva: World Health Organization.

Fallis, George. 1990. *The Urban Housing Market, Housing the Homeless and Poor: New Partnerships among the Private, Public and Third Sectors*, edited by George Fallis and Alex Murray. Toronto: University of Toronto Press.

Government of India (GoI). 1946. *Report of the Health Survey and Development Committee*. Delhi: GoI.

———. 1956. *Housing* (Chapter XXVI), 555–569. Second Five-Year Plan. New Delhi: Planning Commission.

———. 1964. *The Working Group on Housing Cooperatives* (Resolution No 36 (12)/62-HII, 1 October 1962. Delhi: GoI.

———. 1992. *National Housing Policy: 1992*. New Delhi: Ministry of Housing and Urban Development.

———. 1993–1994. *Ministry of Rural Development, Annual Report*. New Delhi: GoI.

———. 1994. *National Housing Policy, Ministry of urban Affairs and Employment*. New Delhi: GoI.

———. 1998. *National Housing and Habitat Policy*. New Delhi: Ministry of Housing and Urban Development.

———. 2003. *Draft National Slum Policy*. New Delhi: Ministry of Housing and Urban Poverty Alleviation.

———. 2007a. *Rajiv Awas Yojana—Guidelines for Slum-Free City Planning*. New Delhi: Ministry of Housing and Urban Poverty Alleviation.

———. 2007b. *National Urban Housing and Habitat Policy (NUHHP)*. New Delhi: Ministry of Housing and Urban Poverty Alleviation.

———. 2009. *Integrated Development of Small and Medium Towns (IDSMT) Scheme: Performance Details, Ministry of Housing and Urban Affairs*. Delhi: GoI.

———. 2016a. *Real Estate (Regulation and Development) Act*. New Delhi: Parliament of India.

———. 2016b. *Pradhan Mantri Awas Yojana: Housing for All (Gramin and Urban)*. Vikaspedia.in/Social - Welfare/Rural - Poverty – Alleviation. https://vikaspedia.in/social-welfare/urban-poverty-alleviation-1/schemes-urban-poverty-alleviation/pradhan-mantri-awas-yojana-housing-for-all-urban

———. 2016c. *Pradhan Mantri Awas Yojana 2021–2022*. New Delhi: Ministry of Housing and Urban Affairs.

———. 2017. *Public–Private Partnership Models for Affordable Housing*. New Delhi: Ministry of Housing and Urban Poverty Alleviation.

———. 2018. *Smart Cities Mission*. Wikipedia. https://en.wikipedia.org/wiki/Smart_Cities_Mission.

Government of Karnataka (GoK). 1985. GO.NO.HUD/113/MNX/85, 18 June. Bangalore: Department of Housing and Urban Development.

Gupta, Devendra B. 1985. 'Urban Housing in India'. World Bank Staff Working Papers (Number 730). Washington, DC: The World Bank.

Hudli, J. 1975. *Housing in Karnataka*, 76. Mysore: Administrative Training Institute.

Hulchanski, David J., Robert A. Murdie, and Philippa Campsie. 2004. *Adequate & Affordable Housing for All*, edited by J. David Hulchanski, Robert A. Murdie, and Philippa Campsie. Research Abstracts from the International Housing Research Conference, University of Toronto. Toronto: Centre for Urban and Community Studies.

Indian Parliament. 1987. *The National Housing Bank Act, 1987*. Number 53 of 1987. New Delhi: Ministry of Law and Justice, Government of India.

———. 1994. *National Housing Policy*. New Delhi: Ministry of Urban Development, Government of India.

Jain, A. K. 2016. 'India: Building 20 Million Homes'. Paper presented at the No Cost Housing Conference, Organised by the ETH Zurich, 30 June to 1 July.

Jorgensen, N. O. 1977. *Housing Finance for Low Income Groups: With Special Reference to Developing Countries*. Rotterdam: Institute of Housing and Urban Studies.

Khurana, M. L. 1986. *Organisation and Management of Housing Cooperatives*. New Delhi: National Cooperative Housing Federation.

Kundu, Amitabh. 1998. 'Access of Urban Poor to Shelter in the Context of Policy Perspective in India'. In *Affordable Housing and Infrastructure in India*, edited by K. P. Bhattacharya. New Delhi: Reliance Publishing House.

Lawrence, Berksmith. 1974. *The Post War Canadian Housing and Residential Mortgage Markets and the Role of Government*. Toronto: University of Toronto Press.

Mahadeva, M. 1992. 'A Study of the Housing Cooperatives in India with Special Reference to Karnataka'. Unpublished Doctoral Dissertation. Mysore University of Mysore.

———. 1993. 'Refinancing Housing Cooperatives: An Illusion'. *Cooperative Perspective* 28, no. 2 (July–September).

———. 1994. 'Housing Policies in India'. *Nagarlok* 2 (April–June): 53–62.

———. 1997. 'Housing Development in India: Challenges Ahead'. *Urban India* 1–2: 117–134.

———. 2002a. 'Canadian Perspectives on Housing Development: Lessons for the Indian Context'. *Indian Journal of Social Development* 2, No. 2.

———. 2002b. 'Reducing Urban Housing Poverty: An Assessment of Policy and Failures'. *Urban India* XXII, no. 2 (July–December).

———. 2003. Third Sector in Urban Housing: Problems and Prospects'. *Urban India* XXIII, no 2 (July-December): 1–31.

———. 2005. 'India's Housing Needs: Towards Pragmatic Strategies'. *Review of Development and Change* X, no. 1: 137–157.

———. 2006. 'Reforms in Housing Sector in India: Impact on Housing Development and Housing Amenities'. *Habitat International* 30: 412–433.

———. 2008. 'Financial Growth in India: Whither Financial Inclusion?' *Margin—The Journal of Applied Economic Research* 2, no, 2: 177–197.

———. 2009. 'Challenges of Sustainable Housing Finance System in India'. *Margin—The Journal of Applied Economic Research* 3, no. 1: 41–61.

Mahadeva, M. 2019. 'Watershed for Rural Housing in India: A Review of the Policy Developments, Changes and Major Issues'. *Journal of Rural Development* 38, no. 2 (April–June). http://nirdprojms.nirdpr.in/index.php/jrd/article/view/146744

Mishra, Ramesh. 1990. 'The Collapse of Welfare Consensus? The Welfare State in the 1980s'. In Housing the Homeless and Poor, edited by George Fallis and Alex Murray. Toronto: University of Toronto Press.

MRCL. 1992. *Model Rent Control Legislation*. New Delhi: Ministry of Housing and Urban Development, Government of India.

Mohan, Rakesh. 1985. 'Urbanization in India's Future'. *Population and Development Review* 11, no. 4: 619–645.

NABARD. 2006. *Statistical Statements Relating to Cooperative Movement in India: Part II—Non-Credit Societies*. Mumbai: National Bank for Agriculture and Rural Development.

Naik, D. D. 1971. *Cooperative Housing in India*. New Delhi: The National Cooperative Housing Federation.

———. 1976. *You and Your Housing Cooperative*. New Delhi: The National Cooperative Housing Federation.

National Housing and Habitat Policy. 1998. *Ministry of Urban Areas and Employment*. New Delhi: Government of India.

NBO. 1988. *Housing Needs*. New Delhi: National Buildings Organisation.

NHB. 2010. *Report on Trend and Progress of Housing in India*. New Delhi: National Housing Bank.

———. 2014. *Report on Trend and Progress of Housing India*. New Delhi: National Housing Bank.

———. 2018. *Booklet on Refinance Schemes of National Housing Bank*. New Delhi: National Housing Bank.

NIUA. 1988. *State of India's Urbanisation*. New Delhi: National Institute of Urban Affairs.

———. 1992. *The Informal Finance for Urban Housing—Status and Prospects*, Research Study Series, Number 47. New Delhi: National Institute of Urban Affairs.

———. 2015. *Urban Solid Waste Management in Indian Cities*. New Delhi: National Institute of Urban Affairs.

NSSO. 1977. *Condition of Slum Areas in Cities*. 31st Round, Report Number 290. New Delhi: National Sample Survey Organisation, Government of India.

———. 1998. *Household Expenditure*. 48th Round, Report Number 437. New Delhi: National Sample Survey Organisation, Government of India.

———. 2003. *Conditions of Urban Slums*. NSS 58th Round. New Delhi: National Sample Survey Organisation, Government of India.

———. 2009. *Some Characteristics of Urban Slums*. NSS 65th Round. New Delhi: National Sample Survey Organisation, Government of India.

Okhpala, Don. 1994. 'Financing Housing in Developing Countries: A Review of the Pitfalls in the Development of Formal Housing Finance Systems'. *Urban Studies* 31, no. 9: 1571–1586.

Papa, Oscar. 1992. *Housing Systems in Europe: Part II A Comparative Study of Housing Finance*. Delft: Delft University Press.

Planning Commission. 1951. *First Five-Year Plan: 1951–56*, 235. New Delhi: Government of India.

———. 1956. *Housing* (Chapter XXVI). Second Five-Year Plan. New Delhi: Government of India.

———. 1960. *Third Five-Year Plan: A Draft Outline*. New Delhi: Government of India.

———. 1978. *Draft Five-Year Plan: 1978–83*, 452. New Delhi: Government of India.

———. 1992–1997. *Eighth Five-Year Plan*. Vol. II, Chapter 14. New Delhi: Government of India.

———. 1998–2002. *Ninth Five-Year Plan*, Vol. II, Chapter 3. New Delhi: Government of India.

Pugh, Cedric. 1990. *Housing and Urbanization*. New Delhi: SAGE Publications.

Raj, Mulkh. 1994. 'Housing Affordability: Land, Finance, Design and Technology'. In *Indo-Swedish Perspectives on Affordable Housing*, edited by R. N, Sharma. Bombay: Tata Institute of Social Sciences.

Rao, Prakash V. L. S. 1983. *Urbanization in India: Spatial Dimensions*. New Delhi: Concept Publishing House.

Rao, Seshagiri Y. 1988. *Housing Needs*. New Delhi: National Buildings Organisation.

Ray, Debraj. 1998. *Development Economics*. New Delhi: Oxford University Press.

RCFI. 2008. *Report of the Committee on Financial Inclusion (Dr C. Rangarajan)*. New Delhi: Government of India.

Reserve Bank of India (RBI). 1950. *Cooperative Housing*. Bombay: Reserve Bank of India.

———. 1956. *Review of the Cooperative Movement in India*. Bombay: Reserve Bank of India.

———. 1978. *Finance for Housing Schemes, Report of the Working Group on Role of the Banking System*. Bombay: Reserve Bank of India.

———. 1988. *A Review of the Agriculture Credit Systems in India*. Bombay: Reserve Bank of India.

Saluja, Vijay K. 2004. 'Informal Housing in Urban Situation in Developing Countries: A Case Study in New Delhi'. In *Adequate & Affordable Housing for All*, edited by J. David Hulchanski, Robert A. Murdie, and Philippa Campsie. Research Abstracts from the International Housing Research Conference, University of Toronto. Toronto: Centre for Urban and Community Studies.

Seetharam, Kala Sridhar, and A. Venugopala Reddy. 2014. *Contribution of the Urban Poor: A Pilot Study from Bengaluru, India*. Inclusive Urban Planning: State of the Urban Poor Report 2013. New Delhi: Ministry of Housing and Urban Poverty Alleviation.

Sen, Kunal. 2014. *Inclusive Growth, Social Exclusion and the Urban Poor: Taking a Production Lens to Informality in India*. Inclusive Urban Planning: State of the Urban Poor Report 2013. New Delhi: Ministry of Housing and Urban Poverty Alleviation.

Sengupta, Urmi. 2004. 'Public–Private Partnership for Housing Delivery in Kolkata'. In Adequate & Affordable Housing for All, edited by J. David

Hulchanski, Robert A. Murdie, and Philippa Campsie. Research Abstracts from the International Housing Research Conference. Toronto: University of Toronto. Toronto: Centre for Urban and Community Studies.

Sharholy, Mufeed, Kafeel Ahmad, Gauhar Mahmood, and R. C. Trivedi. 2008. 'Municipal Solid Waste Management in Indian Cities—A Review'. *Waste Management* 28: 459–467.

Sharma, K. S. R. N., ed. 1989. *Housing Finance in India: Some Issues, Housing Finance in India*. New Delhi: Indian Institute of Public Administration.

Shivalingappa, B. K. 1975. 'Slum Clearance Related Problems and Programmes'. for *Housing in Karnataka*. Mysore: Administrative Training Institute.

Singh, Andrea Menefee. 1978. 'Poverty and Slum Dwellers in Urban India—Some Urgent Research and Policy Considerations'. *Social Action* (April–June): 165.

Smets, Peer. 1997. 'Private Housing Finance in India: Reaching Down Market?' *Habitat International* 21, no. 1: 1–15.

UNGA. 1988. 'Global Strategy for Shelter for the Year 2000 A/RES/43/181, 20 December'. Nairobi: United Nations General Assembly.

UN Habitat. 1976. *Report of United Nations Conference on Human Settlements*. New York: UN Habitat

———. 1996. *An Urbanizing World*. Global Report on Human Settlements. New York: Oxford University Press.

———. 2000. *Shelter for All: Global Strategy for Shelter to the Year 2000*. Nairobi: United Nations Centre for Human Settlements.

———. 2003. *The Challenge of Slums: Global Report on Human Settlements*. United Nations Human Settlement Programme. London: Earthscan.

———. 2005. *Financing Urban Shelter: Global Report on Human Settlements-2005*. London: United Nations Human Settlements Programme.

Union Budget. 1996–1997. *Budget Speech of Finance Minister, Part B*. New Delhi: Ministry of Finance, Government of India.

United Nations Centre for Human Settlements (Habitat) (UNCHS). 1996. *An Urbanizing World: Global Report on Human Settlements*. London: Oxford University Press.

———. 1998. *An Urbanizing World: Global Report on Human Settlements*. London: Oxford University Press.

WHO, and UNICEF. 2000. *Global Water Supply and Sanitation Assessment Report*. New York: World Health Organization and United Nations International Child Emergency Fund.

World Bank. 1984. 'Housing and Financial Institutions in Developing Countries'. Staff Working Paper Number 658. Washington, DC: World Bank.

———. 1999. *Urban Water Supply and Sanitation*. South Asia Rural Development Series. Washington, DC: The World Bank; New Delhi: Allied Publishers.

ABOUT THE AUTHOR

M. Mahadeva is Professor at Institute of Finance and International Management (IFIM), Bengaluru. He was a research faculty of economics in the Centre for Economic Studies and Research and the Centre for Agricultural Development and Rural Transformation at the Institute for Social and Economic Change (ISEC), Bengaluru. He served at the Planning Commission of India as the Chairman of the Sub-Committee (Twelfth Five-Year Plan), Member of the Working Group (Twelfth Five-Year Plan), Member of the Steering Committee (Twelfth Five-Year Plan) and Member of the Mid-Term Appraisal (Eleventh Five-Year Plan). He has both teaching and research experience of about two decades and academic administrative experience of over 15 years.

Professor Mahadeva obtained all three of his degrees from the University of Mysore, including a PhD in Economics (1987–1993) on the theme 'Market and Economics'. He was a visiting academic fellow in the University of Bristol, UK (December 2008 to April 2009); University of Toronto, Canada (October 2000 to January 2001); Institute for Housing and Urban Studies, (December 1997 to January 1998); Institute of Social Studies, the Netherlands (November to December 2010); and Maison des Science de l'Homme, France (December 1998). He has earned five international fellowships, including the Commonwealth Academic Scholarship and has published extensively in the areas of housing poverty and deprivations, housing market and housing development players, financial exclusion/inclusion policies and human settlement issues of poor and vulnerable households in both urban and rural contexts.

INDEX